MW00995743

Enjoy Your Money!
How to Make It
Save It
Invest It
and Give It

*The Adventures of the
Counterculture Club*

By J. Steve Miller

Enjoy Your Money! Copyright © 2009 by J. Steve Miller. All rights reserved. Printed in the United States of America. No part of this publication may be reproduced, stored in or introduced into a retrieval system, or transmitted, in any form or by any means (digital, electronic, mechanical, photocopying, recording, or otherwise), without the prior written permission of the publisher, except for brief reviews. For information contact Wisdom Creek Press, LLC, 5814 Sailboat Pointe, Acworth, Georgia, 30101, www.wisdomcreekpress.com.

Cover design by Carole Maugé-Lewis
Front Cover Photography by Rasmus Rasussen
Author Photo by Christina Cosenza
Typesetting by Callisa Ink & Co. and Carole Maugé-Lewis

Library of Congress Cataloging-in-Publication Data

Miller, J. Steve, 1957-
   Enjoy Your Money! How to Make It, Save It, Invest It and Give It:
The Adventures of the Counterculture Club / by J. Steve Miller
   p. cm.
   Includes bibliographical references and index
   LCCN 2008941060
   ISBN-13: 978-0-9818756-7-5
   ISBN-10: 0-9818756-7-X

   1. Finance, Personal   I. Enjoy Your Money!

   HG179.M4919 2009   332.024
                         QBI09-200015

Bulk Sales, Discounts and Special Printings

Since this book makes an ideal gift or classroom text, Wisdom Creek Press offers discount pricing to those purchasing in bulk for individuals, businesses, government agencies, classrooms, and not-for-profits. Consider this book for graduates, employees, special promotions, etc. We also consider special print runs to personalize *Enjoy Your Money* for your organization. For more information, contact us at www.wisdomcreekpress.com .

Advance Praise

"A comprehensive look at managing your money. For me, the genius of this book is that it gathers wisdom from top financial gurus and uses it to explain clearly and practically how average folks can apply it to everyday living."

Alan Buckler
Allstate Insurance

"I really liked the format! The dramatic layout used a totally different part of my brain when I read it...it's like watching a movie or reading a novel. The story line kept my interest so that I got through it quickly. The content was very inspiring. 'Living differently' and 'starting a financial counterculture' hits home to me. And it was SO PRACTICAL! I think it will also appeal to most of my generation and the one coming up behind me."

Anthony Daniel, age 28
Chemist, *Tiarco Chemical*

"I loved the story and the characters! Read this book and you'll get the practical tools and wisdom to chart your own course toward financial freedom."

Jamie Maddox
Former Senior Business Analyst, *The Coca Cola Company,*
Present Pastor of Stewardship, *NorthStar Church*

"Financial responsibility has reached a state of crisis. This book attacks the problem in a common sense, refreshing manner that anyone can understand and apply to real life. It should be required reading for all young people, before they find themselves broke, deeply in debt and miserable."

William C. Lusk, Jr.
Senior Executive Vice President & Chief Financial Officer, Retired, *Shaw Industries*, a *Fortune 500* company and the world's largest manufacturer of carpet

"A very entertaining, engaging book! The characters are appealing and aid the reader in interacting with the principles taught. Although especially geared to older teens and young adults, all ages will enjoy it and benefit. Meticulously researched and documented. Chock full of financial and lifestyle wisdom. I'll keep plenty of copies in my office to hand out to clients."

Dr. Ken Walker
Psychologist with the *Georgia Department of Juvenile Justice* and Director of *Dalton Counseling Service.* Former regional credit manager

"For me, the section on savings was worth the price of the book, detailing scores of hidden ways to save a fortune over a lifetime. Then, unlike many books, it goes beyond '*having* more' to '*doing* more with what you have.'"

Bryan McIntosh, Ph.D.
Dalyn Corporation

"Clever! The movie script format pulled me into the story and endeared me to the characters. Before I knew it, I found myself thinking about money strategies that I'd have never learned from traditional finance books. Teaching finance through people stories works for me. Rather than staring at obscure charts, I just followed the lives of successful people. Finally! A readable book on personal finance for people who don't want to read a book on personal finance...which of course is me and just about everybody else!"

Mark Hannah
Film Producer

"A fast, fun read with practical and often remarkable insights. Should be required reading for every high school senior and every young adult who's landed his or her first full-time job. I'm incorporating parts of the book into my lectures."

Robert A. Martin, MBA, CPA
Lecturer of Accounting in the prestigious *Coles College of Business* at *Kennesaw State University,* founder of a tax and consulting firm

"Every young person should read this book! It's the first time I ever laughed out loud (repeatedly!) and darn near cried while reading a financial book. And, the content is so practical that I find myself routinely reflecting on the principles in my daily money decisions. I am thoroughly impressed with the scope of information covered in this book and consider it, by far, the most valuable book on finances I've ever read."

Callie C. Brown,
Author of *The Complete Guide to Investing in Gold and Precious Metals*

"Teachers of financial management and life skills will be thrilled to discover this book! Miller uses people stories to breathe life into financial concepts, making lessons both memorable and enjoyable. As an educator, I was impressed that the book:

- goes beyond 'the same old stuff' that students hate.
- *expands* minds with research-based facts.
- *engages* minds with intriguing angles and creative assignments.
- challenges students beyond selfish accumulation to consider service to humanity.
- includes multiple cultures.
- offers hope to those with learning disabilities."

Phillip Page, Ph.D.
Public School Principal

"Financial success is simply having more than you need. Reading this book will put you on your way to achieving that success."

David E. Hultstrom, MBA, CFP, CFA, ChFC
Financial Architects, LLC, *Financial Planning & Wealth Management*

"Had I read this book in my 20's, I'd be financially independent today. It's a remarkable blend of fabulous research with clear and lively writing. You'd pay an expert quite a sum for this caliber of counsel. That's why I say that the best investment you make this year just might be this book. Your second best investment will be the copies you buy for your children."

Dr. Dwight "Ike" Reighard
Executive Vice President and Chief People Officer, HomeBanc – One of Fortune's 100 Best Places to Work, four years in a row

"As a practicing CPA and financial counselor for the past 35 years, I've read scores of books and periodicals on personal finance. Just when you think you've heard it all, something like this comes along. It's rare and refreshing to find a book so enjoyable, so accurate, and so life-changing. I'm purchasing hundreds of copies to give away to graduating seniors."

Larry Winter,
Winter & Scoggins, CPAs
Certified Valuation Analyst, Certified Fraud Examiner, Personal Financial Planning Specialist

For my wife, Cherie: my love and my inspiration. For my seven sons:
Steve, Josh, Andrew, Benjamin, Mark, David and Paul

Table of Contents

Preface

This book will help you to:

- get out of debt and accumulate wealth.
- get ahead, even when the work you love doesn't produce big bucks.
- find your strengths and passions and make a living with them.
- live a more fulfilled life.

You'll discover the wisdom of the great makers and accumulators of wealth, presented in a story form to help you understand, internalize and have fun in the process. You'll learn investing from Warren Buffett, the world's greatest investor and wealthiest man in the world. You'll learn principles of business success from Sam Walton, the uber-successful founder of Wal-Mart. You'll find advice on landing and succeeding in a dream job from experts in career guidance.

Is This Book for Me?

You're never too young or too old to discover these ageless principles. They apply to the seasoned business executive as well as the entrepreneur with his first lemonade stand. Warren Buffet caught his vision at age five and started investing at age 11. My grandmother started multiplying her money in her mid-60's. At age one hundred and two, with her sharp mind intact, she's accumulated a small fortune.

What's Unique About This Book?

Many books teach personal money management. Some of them are good. But, as Paul A. Samuelson (MIT Professor of Economics and Nobel Laureate) said:

> *"The same surgeon general who required cigarette packages to say 'Warning, this product may be dangerous to your health' ought to require that 99 out of 100 books written on personal finance carry that same label. The exceptions are rare."* [1]

I strove to be one of those exceptions by basing my advice not just upon years of personal experience, but upon the knowledge and experiences of well over one hundred wise people. In the process, my house at times bore more resemblance to the famed library of Alexandria than to a home.

But each new book or interview seemed to offer new angles or fresh insights, often pointing to new paths just begging to be traveled. [2]

After writing my first draft, I put it into the hands of over forty smart people I respect, asking them, "If you could put a lifetime of financial wisdom into a book, is this what you'd say? Be ruthlessly honest!" Their input proved invaluable.

Essentially, I distill the wisdom of the wise on working hard, working smart, saving, investing and giving - all the ageless basics - applied to today's world. I was especially fascinated with the counterintuitive nature of so much of their advice. The more you study the successful, the more you see why most people aren't very successful. The path to financial freedom isn't the path that initially appears obvious. Thus, the need for books to challenge the conventional thinking of popular culture.

I cover critical topics often left out of books of this nature. For example, the excellent studies of millionaires by professors Thomas Stanley and William Danko found that character traits such as integrity, diligence and thrift are shared by most who accumulate wealth.[3] The massive Gallup study of managers and people at work helps us discover our passions and strengths and put them to work in a fulfilling career.[4]

Finally, people usually seek money, not as an end in itself, but as a way to find peace and happiness. Funny that so many money books assume that lots of money will automatically cure our ills and put smiles on our faces. When does money help lead us to happiness? When does it hinder our happiness? Social scientists have studied happiness extensively and drawn some fascinating, counterintuitive conclusions.[5] Isn't happiness important to consider in handling your money?

Money management can be exciting! I believe that this story of Antonio, Akashi, James, Amy and their mentors can build some of that excitement. It's fun to beat the system. It's fun to see your money grow. It's fun to feel successful. It's fun to have enough money to help others. To this end, I hope you have fun reading my book.

Introduction: From Cliff Hanger to Hash Brown's

AUGUST 15, 2005, SOMEWHERE IN THE MONTANA ROCKIES...

Dangling off the edge of a massive rock, something had to give. Antonio could no longer hang on to both his well-chalked handhold and his struggling, neophyte climber - a Down 's syndrome teen named Chad.

Antonio shot a piercing glance directly into Chad's fear-filled eyes. "I've got to let go of ya, Chad! Trust in what you've learned and hang on to that rope!"

After the briefest silent prayer, Antonio let go....

Chad let out a blood-curdling scream, which quickly shifted into quiet concentration as he relaxed his death-grip on the rope and let it slide through the carabineers. He pushed off of the rock and began bouncing down the cliff. Rappelling with newly found confidence and his own distinctive style, his silence erupted into laughter. Chad had conquered yet another challenge during his week-long retreat with *Extreme Wisdom Wilderness Adventures.*

Antonio free-climbed his way down the adjacent rock, shouting triumphantly to the cloudless sky, "What a job! The wilderness is my office. My clients love me. I'm changing the world, one person at a time!"

Then, he chuckled to himself as his mind rewound to a decade earlier, to "In School Suspension," "The Counterculture Club," and that loony old Mrs. Kramer, who turned out to have more sense than anyone he'd ever met.

"Without them," Antonio thought, "I could have never landed this dream job. Not the way I handled my money back in high school. When I get back to civilization, I'm calling a reunion of the "The Counterculture Club.""

11:00 PM, TWO MONTHS LATER, HASH BROWN'S BREAKFAST BAR IN ACWORTH, GEORGIA...

Second-shift manager Larry Wiersbe was experiencing a rare lull in customers until four rowdy twenty-somethings suddenly charged in, looking like they'd stepped straight out of a culturally-sensitive brochure: an Asian girl, an African-American guy, an alternative-looking Caucasian girl and a Hispanic guy.

Larry introduced himself, took their orders and retreated to the grill until a sudden movement forced him to glance at the crowd. The Asian had jumped up suddenly and was swinging her glass Ketchup bottle over her shoulder like the start of a tennis serve. Then, she brought it down forcibly toward the table. Before he could intervene, she stepped back just far enough to miss the table. Riotous laughter followed, until an elderly lady appeared in the entranceway. She pointed her cane at the small party and announced at the top of her lungs, "I christen thee, 'The Counterculture Club!'"

"Mrs. Kramer!" the Hispanic shouted, as they sprang from their seats to hug their old mentor and friend. High fives, hand slaps and severely dated hand-shakes followed. After all the commotion, Larry half expected them to boost the old lady overhead and body surf her to the table. Instead, they led her gently by her hands, respectfully seating her at the head.

His curiosity piqued, Larry followed their loud conversation from the grill.

"You crazy kids!" Mrs. Kramer began. "What in the world have you been up to? You kept me up-to-date with e-mails and an occasional meeting for a few short years, but then you fell off the face of the earth, you ungrateful bums!"

"You were never one to beat around the bush," Antonio said sheepishly. "I'll be the first to plead guilty to the charge of not writing…"

"Enough with the boring confessional," Mrs. Kramer broke in. "I'm dying to catch up with your lives!"

For the next hour, Larry listened intently to some incredible success stories. Although far from perfect, these people seemed to "get" something that Larry didn't. They exuded vision, goals, purpose. Much of the conversation revolved around finances – refusing debt, making, saving and investing money. But then the conversation would move seamlessly to finding fulfillment in serving others with their time and money.

Larry knew he didn't fit in. He shared their age, but that was it. The three credit cards in his wallet were stretched to the max. He worked two dead-end jobs just to keep his head above water. At this rate, he'd never own his own home, much less have the time and resources to help others. And he resolved to never marry a girl who was stupid enough to choose such a loser. Finally, he got the nerve to break in.

"OK guys, it's midnight, closing time. But you've obviously got something I desperately need. Unless you're all high or suffering from delusions of grandeur, you've achieved a freedom that's eluded me all of my life. Can you tell me what you learned from this lady that made your lives into something I'm envying?"

They looked at each other and shrugged.

"I'll cut a deal with you," Larry continued. "If you'll tell me in one hour how you've achieved this…"financial freedom" as you call it, I'll let you hang out as long as you like. Plus, I'll serve you whatever you want. No charge."

"Why not?" said the old lady. Obviously the mouthpiece for the group, she seemed to enjoy taking charge once more. "It would be a hoot to reminisce about old times, and a helpful review for these slow learners. Keep that order pad handy, because you'll need to jot some of this down."

"And you'd better pull up your chair," chuckled the black fellow, "because once you get us started, we'll take more than your hour."

In School Suspension

"I'll start," volunteered the alternative-looking blonde. "I remember that first day vividly because I've relived it in my mind a hundred times since. You wouldn't have recognized me back then. As a fifteen-year-old, I didn't have the cheek-ring or tattoos that today help jump-start conversations while volunteering at the Juvenile Center. Back then, I was a reluctant cheerleader. This unlikely group first met in ISS."

"In School Suspension?" queried Larry.

"If you don't know, you must have been one of the good boys!" teased the Asian.

"So, I walked in to find these three students, but no teacher. I'd hoped someone I knew would be there, but no such luck. An assistant principal broke the ice by stepping in and explaining that our teacher would arrive shortly. Then she asked for our names and wrote them on a legal pad:

Antonio, Amy, Akashi, James.

She took another sheet and began to read our crimes, something like this:

Flash Back to High School

"Antonio: Fourteen tardies? We're only into the fifteenth school day!"

"I'm not a morning person," Antonio offered.

"Akashi, sleeping through Algebra again? I figured you'd be good at Math."

"Not all Asians can be Math geniuses, you know," Akashi responded, showing more than a hint of attitude.

"James, caught in the hall without a pass."

"The teacher wasn't around, and when you gotta go, you gotta--"

"Spare me the details. And Amy, what's with parking in the teacher's lot?"

"I was late, and a visitor had taken my spot."

"Typical teens: all victims, none responsible. Anyway, Coach Helms will be in shortly."

As the door closed behind her, Akashi mocked, "Typical teens...all victims, none responsible. And since I'm Asian, of course I sit around studying Math for fun. I'm so tired of this prison of a school. And here I sit in house arrest with a couple of jocks and a cheerleader."

"So you resent being labeled a stereotypical Asian Math whiz but have no problem labeling us as stereotypical preps and jocks?" shot back Antonio. "Can you say 'hypocrite'?"

"We're getting off to a bad start," offered James. "If coach Helms walks in and finds us in a rumble, we'll be stuck in ISS the rest of the year. Obviously, none of us want to crack a book until we have to. Let's break through the stereotypes and get to know each other a bit. Surely we have *something* in common. Amy, you're a cheerleader, right?"

"I hate cheerleading," complained Amy. "It's not me at all."

"What do you mean?" asked Antonio. "You *so* look the part."

"I'm a rebel living in a preppie world. You see, my brother started dressing goth in high school about the same time as he discovered drugs. My parents, fearing the same would happen to me if I got with the 'wrong' crowd, won't let me near a Hot Topic or thrift store. I understand their concern, but I'm not about to do drugs. I see what they've done to my brother. But I'm not comfortable with jocks and preps.

"My parents want the best for me. I don't want to hurt them. But I'm counting the days till I go off to college, shed these Abercrombies and join a punk band. Alone in my bedroom with my bass, I can keep up with almost any song you give me."

"Amazing. And you guys probably think I play Soccer," teased Antonio. "It's never interested me. I'm more into weightlifting and wilderness adventures, like rock climbing and caving."

"If you're into stereotypes, I *do* like basketball and fried chicken," offered James. "But I *don't* like watermelon, and I'm *not* on the school basketball team. I spend my after school hours making money. My parents always fight about money, so I plan to make a million by the time I'm 40 so that it won't be an issue in my family."

"Parents with money problems, now *that's* something we've got in common," replied Akashi. "My parents are so obsessed with 'getting ahead' that they work day and night and weekends. We live in a nice neighborhood and have great cars, but they can't enjoy life. They have to work all the time to pay the bills. I'd much rather live in a one room apartment and have time to travel and hang out with my family. Amy, what about your parents?"

"They'd love to teach at the University and write on the side, but they can't quit their corporate jobs. They need the money. They've never been savers. They max out their credit cards over Christmas, pay them off by the end of summer and start the cycle over again the next Christmas.

When my brother went into drug rehab and insurance wouldn't pay, Mom and Dad had absolutely no savings to draw from. They took out a second loan on the house and are now in worse financial shape than ever. It's depressing. They're always tired and worried. I can't see how they'll ever dig themselves out of this hole. Antonio?"

"Mom works day and night to support the family. Dad's a deadbeat. He's always either looking for a job or complaining about the job he has. Money's definitely a big issue at home. Mom and Dad argue all the time about it. It gets so bad that I fear Dad will eventually pack up and leave."

Enter Coach Helms

"Okay class. Sorry to be late. I recognize all of you from previous suspensions, so I'll dispense with introductory matters. Please open your text books and get to work."

"Coach Helms, we've got problems," interjected Akashi.

"Hello! That's why you're in ISS, Right?" offered Coach Helms.

"Not *those* problems," explained Akashi. "I'm talking about family problems. Our parents suck with their money."

"Tell me about it," said Coach Helms. "I wish I had some answers, but I overslept this morning because I work a night job to make ends meet. I can't seem to make it on my teacher's salary."

"Is everyone in this town hopeless with their money?" asked Akashi. "If you don't give us some answers, we'll end up just like our parents – broke, tired and whining all the time. You're supposed to be our teacher. Give us some direction here."

Coach Helms thought for a moment, tapping his pencil nervously on the desk. Without looking up, he said, "What about Mrs. Kramer?"

"Old widow Kramer, the Social Studies teacher?" asked James. "I had her for a class. She dresses worse than my grandma...and her car isn't anything to brag about."

"She may not look the part," said Coach Helms, "but my banker says she's the best money manager he knows. She's got all kinds of investments going. Besides Social Studies and Business, she also teaches Money Management."

"Come to think of it," continued James, "I remember her being hyped about her world travels. I wondered how she paid for it on a teacher's salary. Maybe she got a big life insurance claim when her husband died. But she can be a little scary... and those riddles...."

"Her personality...," continued Coach Helms. "She's definitely a work of art. More Picasso than Norman Rockwell. Been around students so long that I think she's more comfortable with teens than adults. Hardly ever see her in the teacher's lounge. Speaks your language."

"She eats second lunch. How about this? I'll let you eat second lunch. Try to connect with her. Until then, get out those notebooks. I want to see some progress."

- What are your friends and relatives doing right with their finances that you'd like to emulate?

- What are your friends and relatives doing wrong with their finances that you'd like to avoid?

- What would you like to learn most about making and managing your money?

- For more free discussions and activities for each chapter, visit www.enjoyyourmoney.org.

OLD WIDOW KRAMER

Fast Forward Reunion

"So we met her for lunch, and she told us her story," Amy continued. "Tell him about it, Mrs. Kramer."

"At thirty years of age, my husband died of cancer, leaving me, not with a fat life insurance pay out, but with over $20,000 in credit card debt and funeral expenses. The monthly payments on those debts were killing me. Every time the phone rang, I knew a debt collector would be on the other end, hounding and threatening me.

So I sold my house and moved into a condo to pay down my debts and reduce my expenses (and avoid mowing that blasted yard). Then, I took a weekend job. The extra job also helped keep my mind off of my grief. I worked like a dog to dig my way out of debt and get those accursed creditors off my back. In a little over four years, I paid those debts in full, on a day I refer to as 'one of the best days of my life.' I felt soooo free!

From that experience, I got a bad taste in my mouth about debt. I avoided it like the plague. I vowed to never again make credit card payments unless it was absolutely necessary.
I still owed about $15,000 on the condo, so I kept my weekend job, putting all my extra money into paying it down. I was amazed at how quickly I paid it off. I was totally debt free! Nobody could take my home from me. It was mine.

With very few expenses, I quit my weekend job and divided the money I used to make in payments into investments, travel and giving to worthy causes. So far, I've saved up about $500,000 toward an early retirement."

"From $20,000 in debt to $500,000 in savings!" reiterated Amy. "That was quite an impressive story – actually, a bit unbelievable at the time."

Amy continued. "From that short lunch, we knew that there was a lot more wisdom where that came from. And it was more than book wisdom. It came from her experience. She had beaten the system that was killing our parents. If we could learn her lessons at age 18, she could save us tons of headaches along the way."

"More than that," added James, "I decided that she just might hold the key to my dream of making a million dollars by my fortieth birthday and taking early retirement."

"My needs were more emotional," admitted Akashi. "My older siblings were academic overachievers. My parents drilled into me that 'A's in school would set me up for an 'A' career and an 'A' life. But somehow I'd botch up every class with 'C's and 'D's, which I thought would guarantee me a 'C-Minus' life. I was a loser, and felt that everyone saw a huge 'L' tattooed on my forehead. I acted tough, but was scared stiff at the thought of meeting with Mrs. Kramer. Yet, I felt that she offered a glimmer of hope. I was desperate. What did I have to lose?"

"We asked her if she would meet us for breakfast once a week," continued Amy, "to ask questions and learn more. She said that she'd love to, if we'd pay her $5.00 each per breakfast. She explained that it would be a good lesson for us to pay for wise counsel.

For the next year, we met with her every Saturday morning, here at *Hash Brown's*. Sometimes, we'd discuss a book for a month of meetings. Other times, we'd just ask questions. We'll just tell you about the meetings where she pulled out her notebook and covered new topics. Each week, she exposed us to stuff we'd never learned, either at school or at home. Those meetings changed our lives."

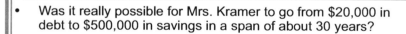

- Was it really possible for Mrs. Kramer to go from $20,000 in debt to $500,000 in savings in a span of about 30 years?

- What keeps most people from making such a dramatic turnaround?

- What could have kept Mrs. Kramer from getting into her predicament in the first place?

PART ONE

INVESTING MONEY

Breakfast #1: Discover the Basics

"I remember that first meeting well," volunteered Antonio, wincing. "I'll tell about the first two breakfasts.

So, I stroll in at 9:04 to find everyone there, waiting on me."

Flashback

Kramer: You're four minutes late!

Antonio: I have a hard time getting places on time.

Kramer: When you're late, you waste our time. Half of success, financial or otherwise, is showing up...*on time*. It's so important that I'll lay out some incentive. If you're late next week, you pay for the entire breakfast by yourself.

Fast Forward Reunion

"Everyone but me thought it a splendid idea, so my resistance was outvoted. I was more than a little ticked off, threatening that I just might not show up at all next week. Kramer nonchalantly replied that it was my choice. We learned quickly that if we wanted her advice, it would be on her terms, not ours. She ignored my pouty expression and continued."

Flashback

Kramer: So you want to learn how to handle your money. Well, if I talk the entire time, I don't get to eat. So let's do it this way. We order our food. While we wait for it to come, I tell a story or throw out five to ten minutes of advice while you think and jot down notes.

After the food comes, everyone throws in their thoughts. I want to know *your* experiences with the concept, good or bad. Take your best shots at my ideas. Too much education these days is merely transferring a set of notes from the teacher to the students, without it going through the minds of either.

I'm not easily offended. Tell me why it won't work for you. Your objections and comments will help us distill each concept into something that will work for *you*. At the end of each session, tell us what you want to deal with the next week. That way, we stay practical. Sound good to you?

(Everyone agreed as the waiter arrived to take our orders.)

Kramer: First, I'll pass out a sheet that should help you to lighten up on your parents. I know that you think they're totally incompetent buffoons with finances. I want you to understand the bigger picture of our culture, a big part of the reason for their money issues. Your parents' neighbors, friends and relatives probably handle their money the same way. They're just doing what their culture has taught them. When everybody's doing it, it's hard to question your way of life.

James: You're saying that if I were to live with my neighbors for awhile, I'd likely find the same financial problems that Mom and Dad have? I've assumed that their nice cars and smiling faces meant that they were better off than me.

Kramer: Wrong assumption. Here's the way many of your friends and neighbors manage their money.

Personal Finances in America

According to surveys:

- Ninety-seven percent of workers over 45 say they regret how they spent their money, in light of how much they could have saved.[1]

- Almost one in four adults live paycheck to paycheck.[2]

- Fifty-nine percent of Americans don't save regularly.[3]

- We're getting worse and worse at saving.[4]

    Twenty-five years ago, Americans saved over ten percent of their income.

    Ten years ago, we saved 4.5 percent.

    By 2005, for the first time since the Great Depression, we spent more than we earned.

- Approximately 1,500,000 Americans declare personal bankruptcy each year.[5]

- The average college student graduates with over $20,000 in debt.[6]

- Most Americans haven't even calculated how much money they need to retire.[7]

- Personal debt is reaching record highs, and personal savings is reaching all time lows.[8]

James: That's insane! I'd hoped that retirement would be the time for me to say goodbye to the eight to five grind and relax at a beach house. If I follow the crowd in finances, I'll be worrying about money the rest of my life!

Akashi: One in four adults living paycheck to paycheck? Talk about risky living! And adults complain about teens' risky behaviors! A short-term job loss or illness could put them in serious debt and make them lose their houses.

Amy: The scary side of it for me is that if we don't do something different, we'll all be over $20,000 in debt in about six years. Then we'll go to work and live paycheck to paycheck, until we retire in a low rent district, watching *Wheel of Fortune* on one of our four antenna stations, constantly whining about how we regret the way we lived our lives and don't have enough money to have any fun.

Akashi: Our kids will probably hate our visits, assuming we're there to ask for another handout!

Kramer: Exactly! Somehow, you've got to break loose from a culture that's gone crazy with its finances. Many dig themselves into a deeper hole every day, enjoying life less and less as they spend everything they've got to pay off past debts. In the land of the free, they've become financially enslaved.

(Kramer gets a wild look in her eyes, more animated with each sentence as she rises from her seat.)

You're already different from the mainstream. That's why I relate to you. I challenge you to extend your independent thinking and counterculture attitudes to your finances.

And to that end (she pulls back a glass ketchup bottle high overhead with both hands, waving it menacingly in the air), I christen this group (she brings the bottle back down with increasing speed, aimed directly at the table), THE COUNTERCULTURE CLUB!

(She pulls back the bottle at the last second, missing the table, but sending her students scattering all directions. Kramer erupts into laughter.)

Amy: You scared me to death! Did you really have to embarrass us in front of all these people to make that point?

Kramer: A little adrenaline is good to help cement points in your memory. You'll never forget this moment. Plus, if you never get over the "Oh my gosh, what's everybody gonna think?" thing, you'll find yourself living everyone else's life, the life of your culture, rather than your own life. I like a little drama now and again to spice things up. Later today I'll get a good laugh out of picturing your faces as you envisioned ketchup exploding all over the restaurant.

James: (Settling back into his chair.) A good laugh at our expense! Don't be surprised if you find toilet paper in your yard from your favorite club to test your own embarrassment index. So where were we? Something about how our culture sucks at finances?

Kramer: From the stats on my handout, you know how NOT to handle your finances – the way most others handle *their* finances. You've seen it in your parents and now in the culture at large. Let's transition to how we can do finances *right*. This being the first breakfast, let's start with an overview – some basics of financial wisdom. In the coming weeks, we'll devote entire breakfasts to each principle.

But instead of handing out the list, I want you to draw out the basics from a real person who went counterculture with her finances. From decades of teaching, I've found that students remember stories better than lists; plus, stories are more interesting. As I tell the story, jot down the principles that you think made the person successful.

Osceola Enjoys Life and Saves a Fortune

Some of us might fear that we'll never have enough money to make ends meet and enjoy life. What if your job doesn't pay well, and you can't seem to get ahead? I want to introduce you to Oseola, who has a lot to teach us. She didn't have the advantages of most of us, yet she enjoyed life and saved a ton.

Oseola grew up in a simple house with her grandmother, mother and an aunt. As an eight-year-old, she would wash clothes after school to help make ends meet. Her school education ended at age 12, when she dropped out to care for her sick aunt and work full time at washing.

So far, she's not on anyone's "most likely to succeed" list.

Her work was hard, but she enjoyed it. She washed the old-fashioned way: building a fire under her wash pot, then soaking, washing and boiling a bundle of clothes. Rub. Wrench. Rub again. Rinse. Starch. Hang out to dry. She worked Monday through Saturday, for 75 years, until arthritis forced her into retirement at age 86. She never got to finish school, never had a car and owned few possessions. Her TV received only one station. But that didn't bother her because she never watched it very much anyway.

I can hear you thinking, "Get a life, woman!" But, you see, Oseola *did* have a life – a great life. She didn't desire travel or possessions. She loved her God, her family and her work. Singing and storytelling filled her days with joy and laughter.

She never bought on credit so that she would be financially free. And since she didn't need money for a lot of possessions or travel, she invested it, a little each month. By July 1995, a half year after her retirement, she had saved – get this – $280,000. That's over a quarter of a million dollars! Then, she stunned the world by giving away over half of it, $150,000, to establish a college scholarship for needy students, offering others the education she never had.

Until recently, Oseola McCarty referred to herself as a "poor little old colored woman who walked everywhere." No one paid her much attention when she was out. But when the word leaked out about her donation, the world took notice.

She has since received numerous awards, been interviewed on ABC, CNN, NBC, BET and MTV. She's béen featured in *Newsweek*, *The New York Times*, *People*, *Life*, *Ebony*, *Essence* and *Jet*. But all that recognition never changed her simple life. You see, she didn't *need* all the recognition. In her own words, "I think my secret was contentment. I was happy with what I had."[9]

Now, compare her to most Americans. Many with huge salaries haven't managed to save a cent. Many are worth less than nothing, worrying constantly about their debts. But Oseola shows me that if she can save over a quarter of a million dollars by washing people's clothes in boiling water over a fire, I can save money as a schoolteacher.

So, what do you think?

Reflections on Oseola

Akashi: I'll start. I think her life sucked. She spent her entire life in a hovel working the same crappy job day in and day out, with only one TV channel for entertainment. She didn't even own a car. What kind of life is that?

Antonio: Akashi! Mrs. Kramer is trying to help us out here. Don't be so hard on her!

Kramer: I'm the one who sets the ground rules, and I challenge you to be just as outspoken as Akashi. If you other three sit there smiling at each other and sipping your juice while disagreeing in your gut, we're getting nowhere. Say what you think. Be ruthless.

Jack Welch, one of the greatest business leaders of our time, devoted an entire chapter of his book *Winning* to push for *candor*.[10] He observes that we usually don't tell it like it is, fearing we'll hurt people's feelings. He thinks lack of candor is deadly to business.

Lack of candor may be easier in the short-run, but it hurts us in the long-run. Without candor, we don't face reality. Be honest, guys! Do you agree with Akashi?

Antonio: I'll be candid with you, Akashi. In ISS you complained about your parents being so wrapped up in their work and living in a ritzy neighborhood that they didn't have time for the important stuff, like family.

Oseola chose relationships over things. She enjoyed working at home, spending time with her relatives and helping others. She didn't secretly desire to get the latest version of Halo or go to Disneyland. She lived life the way she wanted to, had lots of fun and can look back with the satisfaction of knowing she helped others along the way.

Think of Einstein. He never drove a car. He enjoyed thinking more than mansions and hot cars.

Akashi: You nailed me. As much as I complain about my parents' obsession with things and money, I'm pretty hooked on some of my things, like always upgrading to the latest cell phone, playing online games till late at night and the freedom that my car gives me.

But fun is different for everyone. I *do* admire Oseola for bucking the crowd, choosing her own path, finding financial freedom and putting people first.

Kramer: We don't have to adopt *everything* about her life. But what *can* we learn from her financial success?

James: I'm astounded that she could accumulate such wealth from what must have been a pitiful salary.

Amy: I think it's actually pretty simple. She spent less than she made. With no car, low-cost housing and no frivolous spending, she could save more than a lawyer who has a great salary but spends it all on his ritzy house and payments on his Porsche. The first thing I learned from Oseola is: **Live beneath your means.** All of our parents make tons more than Oseola, but I'll bet you that everything they get on Friday is spent by the next Thursday. You can't save if you spend all that you make.

Akashi: Look not only at what she *did*, but what she *didn't* do. She didn't own even one credit card. Whereas most of us spend outrageous money in interest, she waited till she could pay cash. I'll bet that one habit saved her thousands and thousands of dollars.

Kramer: You bet right, Akashi. In Oseola's own words,

> *"I save my money till I can buy something outright."*[11]

Akashi: So, principle number two is: **Avoid paying interest.**

Antonio: Principle number three: **Save for the future.** If she had a medical emergency, she wouldn't have to sell her house to pay for it.

James: She took the money that she would have been paying the credit card companies and invested it, so that she was *receiving* interest rather than giving it away. Over time, it all added up. Principle number four: **Invest over time.**

Antonio: She worked hard at something she enjoyed. Even a small salary adds up when you put in the hours.

Kramer: I think you've summed up the basics of financial wisdom. Think about those principles this week, and see how they apply to your personal finances. In future weeks, we'll talk in much more depth about each principle. What do you want to cover next week?

James: I'm fascinated with how Oseola multiplied her money. I want to be financially independent as quickly as possible. How can investments multiply my money so that I can retire in my 40's?

Kramer: Is that okay with everyone else?

(Nods all around)

Hmmmmm...

- What facts from the "Personal Finances in America" sheet bother you the most? Why?

- Why do you think Americans struggle with their finances?

- How would your personal finances be different if you handled them more like Oseola?

- Are you living above or below your means? How could you begin living below your means and saving some money each week?

- What can you do this week to start handling your money better?

Resource to Take You Deeper

**Read Oseola McCarty, *Simple Wisdom for Rich Living*
(Atlanta: Longstreet Press, 1996).**

Assignment

This week, ask your parents to tell you what they know about investments. Go on the Internet and read some basic articles on stocks and mutual funds. Next week, bring your calculators. What I'll tell you is so extraordinary that you won't believe it unless you see the numbers yourselves.

One more thing! I have a riddle for you to solve:

To some I'm their greatest nightmare
To others their greatest friend.
Neither spirit nor flesh
I'm not hard to comprehend.

I increase the wealth
Of both paupers and kings,
Rewarding the wise,
Robbing fools of their dreams.

I work when you work
Just as hard when you sleep.
With me Buffett made billions
If you sow, you can also reap.

I'm slow at the beginning
'Till my power is unfurled.
It's why bankers and investors say,
"You're the eighth wonder of the world."

Breakfast #2: Catch the Vision

HASH BROWN'S BREAKFAST BAR, SATURDAY MORNING, 9:00 AM.

(Antonio enters, wearing a white button down shirt, a shirt-tail hanging out, glasses cocked up on one side, hair frazzled, a massive pocket saver with colored pencils and a killer calculator fit for an aerospace engineer.)

Kramer: So, you decided to dress for success as an accountant?

Antonio: That's right. If we're using calculators, I should dress the part.

Akashi: Scary. It looks almost natural for you. Is that the real you, Antonio?

Antonio: I assumed that the *real* you wouldn't even *own* a calculator. Did you grab one at Wal-Mart on the way?

Akashi: Quite perceptive, Antonio. I sacrificed an entire $2.95.

Antonio: Are you sure it will do all the advanced functions, like subtraction and multiplication?

(Mrs. Kramer followed Antonio and Akashi's bantering with interest. "More playful than mean-spirited," she thought. "Hmmm…. Was that a flash of resentment in her eye…or perhaps…a twinkle?")

Kramer: I think you two ought to settle your differences outside of this meeting, say, a Sunday picnic at Lake Acworth. What do you think?

Antonio: *(Obviously taken off guard.)* I…I…I'm not sure Akashi would be into a picnic.

Akashi: Why not? 1:00 Sunday at the Pavilion. Pick me up at 12:45. Don't be late and don't *dare* wear that outfit.

Antonio: Fine!...I guess….

Kramer: Risk. Antonio and Akashi just took a calculated risk. Maybe the picnic won't go so well. But maybe it will. One thing's for certain, if you're not willing to diversify your friendships by getting to know new people, you may never find the right person.

That's a great introduction to investing. Not all investments turn out great. They all require a degree of risk. But *not* investing also carries risk, just like not meeting new people. With investing, you've got to start somewhere, take a calculated risk and diversify so that if two investments bomb, the other eight will make up for them.

You minimize your risk with your knowledge. You've simply *got* to understand what you're doing.

But here I go, rambling on without a story to base it on. As we wait for our food, let me tell you about a little boy named Warren. Jot down lessons from his life on your napkins as I talk.

Warren Loves Investing

Warren was born in 1930, in the midst of the Great Depression, which stripped his dad of his job and savings. They had food to eat, but that was about all. Perhaps those bleak years built into Warren an early passion to pursue money.

He decided to get rich, very rich. The vision took hold of him before he was five and never left him. From that early age, he passionately pursued his goal.[1]

Seriously ill at age seven, he prophetically told a nurse, "I don't have much money now, but someday I will and I'll have my picture in the paper." In elementary school, he'd tell his classmates that he planned to be rich before his 35th birthday.[2]

His early pursuits seemed endless:

- At age five, he set up a stand in front of his house and sold Chicklets – those tiny, candy-coated pieces of chewing gum. Then he progressed to lemonade, finding a better location at his friend's house on a busier street.[3]

- On vacation at Lake Okoboji at age six, he bought a six-pack of Cokes and sold them at a profit of five cents per Coke.. (Interestingly, as an adult, he would buy up a huge chunk of the Coca Cola Company, one of his greatest investments.[4]

- Before age 11, he hired neighborhood kids to find golf balls and paid others to sell them, taking his cut. He caddied for golfers at the Omaha Country Club for $3 a day.[5]

But Warren's interest went further than merely *making* money. He thought long and hard about *investing* money. By age 11, he'd earned enough to begin investing, so he bought three shares of Cities Service preferred **stock** for $114 (that's over $1,500 in 2008 dollars!)[6], which he later sold at a profit.

In the 8th grade, a family friend asked Warren about his drive to make money. "It's not that I *want* money," he explained. "It's the fun of making money and watching it grow."[7]

He continued the pattern of working, saving and investing. And he read everything he could find about business and finance. He grew a paper route into a profitable business, so that at the age of 14, he invested $1,200 (over $12,000 in today's money) in forty acres of Nebraska farmland.[8]

Define: Stock

A single bit of a company that investors buy and sell. If you own 100 percent of a company's stock, you own the entire company. Stocks are also called "equities."

You probably picture Warren at this point as wearing the sharpest clothes, having the best toys and flashing his wealth around. But Warren couldn't have cared less about impressing others. Norma Jean Thurston, a high school classmate, remembers that Warren wore the same tennis shoes year-round, which made him come across as a country bumpkin. Fellow students would joke about it. Norma Jean noted,

> *"Most of us were trying to be like everyone else. ...I think he liked being different. ...He was what he was and he never tried to be anything else."*[9]

Before Reading On...

Reflect: What you can learn from the story?

Warren and a friend, Donald Danley, bought a used pinball machine and enjoyed playing it for hours. Then, they decided to put it in a barber shop and split the profits with the barber. Donald was mechanically inclined, so he fixed the machine when it broke. Warren did the accounting. It went so well that they bought two more and placed them in other barber shops.[10]

By high school graduation, Warren had read over 100 business books and earned over $5,000 (over $47,000 in today's money) during summers and after school. From his paper routes, pinball machines and rent from a tenant farmer, he was earning more money than his teachers.[11]

In college, he studied investing under Benjamin Graham, a respected authority on investing. Graham later became his mentor. By college graduation, Warren had saved $9,800 (over $75,000 in today's money), which he spent full-time investing, along with other people's money.[12]

By age 31, four years ahead of his elementary school goal, he'd multiplied his savings to $1,000,000.[13] He kept multiplying that money with rapidly compounding interest until he became the wealthiest man in the world, with a net worth of $62 Billion in 2008. His full name is Warren Buffet.

He never spent the money on extravagant living, always intending to give the bulk of it away. Today he lives in a modest house, the same one he bought in 1958 for $31,500.[14] He drives a modest car and buys his Cokes when they're on sale.[15]

He loves his work of researching companies so much that he describes his typical workday as beginning with tap-dancing into the office. Besides his work, his pleasures are simple: playing bridge with his friends, eating a good hamburger at Dairy Queen and washing it down with a Cherry Coke. He probably enjoys it all the more, knowing that he owns a huge portion of both The Coca Cola Company and DQ. So if his tastes are simple, what does he want to do with all that money? His intent from the start was to use his wealth to make a positive impact on the world. He recently committed to give away billions to worthy causes.[16]

So, my budding financial wizards, what can we learn from Warren?

Amy: Start early. Think about it. As a kid, he had no expenses: no car, no house payments, no children to feed and his tax rate would have been low. At an age when most of us were watching hours of TV and playing video games, he was saving mounds of cash. I can't imagine someone today saving $47,000 by high school graduation! By starting so early, his money had more time to grow.[17]

Antonio: **Work hard.** Think of the physical and mental energy he put into his work.

James: The mental energy…I suppose that stood out to me. I work a lot, but I don't *study* business. He didn't just work *hard*; he worked *smart*. Devoured one hundred business books by graduation? I've not read even one. **He had a passion to grow in wisdom and found a mentor he could learn from.**

Akashi: He was his own person, doing what he loved, regardless of what anyone else thought. Although, in my opinion, he seemed overly obsessed with money, I admire him for charting his own course.

James: I like how **he tried various ventures**, from selling Chiclets to putting video games in barber shops to running a paper route to finding and selling golf balls. If one business didn't go well, maybe another would. And hey, these are all ventures that *I* could do. It's not like he programmed a computer operating system or invented the microchip.

Amy: He lived way beneath his means so that he could save, something my parents haven't learned to this day. Honestly, it would be difficult for me to have $1,000 lying around and not find something cool to buy with it.

Antonio: And what he saved, **he invested** in land and stocks. But I don't get it. How could $9,800 grow to billions through investing?

Kramer: It's called compounding interest. You won't believe it unless you figure it out yourselves on your calculators. Antonio, you won't need all those higher functions. **Basically, all you need to know is the difference between addition and multiplication**, something that most people haven't thought through. Let's start with a couple of examples:

(She pulls out a checkerboard and a zip-lock bag full of wheat grain.)

Multiplying Grain

Let's start with addition. I'm placing one grain of wheat on the first block, two on the second and three on the third. If I continue this pattern of adding one grain per block, how many grains will I have on the 64th block?

Amy: That's easy. Sixty-four grains.

Kramer: Now fasten your seatbelts. We're moving into multiplication. Let's start again with one grain of wheat on the first square, but this time we *double* it for the second square, so that you have two grains on the second square, four on the third square. Now you tell me: how many are on the fourth square?

James: Eight.

Kramer: How many on the fifth square?

Amy: Sixteen.

Kramer: Now let's get out those calculators and have some fun. Put 16 on your calculator and multiply times 2 for the sixth square, times 2 for the seventh square. How many squares until the number's so huge that your calculator display won't even hold it? That's a lot of grain!

Multiplication starts slowly, *deceptively* slowly, but do you see what happens once it starts taking off?

Let's compare addition to multiplication. By *adding* 1 to each square, we ended up with 64 grains on the 64th square. How many grains do you think would be in that 64th square if we kept multiplying times two? The answer?

(Kramer starts getting that wild look in her eyes, as she stands up for dramatic effect.)

Enough grain to cover the entire country of India 50 feet deep! That's the incredible power of multiplication![18]

(Dead silence and incredulous looks from all four students.)

Multiplying Paper

(Kramer doesn't think they get it yet, so she sits back down and takes out a sheet of notebook paper.)

"Let's imagine that this paper is 1/1000 of an inch thick. James, tear it in half and stack one on top of the other. How thick is it now?

James: Two thousandths of an inch.

Kramer: Multiplication starts out *deceptively* slowly. Don't forget that. Tear it again to make it 4/1000 of an inch and again for 8/1000 of an inch.

Amy: That paper's so thin that we're getting nowhere.

Kramer: It starts deceptively slow, Amy. *Deceptively slow.* But imagine that we were to tear it and stack it 50 times. Remember, it's doubling in height each time. How high do you think the paper would be?

Antonio: I'm starting to catch on. As high as the ceiling?

James: I'll guess as high as this building.

Kramer: And the answer is (dramatic pause), approximately 17,000,000 miles high, about the distance of 34 trips to the moon![19]

Antonio: That's hard to believe. From 1/1000 of an inch to 17,000,000 miles in only 50 doubles?

Kramer: Try it on your calculator when you get home. Trust me for now.

Multiplying Money

Let's move on from multiplying grain and paper to multiplying money. How did multiplication allow Warren Buffett to catapult his $9,800 into billions?

With his dogged research and brilliant understanding of companies, he was able to get an extremely high return on his investments. If you double your money every few years, it multiplies beyond your wildest dreams, just like doubling grain and paper. Investors call it "compounding interest," or "compounding growth." It's been called "the eighth wonder of the world."[20] The more you think about it, the more it seems like magic.

Akashi: That's all great for Buffett, who loves studying businesses and can choose just the right stocks. But I can't see myself tap dancing into a lonely office to study businesses all day. I assume you've got to do that to predict which business will do better than average.

Kramer: Actually, you don't have to be a Warren Buffett to get multiplication working for you. I'm with you; I don't want to spend my weekends pouring through the financial reports of businesses. I invest in stocks the lazy, easy way, with **Mutual Funds.**

Akashi: My parents told me about stock mutual funds. So an investment company pools lots of people's money to buy stock in lots of companies. That spreads my risk through many companies. But won't some of those companies go down in value?

Kramer: True, but others will go up. When you average them all together, over the long-haul, the return is still good enough to multiply your money incredibly. I'll give you an example.

A *Total Stock Market Index Fund* tries to track the behavior of the entire stock market by investing in many different types of businesses. If you buy some shares of the fund, you own a little bit of utility companies, real estate companies, hospitals, pharmaceuticals, retail stores, oil companies, high tech companies — well, you get the idea.

Since 1926, stocks have averaged a return of slightly over 10 percent per year.[21] Some years they go down; some years they go up. But if you kept the stocks through the good and bad times, you'd have averaged over 10 percent.

Let's say you save up $5,000 and invest it at the age of twenty in a Total Stock Market Index Fund. In the coming weeks we'll talk more about what this is. Trust me for now.

If it grows at an average of 10 percent per year, how many years will it take that $5,000 to double to $10,000?

You figure it by taking 10 percent of $5,000 (5000 x .10) and adding it back to the $5,000, giving you $5,500 after the first year. To figure the second year, take 10 percent of the $5,500 and add it back in. Do it for each new year until it's doubled. Got it?

Men and women, to your calculators!

(Antonio whips his out of his shirt pocket with bravado.)

HOW THEY CALCULATED IT

Starting with $5,000

Year One: $5,500
($5,000 x .10 = $500. $5,000 + $500 = $5,500)

Year Two: $6,050
($5,500 x .10 = $550. $5,500 + $550 = $6,050)

Year Three: $6,655
Year Four: $7,320
Year Five: $8,052
Year Six: $8,857
Year Seven: $9,742
Year Eight: $10,716

Define: Mutual Funds

Investments where investors pool their money into stocks, bonds, and/or cash equivalents. Mutual funds make investing easier, cheaper and safer.

Amy: (Raising her hand in triumph) It doesn't work out exactly, but it doubles approximately every seven years.

Antonio: OK, so it grew by $5,000 in seven years. It still looks like it's gonna take forever to accumulate anything significant.

Kramer: Like most people, you've been deceived. Remember, *multiplication starts out slowly.* **Don't think of it as *making* $5,000 in seven years. Think of it as *doubling* in seven years.** In each succeeding set of seven years, you'll make increasingly more than $5,000 because you're *multiplying* rather than *adding*.

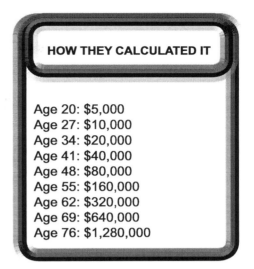

HOW THEY CALCULATED IT

Age 20: $5,000
Age 27: $10,000
Age 34: $20,000
Age 41: $40,000
Age 48: $80,000
Age 55: $160,000
Age 62: $320,000
Age 69: $640,000
Age 76: $1,280,000

Estimating Investment Growth, With Only Three Calculator Keys

Kramer: So at age 20, you started with $5,000. Seven years later, at age 27, you've doubled that to about $10,000. Now it's much easier to figure. It will double approximately every seven years. Back to your calculators! How many years will it take before you have a million dollars?

Akashi: So all I have to do is put $5,000 into my calculator and hit three keys: "x", "2" and "="?

Kramer: Right. It's incredibly easy. For investing, Buffett never uses Algebra. He says that, "If calculus were required, I'd have to go back to delivering papers."[22]

James: (Raising his hand and glancing an "I beat you!" look at Amy) You'll have your million somewhere between the ages of 69 and 76.

The Laws of 10's and 7's

Kramer: We just used the **"Laws of 10's and 7's,"** two of the most useful tools for estimating your return on investments.

Here they are:

MONEY INVESTED AT **10** PERCENT INTEREST DOUBLES APPROXIMATELY EVERY **7** YEARS.

MONEY INVESTED AT **7** PERCENT INTEREST DOUBLES APPROXIMATELY EVERY **10** YEARS.

Remember these. We'll keep using them in the coming weeks so that they'll become second nature to you.

Reflections

Kramer: Okay guys, what are your thoughts?

Akashi: It's not just that we made $1,000,000, but that we made it *with so little effort.* In fact, once we made the investment, there was no effort, time or work needed on our part. It's almost like the money did the work.

Kramer: Killer point, Akashi! It's *passive* rather than *active.* Money gurus put it this way:

Don't just work for your money; get your money working for you.

If a car hit you at the age of 21 and you lay in a coma until the age of 74, you'd wake up and still have your million. While you were sleeping, your money was working, silently but relentlessly, in the background.

The Rule of 72

The "Laws of 10's and 7's" works only for interest rates of 7 percent and 10 percent. To estimate your money's growth at any interest rate, divide 72 by the interest rate to discover how many years it will take your investment to double.

You invested $1000 in a long-term bond that will average 6 percent interest. It will double in 72 / 6 = 12 years. (Note: neither "The Laws of 10's and 7's" nor "The Rule of 72" are exact, but they are close enough to help us estimate returns and grasp the power of doubling.)

Amy: I'm impressed with the difference between the yearly increases from the early years to the latter years. In the first seven years, you made only $5,000. But in the final seven years, your money made $640,000! In the next seven years, it would add well over $1,000,000! It's like your money gets better at making money as the years go by.

Antonio: I'll bet a lot of people get itchy fingers during those slow, early years. They put $5,000 into a fund that makes another $5,000 in seven years and they think, "That's not very much. I'll never get rich at this rate." So they take the money out and buy a country club membership instead.

Amy: (tap, tap, tap) On early investing…let's say that I have a twin sister. I start investing at age 20, but she puts off starting to invest until age 27. Most would think, "Big deal. You'll be investing for 50 years, what difference could a seven year lag mean?" Actually, it means that my money gets to double one more time than hers, so that when we're both age 62 she's got $160,000, and I've got twice that much: $320,000.

Kramer: Since doubling starts out so slowly, few multiply it out to understand **the power of that last double.**[23]

Remember the Oseola story from last week? When someone asked about her secret to multiplying her money she said,

> **"The secret of building a fortune is compounding interest.**
> *It's not the ones who make big money, but the ones who*
> *know how to save who get ahead.* **You've got to leave your**
> **investment alone long enough for it to increase.**"[24]

Very few people can think long term. Buffett was the greatest. He'd have a hard time spending $500 on something trivial today, knowing that it could become over $50,000 in 50 years, if invested at 10% interest.

James: Two problems. First, that's not soon enough for me. I don't want to wait until I'm 74 to get my million dollars. I'm afraid I'll be so old that I can't enjoy it. I'd like to have it at least by the time I'm 45. Second, since I failed to save up as early as Buffett, I think all my early savings will go toward college. Realistically, in four years, I'll graduate with nothing to invest.

Kramer: What do you guys recommend to James?

Antonio: I suppose that after college graduation, at age 22, he could start putting in a portion of his salary each month. Just do the math and see how much he'd have to put in each month to make his million at the age he decides.

Kramer: Good suggestion. Most of us will invest little by little over time, rather than all at once. Let me crank up my computer and surf to one of those online interest calculators. We can thank Hash Brown for making his restaurant into an internet hot spot last year. Amy, would you mind taking the computer and running the numbers? Just Google "interest calculator" and you'll find scads of them.

Amy: My pleasure!

Multiplying an Average Salary

Kramer: The average teacher in the USA made $46,000 this year.[25] Let's assume that James earns a teacher's salary. Of course, he'd make less starting out and more as he got older. But to simplify matters, let's say he makes $46,000 from the start. At age 22, he puts 1/10 of his monthly salary ($383) into a mutual fund which grows at an average of 10 percent per year. At what age can he retire as a millionaire?

Amy: In 31 years, at age 53, he'd have over $1,070,000!

James: Yeeeehaaa! Independence Day! Sooner! Sooner! How can I get my million sooner, say in my 30's?

Amy: Invest more than 10 percent each month, or start investing earlier.

Kramer: That works.

Akashi: What if he could get more than 10 percent interest? Some companies gain 20 percent or more in a year. Why not invest in them?

Kramer: IF you can figure out which companies will beat the market. That's a big "IF." To get higher returns, people take more risk. Some do well at predicting stocks, but the great majority lose money playing the stock market. "Get rich quick" schemes don't usually have happy endings.

But I'll have to admit that some investors beat the market over time. That's the way the great Buffett did it. Incredibly, he averaged over 29 percent per year!

James: Throw that 29 percent into that online interest calculator!

Amy: Let's see. Starting at age 22 with nothing, the average teacher would invest one tenth of her salary at $383 per month. If she got 29 percent interest, she'd be a millionaire in 15 years, at age 37.

James: So *that's* how Buffett did it. He saved his money and invested it early at an incredible rate. It made him a millionaire in his 30's, a billionaire later.

Kramer: But Buffett's the best of the best. He rules the investing world like no other. His mind works in a way that's superbly suited for understanding businesses. Plus, he absolutely loves spending his days thinking about businesses. He's obsessed with it![26]

James: But even if I could get a couple of percentage points above that 10 percent....

Kramer: Perhaps. And some do. We'll talk about that at a later breakfast.

My big point today is this: by starting early and investing 10 percent of a teacher's salary in an index fund to match the market rate, you will likely have a million dollars in your early 50's.

I'll let next week's guest, who knows a lot about investing, tell you about the possibilities and pitfalls of trying to beat the market.

Antonio: Do we need to wear suits?

Kramer: (Laughing.) Not for *this* investor. He'd probably be more comfortable if you dressed like hippies and greeted him with a peace sign.

The Riddle

Amy: Before we leave, may I guess the answer to the riddle?

Kramer: Take a swing.

Amy: Is it "money"?

Antonio: But how does money "rob fools"?

Akashi: I don't understand how every line applies, but is it "compound interest"?

Kramer: Bravo! Let's take apart the riddle with what we learned today.

> ***To some I'm their greatest nightmare***
> ***To others their greatest friend.***

How could compound interest be someone's "greatest nightmare"?

Antonio: When it's working against him, like a huge credit card debt at 16 percent interest.

> ***Neither spirit nor flesh***
> ***I'm not hard to comprehend.***

Akashi: It *is* pretty simple. You're just multiplying times two.

> ***I increase the wealth***
> ***Of both paupers and kings***

James: It works for anyone who invests wisely.

> ***Rewarding the wise***
> ***Robbing fools of their dreams.***

Amy: Again, Buffett *receives* interest while the foolish *pay* interest.

> ***I'll work for you when you work***
> ***Just as hard when you sleep.***

Antonio: If Buffett fell into a coma, compound interest would keep working.

> ***Buffett used me to make his billions.***
> ***If you sow, you can also reap.***
>
> ***I'm slow at the beginning,***
> ***Till my power is unfurled.***

Amy: *Deceptively* slow at the beginning, until it's multiplying greater amounts.

> ***It's why bankers and investors say,***
> ***"You're the eighth wonder of the world."***

Kramer: It's true. Money managers recognize its magic, its wonder. Reflect on it this week. Pound it out on those calculators. Slowly, its magic will dawn upon you as well.

What are the main points you want to walk away with?

Summing it Up

Akashi: *Work hard and save now, while I'm mooching off my parents and don't have a lot of expenses.*

James: *Start investing early so that my money has time to multiply.*

Amy: *Even a little invested regularly grows wildly, crazily, given enough time.*

Antonio: *I don't have to be a lawyer or doctor to make a million.*

The Hand Plan

Akashi, you've just got to let the gang in on that cool memory device you came up with this week.

Akashi: OK. I have a hard time memorizing stuff in classes. So, I make up these crazy visual ways of remembering things. I didn't want to forget what we'd learned from Oseola, so I figured out a way to remember it on my hand. It seems to work with Warren Buffett's life as well. Antonio calls it "The Hand Plan." I took pics of my brother's hand and printed it all on a sheet of paper. Mrs. Kramer helped me word it and added her thoughts.

James: Cool! Let's see it!

Akashi: Here's what it looks like:

Catch a vision! **(Thumbs up)** Most aim at nothing...and hit it every time. Buffett caught his financial vision in elementary school and never let it go. A long-range goal transforms accumulating wealth into a fun game.

Work hard! **(Finger pointing at you like a foreman)** Most first-generation millionaires say they work harder than most people. Buffett and Sam Walton (founder of Wal-Mart) began early with paper routes and odd jobs. Oseola worked hard all her life.

Get Wisdom! **(Central Finger)** This includes sharpening your skills and growing in knowledge. If you're the most skilled in your trade, you'll likely be the best paid and least likely to be fired during a recession. Buffett read over 100 business books by his high school graduation.

Commit Yourself to Live Waaayyy Beneath Your Means! (Ring Finger) Many millionaires work the same jobs as average people, but they have learned to live cheaply so they can save and invest.

Invest Regularly! (Pinky) It may be small, but investing $20 a week starting early in life can multiply into millions.

So what's it all for? To buy bigger toys? To impress people?

HELP OTHERS! (Lend a Hand) The fun of having money goes beyond having more things. Money allows us to help others in need and make a difference in the world. Buffett always planned on giving it away. Many studies show that giving people are happier people.

Kramer: What a "handy" summary! Thanks Akashi!

- What keeps most of us from saving and investing while we're young?

- Which of Buffett's habits have you already adopted?

- Where do you fall short?

- How do you think young Warren managed to buck the crowd and resist spending all his money during his youth?

- What can you take away from this breakfast to help you do better with your money this week?

Assignment
Between Breakfasts

1. Study up on stocks and mutual funds on the web. Know what they are.

2. Ask your parents and friends what they know about investing in stocks.

3. Come up with at least five good questions about investing in stocks.

Resources to Take You Deeper

Alice Schroeder, *The Snowball: Warren Buffett and the Business of Life* (New York, Bantam Books, 2008). Not yet published as I write, this authorized biography (based upon hundreds of hours interviewing Buffett), should give new insights into his remarkable life.

Roger Lowenstein, *Buffett: The Making of an American Capitalist* (New York: Main Street Books, 1995). I'm especially intrigued by the early chapters detailing Buffett's childhood through college years. It's a great example of the power of early earning and investing.

For a more detailed and teachable description of "The Hand Plan," see www.enjoyyourmoney.org.

Breakfast #3: Don't Lose Money in Stocks

COMMON MISTAKES THAT SEPARATE SMART PEOPLE FROM THEIR MONEY

> *"With enough inside information and a million dollars, you can go broke in a year."*
> — **Warren Buffett**[1]

Fast Forward to Reunion

Akashi: Larry, *I'll* tell you about the next session. Antonio and I were becoming a hot item. Plus, Hash Brown's warnings saved me from a lot of expensive mistakes.

Kramer: Not to be rude, Akashi, but I want to warn Larry about something.

If you're not ready to start investing, just skip these two sessions on stocks. They're pretty detailed, and I don't want you to get discouraged and give up rather than hear the rest of the sessions, which are more critical to you right now.

Larry: I'm not ready to start investing, but I'm very curious to understand stocks better. People come in all the time bragging about buying or selling this stock or that. I can't figure out if they're super-smart or just gambling away their money.

Kramer: Well, it's pretty detailed. But the payoff is that if you grasp how stocks work, you can see right through much of the crap that your customers, relatives, newspapers and many financial magazines will throw at you.

Flashback

Kramer: So how did the date go, Antonio and Akashi?

Akashi: He's pretty nice and a lot of fun. With a little training, I think he could be a great guy.

Antonio: You failed to mention my drop dead good looks. The picnic was nice. Then, we played some disc golf and rented a canoe. We only tipped over twice. Glad I'd insisted on life jackets. We both like the outdoors and great conversation. She's cool, but whooo is she opinionated!

(Akashi laughs.)

Antonio: I think if I want to keep seeing her, my two key words need to be, "Yes dear!"

Akashi: OK, so I *am* opinionated and outspoken. But if Antonio could be a little more decisive, *he* could have decided what to eat and where to look for canoes.

Kramer: Sounds like a good start. You're getting to know each other. Even if you never go out again, are you glad you went out once?

Akashi and Antonio together: Sure!

Antonio: It was fun. Much better than spending the afternoon watching TV.

Kramer: Risk. In their case, like a good investment, it paid off. Even if it had gone sour, they'd have learned something about themselves and each other. All they'd have lost would have been a couple of TV shows. Think you'll go out again?

Akashi: We're headed to the movies tonight.

James: Cool! But don't spend all that investment money!

Kramer: Good point! Life's a balancing act. Try to save for tomorrow without cramping today. I think you can achieve both. But, it takes some thought. Many Americans get into such debt that they're financially strapped today *and* worried about tomorrow. That's financial bondage. That's why we're questioning our culture and trying to find a better way. We're going counterculture.

Review

Kramer: So, what have you been mulling over from last week?

James: Wealth isn't just for the privileged few, like lawyers, doctors and movie stars. It's for regular people with regular salaries. The power of multiplication is absolutely crazy, almost unbelievable, magical. I've had to keep pulling out my calculator to run those figures again and again. It's simple, yet I'll bet not one in 1000 people understand it! Somehow, I want to start multiplying my money – the sooner the better.

Kramer: Good summary. I heard that Einstein called compound interest

"The greatest mathematical discovery of all time."[2]

There are many ways to get your money to start multiplying. Next week, we'll talk about some of those ways.

But this week, we'll talk about something that may be even more important than *multiplying* your money. I want to warn you about the common mistakes that *divide* people's money. Not enough is said about how people *lose* money in investments. And I'm not talking about idiots. I'm talking about the mistakes of smart people, like today's guest. As we wait for our food, I'll let him tell you the series of unfortunate events that flushed his inheritance down the toilet.

Fast Forward to Reunion

James: I'll never forget the first time you introduced Hash Brown. Expecting a clean-cut businessman with a white shirt and tie, I glanced up from my pancake to find this relic of the 60's, complete with unkempt hair, a graying beard and Grateful Dead T-Shirt – sort of like Jerry Garcia with a chef's apron.

Larry: Garcia?

Amy: Front man for "The Dead," you know, the Grateful Dead. Their followers were called "Dead Heads."

Flash Back

Kramer: I want to introduce you to a great friend, Mr. Hash Brown, the owner of this fine breakfast establishment. He's got plenty of fascinating life experience, and he shares your outside-of-the-box thinking.

Hash: Nice to meet you guys! Mrs. Kramer and I have had many great conversations about money and investing. We're good sounding boards for each other. By sharing ideas, we double our experience and knowledge. We've kept each other out of some bad investments and tipped each other off to some great ones, kind of like Warren Buffett's relationship with Charlie Munger.

Antonio: Who's Munger?

Hash: Kramer didn't tell you? As brilliant as Buffett is, he wouldn't dream of making an investment without running it by Charlie Munger. Having at least one straight-thinking sounding board would save many people from stupid investments.[3] But I didn't learn that soon enough. I'll give you a little background.

I'm a child of the 60's, the hippie generation. I still hold a lot of those 60's ideals: love, freedom, question authority, trash the materialistic rat race.

So in the mid-60's I was studying business and finance at Berkeley, when I joined a student movement protesting the Vietnam War. My senior year, I decided to drop out of the race for privilege and prestige, going to live in a commune with some of my buddies near Santa Cruz. Thought we were all pretty smart…you know, enlightened.

But at the end of the 60's, it all fell apart for me. Within about a year, three of my musical heroes − Janis Joplin, Jim Morrison of *The Doors* and Jimi Hendrix − all died of drug/alcohol related causes. I didn't feel so good myself.

I'd rejected the *adult* culture, but unthinkingly swallowed the *youth* culture. By 1971, I decided that drugs produced more selfishness than love, more stupidity than enlightenment. As that great philosopher Ozzy Osbourne once said,

> *"All my mistakes - all my stupid f---ups - I can categorically tell you are a direct result of alcohol and drugs or both."*[4]

I decided that as bad as materialism sucks, so does laziness. It's not *money* that's the root of all evil; it's the worship of it.

Anyway, after six months of drug rehab, I packed up my hippie van with a few belongings and a couple of buddies. We headed east, not stopping till we got to Kennesaw, Georgia, where we landed a job at a Waffle House. Our expenses were low. The van was paid for. We shared one of those old houses in downtown Kennesaw that needed some rehab itself. I worked hard, saved like crazy and was soon manager. I eventually took what I learned and bought my own restaurant.

With its 60's décor, I celebrate the good of the hippie movement. With a cup of coffee and a listening ear, I help people to overcome the downfalls of that generation, referring many to a local drug rehab program or financial management support group.

Kramer: Hash, save some of your life story for another day. We've got to help these kids with their finances. You eventually began investing in stocks and later in mutual funds. I'm throwing you to the lions. Kids, ask your questions.

MONEY LOSING TIP #1: Invest in Stocks Before Establishing Your Emergency Fund

James: How early did you start investing?

Hash: Too early…and not early enough.

Antonio: What the …?

Hash: *Not early enough* in that I should have been saving and investing at your age. I'd inherited $40,000 back in California when my parents died in a car wreck, but I blew half of it on drugs. If I'd invested it in a stock mutual fund at age 20 and kept it there, I'd have over $1,000,000 today.

Antonio: That's the "not early enough" part. What about the "too early" part?

Define: Bull and Bear Markets

- **Bull Market:** The Market has been going up for a long time (Think of an active, raging bull.)

- **Bear Market:** The Market has been going down for a long time. (Think of a hibernating, sluggish bear.)

Hash: After migrating to Georgia, I went to this financial seminar in Atlanta that enlightened me about multiplying my money through investments. Got all excited and dumped the remaining $20,000 into the stock market.

Antonio: Sounds wise. You started early. More time to multiply.

Hash: Just one problem. **Stocks are long-term investments. Don't start investing in them until you have a good emergency fund: several months of salary put in a conservative cash reserve, like a money market fund.** It won't get much interest, but you can write a check on it without penalty, and it's not likely to go down in value.

You see, most of us go through some sort of crisis every ten years.[5] For example, this year, over 1,000,000 Americans' homes are to be foreclosed upon because they can't make the payments.[6] Half of those who lose their homes do so because of an unexpected medical problem.[7] Of course, the seminar speaker "forgot" to mention preparing for crises. The realities of life aren't nearly as interesting as multiplying your money to millions.

Stocks are long-term investments because over the short haul the market can fluctuate wildly. I invested my $20,000 in the stock market in 1972, thinking I'd let it sit there and grow long term. So, it didn't really bother me when a **bear market** hit in 1973.

If not for my personal crisis, I could have left the money in the stocks and waited for the market to rebound. But noooo! I had to sell the stocks during the bear market for $12,600[8]. It took all that to pay for rehab. So much for my inheritance. I learned Murphy's Law of Investing:

> ***"If the odds of having an expensive emergency in any given year are 1 out of 10, the odds of it occurring during a bear market are almost certain."***

So maybe you don't struggle with drugs, but what if you break your arms and can't work for three months, or crash your car and need the money to buy a new one, or your kid gets seriously sick and you're out some medical bills or your company downsizes and you get laid off.

Look me in the eyes: **build yourselves several months of cash reserves before making any long term investments.** It's cool having multiplication work for you, but heartbreaking when division works against you.

James: But you got back into stocks?

Hash: *After* saving up an emergency fund. My mistakes were costly, but I *did* learn from them. Other emergencies keep coming up to make me glad I've got that available cash.

James: So what *did* you invest in? Roaming around on the Internet and talking to people, I'm getting tips on stocks that are just about to go up.

MONEY LOSING TIP #2: Get Money Quicker by Trading Stocks for Short-Term Gains

Hash: So people would come into the restaurant giving tips about stocks: "This video game company is coming out with a much-anticipated game next month. The stock is bound to skyrocket!"

Operating off a hot tip, I bought stock in a new technology company, and the worst possible thing happened.

Antonio: The stock went down.

Hash: No, it doubled in a month, and I sold it at a huge profit.

Antonio: Isn't that good news?

Hash: In the short run, sure. But after that success, I thought I'd found an easy way to make money and that I was smart enough to pick great stocks every time.

I was like the guy in Vegas who hits a jackpot on the first try and deceives himself into thinking he can do it again and again. He goes through all his winnings and more trying to hit another jackpot. I was lucky that I didn't lose it all.[9]

Over the next year, I bought and sold stocks like crazy, trading success stories with my customers.

I spent a lot of time studying stocks. I'd research a company, pulling reports and seeing whether the experts were recommending to buy or sell. I'd get the advice of my experienced stock broker. I was searching for hot companies that I thought would go up quickly so that I could sell at a profit.

I was always asking my **stock broker** if I needed to trade something, and there always seemed to be something good out there. It never occurred to me that my broker made his money when

Define: Beating the Market

- If the news states, "The stock market was up 12 percent this year," it's usually speaking of the average of all the publicly-traded stocks in the USA, as measured by an index such as the Dow Jones Industrial Average or the S&P 500.

- Had you "beat the market," your personal selection of stocks or funds would have grown more than 12 percent that year.

Define: Stock Broker

A person who sells securities, such as stocks and mutual funds. He works at a "brokerage."

people bought and sold. Later, I understood what Buffett meant when he said,

"Never ask the barber if you need a haircut."[10]

But I've got to admit, it was pretty exciting! People would sit around at the restaurant, lay out their *Wall Street Journals* and we'd talk about what was up or down. I even put a TV in that corner so we could get an up-to-the-minute ticker of stock prices. We thought we were big time *investors*. Actually, we were *speculators,* gamblers. There's a big difference.[11]

One of my sharp Friday morning regulars overheard us bragging about short-term trading week after week and got sick of it. She shared a few studies with me that brought me down to earth with a thud. Here are the basics:

Study #1 Are You Really Beating the Market?

Money Magazine asked over 500 people if their investments were **beating the market.** Although one out of four said "yes," when they were asked for specifics, the surveyors discovered that 80 percent lagged the market! That's a huge self-deception![12] I wondered, "Have I been deceiving myself?"

I sat down and counted every stock related profit and expense over the last year. It was depressing. I'd remembered my successes and minimized my failures. Although I generally bought low and sold high, when I counted in my losses, broker fees and taxes, I made a measly four percent that year, when the market as a whole increased by 10 percent. I'd have done better by putting the money in an index fund that tracked the market. For me, the old saying was true:

> *"Holding stocks makes investors wealthy. Trading stocks makes brokers wealthy."*

All that time and energy. Instead of obsessing on studying hot stocks, I could have spent my weekends riding Harleys up the Blue Ridge Parkway.

Remember *The Emperor's New Clothes?* I'd been prancing about the restaurant as if I were a finely dressed Wall Street investor. My new friend had the guts to tell me I was naked.

Study #2 How Many Really Profit on Short Term Trading?

Akashi: Mrs. Kramer…I'll bet your new friend was Mrs. Kramer.

Hash: You're sharp, Akashi! She's been a great friend and adviser ever since. And, she told me more.

Even if you're buying low and selling high, you're likely to lose in the long run because of the expenses of buying and selling.

- **Expense #1: Taxes.** Every time you sell at a profit, you pay taxes. And you pay more taxes for short term gains than long term gains. Had I bought and held, that money would have kept multiplying my entire lifetime with largely pretax dollars. The difference over time is huge!

- **Expense #2: Fees.** You pay when you buy. You pay when you sell.

Some smart professors at the University of California followed 66,000 stock buyers for five years. The most active traders lagged the market by 6.4 percent per year![13]

James: That sucks!

Hash: As Zweig summed up the frequent trading strategy:

> *"Thousands of people have tried, and the evidence is clear: The more you trade, the less you keep."*[14]

The good news was, I learned that lesson in one year and didn't lose my shirt in the process.

Study #3 Don't Keep Checking the Market!

The more I read respectable, sane money managers, the better I understood my problem. It wasn't that I was a poor trader; I was playing a losing game. I shouldn't have been doing short term trading at all.

I discovered that Buffett didn't have a working ticker in his office. He's not concerned about hourly fluctuations in the market. Mr. Market (the stock market as a whole) is fickle, going up and down for reasons that often have nothing to do with the real value of a company.

So Buffett doesn't buy stocks for a quick trade; he buys into good companies for the long haul. He doesn't really care what Mr. Market thinks about his stock.[15] If it's a good company, he holds it whether the stock is up or down.

Jason Zweig, senior editor of *Money* magazine, tells of a Harvard psychologist who found that investors receiving frequent news updates on their stocks earned half the returns of investors who got no news updates at all.[16]

The day I read that, I banished the TV from the restaurant and gave up short-term trading.

Introductions by Hash

Here are some people I refer to over and over and why we should listen to them.

Warren Buffett: Anyone who questions his authority on investing must answer the question, "Why is he the most successful investor on earth?"

Benjamin Graham: Buffett's mentor and another of the world's greatest investors. Buffett calls Graham's book, *The Intelligent Investor,* "By far the best book on investing ever written."

John Bogle: Authority on Mutual Funds. He founded the Vanguard Group, a leading Mutual Fund company. Buffett recommends *Bogle on Mutual Funds* as "the definitive book on mutual funds."

Jason Zweig: Personal finance columnist for *The Wall Street Journal.* Recipient of a Lifetime Achievement Award in Investor Education from the Mutual Fund Education Alliance. He wrote *Your Money and Your Brain*.

Are you gonna trust these guys or the guy on the internet site with meager credentials who wants to sell you his secret formula to beat the market?

James: Got your point: don't get caught up in the excitement of short-term trading. Too much time. Too much risk. It's speculating, not investing. Stocks are long term investments. Buy stocks you can keep for the long haul.

Hash: Exactly!

James: So if we're gonna pick good companies for the long term, the question is, "Which stocks do I buy?" I've been following a tech company that makes most of the video games I like. I really, really like the company.

MONEY LOSING TIP #3: Pick Your Own Stocks for the Long Haul and Easily Beat the Market

Hash: James, you might be onto something, but you might not. Just think of how quickly the video game industry changes. I've heard that one third of *Fortune 500* companies, those that are tops in earnings for that year, disappear within seven years.[17] It's hard to know how any of this year's great companies will do next year.

Let's say you buy the stock in your video game company. What if, although they employ 520 people, they're kept on top of the industry by, one brilliant accountant, five key programmers, and two great visionaries. What if those key players decide to quit and form their own video game company?[18]

James: It's like I invest in the *Atlanta Falcons* and the next week they lose their six key players to serious injuries, including their star quarterback, first string running back, an All Pro tackle and two top receivers.

Hash: Precisely! Now since you don't work for the video game company, or read all the trade journals for the gaming industry, you have no idea how important these key players are.

Over the next few years, the company puts out some boring games, and the stock starts going down. Now you're thinking, "Were these recent loser games just flukes? Companies can't hit home runs every time. Besides, I hate to sell the stock while it's down and take a loss." Within a year, the company announces it's going belly up, and you've lost all your money.

Antonio: But look at Wal-Mart. Surely if I'd been around when Wal-Mart rolled out its first stores, I could have looked at them and said, "I'd be crazy not to buy into this business!"

Hash: Antonio, here are a few things I've learned from experience about choosing individual stocks, even for the long-haul:

Stock Lesson #1: Very Few People Can Consistently Pick Good Stocks

WOULD YOU HAVE PICKED WAL-MART?

Hash: Mrs. Kramer, I know that you did some study on the history of Wal-Mart. Do you think we could have spotted Wal-Mart as a great stock pick in its early days?

Kramer: What's crystal clear in the rearview mirror isn't usually so obvious looking

Define: Actively Managed Mutual Fund

A mutual fund in which a manager tries to beat the market by buying and selling securities (stocks, bonds, etc.). Compare to an Index Fund, which is passively managed and doesn't try to beat the market.

forward. I don't think I would have invested in Wal-Mart during those early years. One businessman visited an early Wal-Mart opening on a bad day and reported that it was "the worst retail store I had ever seen."[19] Five years later, Kmart had 250 stores to Wal-Mart's nineteen. And Kmart was far ahead in quality. I'd have put my money on Kmart coming out on top.

Sam Walton himself says that it would have been "absolutely impossible" to convince anyone in the early days that of all the discount chains, Wal-Mart would end up on top.[20] Of the top 100 discounters in business in 1976, 76 of them eventually disappeared.[21] Who would have picked Wal-Mart as being in the bunch that survived, much less the one that would dominate?

What were expert analysts saying about them? Some believed in them while others felt they could fall at any second.[22] One analyst visited Sam and his son Jim in the mid-70's, only to write up a scathing review and advise investors that if they hadn't already sold their Wal-Mart stock, it was probably too late.[23]

THE RESULTS OF MOST EXPERT STOCK PICKERS

Hash: Managers of **actively managed mutual funds** are expert investors with training in their field. They sit around all day analyzing the economy and studying companies to determine which companies to buy and which to sell. But even with their training, experience and time to study companies, how sure can they be about a company's future?

Not very sure, based on their long term records. **Over twenty years, only 37 of 248 (14.9 percent) actively managed funds beat the market.** This record is actually more optimistic than it should be, since it doesn't account for hundreds of funds that folded during that period.[24]

Now let that sink in for a minute. While I spend my days scrambling eggs, these highly-trained, brilliant fund managers spend all day studying investments. **If the vast majority of those experts can't beat the market, what are *my* chances of beating the market?**

One of our problems is that most of us overestimate our intelligence and ability.[25]

I'll put it to you simply: most of us aren't smarter than average. If most of us *were* smarter than average, then average would be higher than it is now, and we'd still be stuck with average. Get it? And it's *certainly* not likely that we're sharper than most experts.

THE EXPERTS SPEAK

Antonio: So if the experts can't pick the top companies, how can I expect to?

Hash: Right. And don't trust the experts when they start predicting the future with authority. A couple of examples:

On March 10, 2000, the NASDAQ (heavily weighted in tech stocks) hit an all-time high of 5,048.62. That day, a respected securities' analyst declared that he expected the NASDAQ to hit 6000 within 12 to 18 months. Instead, five weeks later, it went down to 3321.29.

But no worry, another great market strategist said that although it might go down as much as 200 or 300 points from there, it could possibly go *up* by 2,000. Actually, it crashed to 1114.11 by Oct. 9, 2002.[26]

Had you followed those experts and put $5000 in the NASDAQ on March 10, 2000, you'd have lost about $4,000 by October of 2002.

Kramer: Here's another example of flawed expert advice. Enron has become the poster child for greed and corruption. Don't get me wrong. A lot of great people worked there. But at the top, a group of smart schemers hid losses and invented huge profits with their creative accounting. The bad guys were so sneaky that virtually no investors suspected corporate cancer until it had spread too far. When the truth hit the fan, Enron unraveled and died, taking down the investors with it.

Now here's what should make us go "Hmmm…." Before Enron's fall, experts couldn't say enough good things about it. One respected financial magazine crowned it repeatedly "America's Most Innovative Company" and scored it highest in "Quality of Management." Huge mutual fund companies, which use their own professional analysts, bought big time into Enron. Respected firms were still recommending Enron within months of its demise. As a blue chip stock, it attracted investors with its perceived safety and stability.[27]

My point?

Antonio: If the "experts" are so dismally wrong so often, how can I expect to do better?

Stock Lesson #2: It Takes a Lot of Time and Skill to Consistently Pick and Keep Good Stocks

FALLING FOR "THE EASY WAY": FINDING PAST PATTERNS IN STOCKS (TECHNICAL ANALYSIS)[28]

Hash: Lots of people will try to sell you their "easy formula" for picking stocks. It's usually based on patterns they've found in stocks that have beat the market in the past. But unless you can prove that the pattern "caused" those stocks to beat the market, *and* that the pattern should hold true in the future, you haven't proven anything.

Jason Zweig showed the futility of this approach by looking to the past and discovering that "stocks whose names contained no repeating letters" beat the market soundly over the past 25 years. Does that mean that we should invest in only stocks with repeating letters? Of course not! Repeating letters had nothing whatsoever to do with their stellar returns![29]

Amy: When I start a company, I'm naming it something with repeating letters!

Hash: Great idea! Makes about as much sense as stock pickers making decisions on those past patterns!

WHAT IT TAKES TO BEAT THE MARKET

When Warren Buffett appeared on the TV show *Money World*, he was asked what investment advice he'd give a money manager who was just getting started. He replied,

> *"I'd tell him to do exactly what I did 40-odd years ago, which is to learn about every company in the United States that has publicly traded securities."*

The moderator responded in disbelief: "But there's 27,000 public companies."

"Well," said Buffett, "start with the A's."[30]

Buffett doesn't predict the future of a stock by its past selling prices. Rather, he studies companies to determine which ones are likely to stay healthier than others and out-earn others over time. He has a brilliant mind with almost total recall of numbers and an unsurpassed understanding of how businesses work. He studies companies every day and might go several years before making a major stock purchase. I asked myself, "Do I really want to spend the time it would take to choose and follow the right companies?"

Stock Lesson #3: The Fewer Stocks You Own, The Less Diversified You Are

If you own stock in five companies, and one of them dies, that's a huge loss. What if you'd chosen, like many great stock pickers in the 1990's, Enron as one of your companies?

So let's imagine that, knowing you'll probably pick some loser stocks along the way, you decide to buy lots of individual stocks to diversify and soften the blow of the losers. Benjamin Graham recommended holding between 10 and 30 stocks.[31] But then you've got another problem.

Stock Lesson #4: The More Stocks You Own, The More Time It Takes to Follow the Companies

To help you understand the information you should know to follow just one company, let's have a little debate. Divide into two teams: Akashi, Antonio and I versus Kramer, Amy and James. Let's imagine that James has been looking around for a stock to buy that will outpace the market. He's considering *General's General Store*, which sells a little bit of everything, kind of like a little Wal-Mart.

He knows the store firsthand, since it's the closest variety store to his house – his obvious first stop when he runs out of milk or light bulbs. They have great prices, friendly workers and his favorite blue jeans.

He follows the stock for several months. It's been going up 15 percent per year, beating the market by a significant five percent. That's a good sign. Others think it's a good company and are buying. All the popular money magazines recommend it as a "buy."

You decide to run it by your wise counselors. Let's debate!

James: It's an incredible store! Maybe I'm catching the next Wal-Mart while it's small!

Hash: How many discount stores looked greater than Wal-Mart in those early years, but later went belly up? How do you know this one will last?

Amy: Convenience. Wal-Mart is too big to be put near everyone.

Akashi: But what if another small general store sees how profitable your store is and builds another one across the street, taking half of your customers?

James: But look at those great prices! I don't see how anyone could beat them!

Antonio: But how do they *get* those prices? Maybe they have an employee who has a special relationship with suppliers, getting better deals than the competition. What if a competitor hires him and takes the cheap suppliers?

Kramer: I think their CEO is awesome: a brilliant fireball. I can't imagine him not being able to handle any crises.

Akashi: What if the CEO decides he's got enough money and retires to Tahiti? What if his idiot son takes over?

Antonio: What if the main profit item, like a certain brand of jeans, suddenly goes out of style?

James: But look at how the stock's been rising over the years! Lots of brilliant investors must believe in it.

Hash: Since so many are buying it, Buffett would probably say it's overpriced. He'd say it's very risky to buy a stock that's selling for more than its value.[32]

James: Whoo! Look at the ticker! The price is going way down! Now it's a *great* value!

Akashi: Buy *why* is it going down? Maybe those who are selling know something bad about the company that you don't.

James: Look! Now it's going back up! Let's catch it on the rise!

Hash: If it's such a great deal, why haven't all the mutual fund managers already chipped in their millions, driving the prices sky high? Maybe that's as far up as it'll go, just before it plunges into stock market oblivion. Past performance doesn't guarantee future performance.

Amy: Enough! I get the point. Is everyone else's head spinning like mine?

Hash: I'm gonna spin it a little more. I want you to understand the bewildering complexity of guessing which direction a company and its stock will go. Here are more questions I was constantly asking myself when I was trying to pick my own stocks:

- What if their competition gets better funding and outgrows them?

- What if the suppliers go belly-up, forcing them to pay other suppliers more?

- What if the accountants have been reporting false profits and it's all about to unravel?

- What if an incompetent accountant filled out the tax forms wrong for the past five years and the Fed comes after them?

- What if they expand too quickly with borrowed money, a recession sets in, they can't make their payments and go bankrupt?

- What if the company makes such good profits that they decide to invest in other businesses, but those businesses fail?

- What if the suppliers of clothes in India are mistreating their employees, *60 Minutes* does a special and all the humanitarian organizations stage a highly publicized boycott of your store?

Not only should the wise investor know answers to most of these questions, but she must know how to judge which answers are the most significant.

So, Amy, is your head *really* spinning now? Can't you see why so few stock pickers can consistently beat the market?

When I saw *The Lord of the Rings*, I could identify with poor Smeagol. I'd look into the water in my sink and see a face saying "Buy! Buy! Buy!" Then I'd look up in the mirror to see a face saying, "Don't buy! Don't buy! Don't buy!"

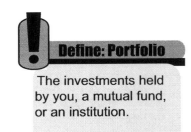

Define: Portfolio

The investments held by you, a mutual fund, or an institution.

Wise investing in companies takes lots of skill, time, effort and a measure of good luck.[33]

> **Stock Lesson #5: Good Quality Mutual Funds are Better Diversified (Thus Safer) and Will Generally Give You Better Returns than Dealing with Individual Stocks**

James: OK, so let's say that I don't have the time, skill or interest to study individual companies and buy their stock. I don't want to spend all that time researching only to end up with the next Enron in my **portfolio**. I'll go with mutual funds instead. How can I pick the best funds?

Hash: I'll tell you that next week. Today, I'll tell you how *not* to pick one.

MONEY LOSING TIP #4: Choose Funds by Their Past Performance

By 1990, I'd learned my costly lessons about saving into an emergency fund, avoiding short-term trading and the need to diversify through mutual funds. So I started flipping through financial magazines and the business sections of newspapers to find the best mutual funds. I found an advertisement for a mutual fund of technology stocks that was beating the pants off both the stock market average and all other technology **sector funds** for the past two years.

So I thought, "Why would I want to go with anything less than the best? The fund manager must be brilliant to achieve that kind of return."[34]

Define: Sector Fund

A mutual fund that invests exclusively in a certain sector of the economy, such as energy companies or health care companies.

Antonio: Makes sense to me. Pick the best-performing fund of the last year. Its managers must be doing *something* right.

Hash: Seemed wise to me, too. And nothing personal, Antonio, but it's stupid, stupid, stupid.

First of all, the top fund of any given year is rarely the top fund the next year. Maybe the managers just got lucky. Maybe they invested in some risky companies that happened to have a good year. Whatever the case, last year's performance tells us hardly anything about next year's performance.[35]

Second, the top funds of any given year are rarely the top funds *over the long haul.* I should have looked for a respected mutual fund company that invested wisely, with a long term strategy, low costs and minimal trading.[36]

Sure, don't pick a fund that consistently lags similar funds over the past ten years.[37] The manager may be an idiot. But rather than looking for past stellar performance, I should have looked at their goals, objectives and strategy. The best funds over the long haul are seldom number one in any given year.

So the next year, my fund didn't do nearly as well as most other technology sector funds. But I wasn't too concerned because technology stocks were still beating the market in general, shooting up well over 20 percent that year.[38]

Boy! Was I looking cool among my breakfast buddies! Some of them were investing in individual tech companies, although I warned them about the need to diversify through a mutual fund.

We'd read some experts warning that the tech bubble would eventually burst. But then we'd read another expert who'd say, "We're in the midst of an unprecedented technology revolution. The old rules don't apply. These stocks will certainly keep going up. It's a 'new economy.'" Experts like that made us feel really smart, like we'd caught the wave of the future. But we were all suffering from the "Duck Delusion."

Antonio: The "Duck Delusion"?

Hash: Munger warns that bull markets go to investors' heads. He puts it this way:

> *"If you're a duck on a pond, and it's rising due to a downpour, you start going up in the world. But you think it's you, not the pond."*[39]

We were all ducks in those days – ducks with big heads. My customers who invested most heavily in tech stocks made the most each year. They showed off their stellar earnings each month, making them the most envied investors among us pancake eaters. So, I invested more and more in tech stocks.

Looking back, our emotions were carrying us away, while we justified our decisions with half-baked arguments. Here's what we should have known:

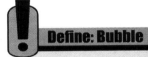

Define: Bubble

When the prices of a sector of the economy, such as real estate or technology, keep inflating wildly beyond reasonable prices, they are said to be in a bubble, which will eventually burst.

First, just because there's some new, hot industry doesn't mean it's going to be profitable. If you'd invested in the airline industry when Orville and Wilbur flew their first plane, you'd have gotten a horrid return over the decades. The airline industry has been extremely useful, but dismally unprofitable. As Buffett put it,

> *"...the net return to owners for the entire airline industry...is less than zero. If there had been a capitalist down there, the guy should have shot down Wilbur."*[40]

Second, if I'd been reading Buffett and Graham at the time, I'd have known that technology stocks were selling for far more than their profits justified. There was no **margin of safety**. Rather than investing in sound companies at a reasonable price, we were buying at outlandish prices, speculating that the price of technology stocks would keep going up.

Define: Margin of Safety

The difference between the price of a stock and the worth of the company. By paying only bargain prices for stocks, Graham greatly reduced the risk of losing money.

Third, in the stock market, what goes up usually comes down.[41] If you get excited about a stock or a fund, always find out how it fares in bad markets as well as good.

Akashi: So the stock went down?

Hash: Like a lead zeppelin.

Akashi: The band?

Hash: No! The big gas filled transport – like a blimp. But that *is* what Led Zeppelin was named after. Let's see, when Jimmy Page was talking about forming a new band, the drummer of "The Who" predicted that they would go down like a lead zeppelin...[42]

Kramer: Getting back to stocks...

Hash: Oh yeah. So the herd psychology goes like this. It's how so many lose money in stocks or mutual funds. You buy a fund when everybody (the herd) is buying – when it's going up and everybody at the restaurant has a story of all the money they've made over the past months in the fund. You don't want to miss out, so *you* start buying too.

Then prominent analysts start raising fears that the price of the stocks in the fund has gone too high, or quarterly reports from several of the major companies record that earnings are down. By the time you've noticed, big time investors have already bailed so that the stock has plummeted. You resist selling for awhile because some experts are predicting that it's probably reached the bottom and will rise again. But it keeps going down. Finally, you panic and sell.[43]

The end result? You bought high and sold low, the classic way of losing money in the stock market.

Sure enough, with way too much of my investments tied up in technology, the sector crashed, leaving me with one fourth of my original investment. I wasn't alone. *Money* magazine surveyed 1,338 Americans in 1999 and found that nearly one-tenth of them had at least 85 percent of their money in Internet stocks.[44] That's foolishness, and I was right in the middle of it all.

What I just described happens over and over and over. A fund starts going up. The fund gets great press as "the best fund over the last year." New investors buy into this "winning" fund, paying outlandish prices for the overvalued stocks. More get on board. It keeps going up. Something bad happens in some of the fund's key businesses. Investors get scared. They hang on for awhile, hoping it will go back up, but then bail out near the bottom.

As Jason Zweig warns us,

> *"The people who take the biggest gambles and make the biggest gains in a bull market are almost always the ones who get hurt in the bear market that inevitably follows."*[45]

As Santayana said,

> *"Those who cannot learn from the past are condemned to repeat it."*

Or, to paraphrase a more pessimistic Hegel,

> *"The only thing we learn from history is that we can't learn anything from history."*[46]

Here are a couple of quotes to sum up what I learned about trying to buy stocks and funds based on past performance:

> *"The dumbest reason in the world to buy a stock is because it's going up."* – **Warren Buffett**[47]

> *"Your chances of selecting the top-performing funds of the future on the basis of their returns in the past are about as high as the odds that Bigfoot and the Abominable Snowman will both show up in pink ballet slippers at your next cocktail party."* – **Jason Zweig**[48]

Had I known back then what you know now, and what you *will know* next week, I could have accumulated well over $1,000,000 by now, with fairly little effort. I'm giving you a million dollar education.

Akashi: So now I'm confused. I came out of last week's breakfast all fired up about multiplying my money with stocks. At this point, I don't ever want to hear the word "stock" again. Look at how much money you lost!

Hash: The problem isn't stocks. The market has great returns over time. It's people's uneducated approaches to stocks that get them into trouble. Or, I should say, it's what people think they know about stocks that they don't. Mark Twain put it well:

> *"It's not so much what people don't know that hurts them. It's what they do know that ain't so."*

I knew so much that wasn't so. To protect yourself from making foolish decisions, you've simply got to read the right people and hang around the right people.

But now that you've learned from my foolishness, you're set to make a killing on stocks. Next week, I'll tell you how.

Summing It Up

Kramer: So from Hash Brown we've learned…

Amy: Save up three or four months' salary in a place I can get to it in case of an emergency – like a money market fund.

James: Don't trust people when they say that they know a stock or fund will beat the market. Even experts are wrong over and over.

Akashi: Don't choose a stock or fund just because it went up a lot last year. Last year's winners are often this year's losers.

Antonio: Buying and selling stocks over the short term is gambling, not investing. Trying to beat the market by picking individual stocks for the long term requires a lot of time and skill.

Akashi: Beware of joining the latest investment fad where everyone is making big money. Maybe it's a bubble that's just about to burst. I need to thoroughly understand something before I jump into it.

Amy: Let's see…here's a key thought from Hash that I wrote down about choosing good funds: "Look for a respected mutual fund company that invests wisely, with a long term strategy, low costs and minimal trading."

Kramer: Great insights! Here are your assignments.

- Many advertisements and articles recommend funds that grew spectacularly over the past year. Why should you question these recommendations?

- A recent article recommended investing in the cell phone industry and hand-held computer devices, since they are the hot new industries. Do you think their stocks will grow faster than other stocks over time? Why or why not?

- An investment magazine is recommending one company as "the next Microsoft" and another as "the next Wal-Mart." What questions would you want answered about these companies and the person who is doing the recommending?

Assignment
Between Breakfasts

1. Define "stock," "bond," "mutual fund" and "index fund." (Try Googling "define: stock"; "define: bond") Don't just memorize definitions. Understand them well enough to be able to talk intelligently about them at the next breakfast.

2. Read an article or two on index funds at a respected mutual fund site like www.vanguard.com or www.americancentury.com (both respectable as I write).

3. Talk to your parents about their investments and plans for retirement.

Akashi: Did you forget? Our parents suck at finances. That's why we're here.

Hash: Learn from your parents' successes. Learn from their mistakes. They are a great source of wisdom and it's less costly to learn from *their* mistakes than your own.

Resource to Take You Deeper

Ben Stein, *How to Ruin Your Financial Life* (California: Hay House, 2004). Stein has done it all - studied finance at Yale, practiced law, wrote columns for *The Wall Street Journal*, played a role in the movie *Ferris Bueller's Day Off*, and ran his own game show: Win Ben Stein's Money. In this short book, he draws from his vast wisdom on finance to give brief, entertaining tips on how to lose money.

Breakfast #4: Make Money in Mutual Funds

"If a graduating MBA were to ask me, 'How do I get rich in a hurry?' I would...
hold my nose with one hand and point with the other toward Wall Street."

— **Warren Buffett**[1]

Fast Forward to Reunion

Larry: That last session makes me want to avoid stocks.

Antonio: I thought the same thing after that breakfast.

Amy: Ditto.

James: Hey, Larry, can you throw a couple of bacon strips on the grill? And I'll go with French toast this round.

Akashi: I'll take another coffee.

Larry: No problem. Just talk loudly, so I can hear you from the grill.

James: Let me tell about the third breakfast. For me, it cut through all the bogus noise you hear about stocks and bonds and gave me a clear, simple direction – just what I needed. I followed that advice, and it's serving me well.

Akashi: Just don't be too hard on me. If you remember, Antonio and I had hit some relational rough spots, and I was afraid that Amy might be moving in.

James: I'd forgotten all about that! You guys started the meeting early, in the parking lot!

Flashback

HASH BROWN'S PARKING LOT, 8:50 AM

Akashi: (Arriving to find Antonio and Amy leaning on his car, talking.) Hey guys! You and Antonio seem awful chummy this morning. Am I interrupting anything?

Amy: Naaa. I was just admiring his new wheels, or didn't you notice?

Akashi: Of course I knew he'd gotten new wheels! He's been agonizing for two weeks over what kind to get.

Amy: Hey, you don't have to get defensive. We just happened to both get here early.

Akashi: It's just a little odd for Antonio to show up early for anything. I know you've been eating together in second lunch shift.

Amy: If you had second lunch, we could all eat together. Antonio and I like to talk, often about what we discussed at the last "Counterculture Club" breakfast. There's only so many people who'd understand this stuff. Plus, Antonio and I are so laid back. We can talk about anything.

Akashi: And I'm NOT laid back and easy to talk to?

Amy: If you think I'm after Antonio…

Kramer: (Calling from the entranceway) Kids, let's get started!

Review

Kramer: Whatever's going on with you guys, leave it outside. This breakfast is key to your financial success. Today, we lay out THE PLAN.

But first, what are your thoughts after reflecting on last week's breakfast?

Antionio: What Hash said goes right along with this counterculture idea. Everything he did to lose money seemed so reasonable at the time. It seemed like everybody who was anybody was doing it. But the "everybody" he was hanging out with was wrong. To succeed in stocks, he needed to ignore the herd and go counterculture.

Hash: You don't have to listen to Buffett and Graham very long before you hear them repeating themselves, warning us over and over, "Buck the crowd. Don't listen to Mr. Market when he says to buy or sell. If you follow the crowd, you'll end up buying high and selling low. Do what makes sense, not what's popular."[2]

James: Now I understand why my parents are so wary of stocks. Every time they see something on TV about the stock market going down, they say, "A lot of people are learning today what I learned years ago. You can lose everything on Wall Street just as easily as you can lose everything at Las Vegas."

Akashi: Hash, you're a pretty smart guy.

Hash: Thanks!

Akashi: You're welcome. But all I could think about this week was, "If Hash Brown is so smart and could lose so much on stocks, how much easier could *I* lose all *my* money in the market. If he'd just hidden all that money under his mattress or in a savings account at his bank, he'd still have it today."

Why Invest in Stocks?

Hash: But that's not safe either. Put it under your bed, or in a low yielding account, and you're almost *guaranteed* to lose. You're not taking inflation into account.

You see, the cost of living has a bad habit of going up each year. You'll hear your parents complaining about how, years ago, they could buy a house for half the price people are paying today. They're not exaggerating. Over time, the prices of things keep *inflating*, eroding your money's buying power. That's why they call it **inflation**.

Even if inflation stays at a low rate, say three percent, it will cut the purchasing power of your money in half in just 24 years. If inflation gets out of hand, like it did from 1973 to 1982, the buying power of that money under your bed could be cut in half in a decade.[3]

Amy: So if you ignore inflation and refuse to invest, you're throwing away half your savings!

Define: Inflation

A condition of increasing prices on goods and services, as measured by the Consumer Price Index.

Hash: So you've got to find a way to stay ahead of inflation. Historically, stocks have been the best way to beat it. Sure, in any given day or year, inflation may beat the market. But eventually, it always roars back and leaves inflation sitting in the dust. Other investments, like money markets, CD's and bonds, don't tend to multiply your money fast enough to beat inflation over the long haul.[4]

Akashi: Nothing personal, but while the market was doing all this going up stuff, you applied your brilliant Berkeley brain to the market and managed to lose a ton of money.

Hash: I can tell that Kramer has already covered the candor thing.

Kramer: I told them you could take it.

Can I Invest More Safely In Stocks?

Hash: There's a way to invest in stocks that's much safer and smarter than how I was going about it. I've learned a lot since those mistakes. Learn from my experience. I was going about it all wrong. It wasn't that stocks were a bad investment. During those years, the stock market as a whole went up over 10 percent per year. I was investing in stocks the wrong *way*. Actually, although I *thought* I was investing, I was *actually* speculating.

I'd been listening to the wrong people - my customers who constantly talked about how well their stocks were doing. I read the publications *they* read, surfed the websites *they* surfed.

As you recall from last week, when Mrs. Kramer brought me the studies that show how few people, even professionals, actually beat the market over time, I started reading different books and changing my strategy.

I should have been listening to people who have a public record of doing exceptionally well with stocks over the long run — people with proven records.

Who to Listen to

Amy: From what we learned last week, I'll guess…Warren Buffett and Benjamin Graham on stocks. Then John Bogle, the innovative leader at *Vanguard* who's had such success with mutual funds.

Hash: Bingo! And I also rely a lot on Jason Zweig, personal finance columnist for *The Wall Street Journal*, who's one of the best writers about the approaches of Graham, Buffett and Bogle. He brings together all the current research and then tells it like it is.

When I began reading these guys, and people who think like them, I realized that intellectually I'd been hanging around the wrong crowd. It's not enough to read books. You've got to read the *right* books.

I'll admit, these books cover a lot of ground and aren't nearly as entertaining as *Marvel Comics*. So I'll just give you the tips from the masters that you need to get started with intelligent investing. When you've finished your breakfast, I'll recommend some reading.

1. Save Four Month's Salary in an Emergency Fund.

Wisdom from the Money Masters

This will keep you from having to pull out your investment money in a crisis, like a job loss, a medical emergency or a large meteor landing in your driveway.[5]

WHERE TO PUT IT

This money needs to be liquid, meaning you can get at it quickly and easily. Also, it needs to be relatively stable, not fluctuating wildly in value, so that you don't have to pull it out when the value is down. Most recommend **Money Market funds,** either through your bank or a mutual fund company. They earn interest, plus you can write a check on them.

Other relatively safe and liquid places for cash reserves include

- **Liquid Certificates of Deposit (CD's)** (a relatively new type of CD that you can draw from without penalty. **Insured by the government [FDIC])**

- **Savings Accounts** (also insured by the FDIC)

- **Short Term Bond Funds** (They fluctuate in value, but less than stocks or medium and long-term bonds. They tend to get better interest than the above investments. For added safety, buy short-term government bonds.)[6]

HOW TO SAVE IT: PAY YOURSELF FIRST

Mrs. Kramer will deal with this concept more during your breakfasts on saving, but I'll introduce it here. James, when you get a paycheck for $200, how much of that $200 is yours?

James: All of it.

Hash: Are you sure? Part of it has to go for food. Another part to gas. Still more to car insurance.

James: I'm with you.

Hash: For most people, this week's paycheck is spent by the next paycheck. When it's spent, they have nothing left for themselves. That's why financial advisers suggest that you set aside some of that paycheck for yourself, first to build your emergency fund, second to invest for the long haul. **Pay yourself first, before you pay anyone else. Try to set aside at least 10 percent, much more if you can.**[7]

I'll say it one more time, a little louder: **DON'T START INVESTING LONG TERM UNTIL YOU'VE SET ASIDE FOUR MONTHS SALARY IN AN EMERGENCY FUND!**

Akashi: That would have saved you from your first failure. Instead, you put all your savings in stocks, and the market took a dive. Then, you needed the money for rehab. If you'd had an emergency fund, you could have grabbed it and left your investment money in the market until stocks regained their value.

Hash: Sad, but true. Tell your local banker you want to keep four months of salary for an emergency fund, and ask where he'd recommend that you put the money. Talk to a mutual fund group about your goal, and ask the same question. You learn a lot by continually asking questions – often the same questions – to different wise people.

The good thing about a mutual fund group is that you can probably get a better interest rate than your local bank in its money market fund.

The good thing about dealing with local bankers is that you can get to know them personally, which often comes in handy throughout your life. Also, your money will be insured by the FDIC up to $100,000. If the bank goes broke, the U.S. government will give you your money back.

Akashi: What if our government dies?

Hash: Then none of your money, even the stash under your bed, will be worth anything anyway. We'd probably go back to trading food, guns, pigs and Pokemon cards.

2. Invest in a Total Stock Market Index Mutual Fund for the Long Term.

Amy: So let's say I've got four months' salary saved in a money market fund. What next?

Index funds (or a close relative, Exchange Traded Funds) are a wonderful way to diversify your investment dollars for the long haul. Buffett says they're the best investment tool for the great majority of investors. All the smart investors I'm reading now sing their praises.[8]

Define: Total Stock Market Index Fund

A whole bunch of stocks of all kinds of companies that the fund manager thinks will match the returns of the entire stock market.

I lost money by investing for the short term in small parts of the market. Had I been invested in a total stock market index fund during the tech stock crash, I wouldn't have done so badly. Tech stocks would have been just one part of my well-diversified stock holdings.

Akashi: So what exactly is an **Index Fund**?

Hash: The manager isn't trying to beat the market. He just wants to match it.

Akashi: Why just keep up with the market?

Hash: First, we've seen that the rise of the market as a whole over the last 100 years provides plenty of growth to get our money multiplying. Why take extra risk by trying to beat the market?

Second, as we saw last week, less than 15 percent of actively managed funds end up beating the market after twenty years.[9] What are my odds of picking that 15 percent?

That's why so many wise, respected investors think that index funds are the greatest invention since underarm deodorant.[10]

Here are some other benefits.

- **You don't have to waste lots of time thinking about it.** The market will go up drastically some years, down drastically others. With an index fund, you couldn't care less. You're in for the long haul. Instead of spending your weekends studying businesses and funds to try to beat the market, you can spend your time dating, kayaking, going to concerts or chilling with your friends.

- **You pay less in taxes.** Every time you or your mutual fund manager trades stocks, (unless it's in a retirement account) you have to pay taxes on your gains. Managers of index funds trade very little, holding down your taxes to a minimum. That way, money you would have spent in taxes stays in the fund, working harder for you.

- **You have fewer expenses.** Mutual fund managers charge for their services. They charge a lot less to manage an index fund because it requires less work. The difference this makes in total returns can be huge![11]

- **You're broadly diversified.** With investing, you don't want to put all your eggs in one basket. In the 1990's, some people put way too much of their money into Enron, which seemed like a great bet at the time – a Fortune 500 company, a Blue Chip stock, awards for innovation and management. Of course, it crashed and the investors lost their money. With an index fund, you own scores of businesses of different types, from oil companies to healthcare companies to Wal-Mart to Microsoft, so that if one sector of the economy slumps, another may do great. If one company fails, another succeeds.

Amy: Sounds cool! But I've been reading investing news in a couple of newspapers and financial magazines. If index funds are the way to go for our core investment, how come they don't talk more about them?

Hash: Index funds are boring. Let's say you own a financial magazine and need new, fresh articles every week. If someone's actively managed fund beat the market by 10 percent last year, that's news. If Microsoft doubled the market average, that's news. Put it on the front cover!

But who'd subscribe to your magazine if every week the cover highlighted an article entitled: "Just Buy an Index Fund, You Idiot!" Hey, how about this "exciting" newspaper article at the end of each year: "American Century Index Fund Almost Equals the Market for Ten Years Running!"

Index funds aren't typically spectacular in any given year. They're just lean, steady workhorses that have slowly and steadily beat 85 percent of the managed funds over the long haul.

Choosing the Best Companies and Best Funds

Amy: So how do I choose the best mutual fund company and the best index fund?

Hash: Here are a few things to look for in a mutual fund company:

- **Minimal trading (to minimize taxes)**
- **Low costs (to maximize returns)**
- **Keeps close to the market index it's trying to track (since that's the goal)**
- **No up front fees ("No Load") to keep that money working for you**
- **Known for candor and integrity**

I want to emphasize that while one index fund may look like another on the surface, these factors can make a huge difference over time.

James: Do I really have to look at all those factors for a fund? What about this for a shortcut? Look at these Morningstar fund ratings in the *Wall Street Journal*. Can't I just choose this fund that gets five stars for last year's performance?

Hash: Morningstar is a great group that offers valuable statistics. But those one year ratings are heavily influenced by the percentage increase of that fund over the last year.

Akashi: And last year's high performers are seldom this year's high performers.

Define: Prospectus

A document explaining the goals and methods of a fund.

Hash: Exactly! Those rating stars tell us something about the past of a fund but are rather dismal predictors of the future of a fund.[12] If it's only got one or two stars, especially over a five-year period, that may warn you that something's wrong. But even if it's got a great rating for the past five years, go to the fund's website and read its **prospectus** carefully to make sure its costs are low, to find out how long the company and fund have been in business, etc. Basically, you want to know the five indicators I mentioned earlier.

Akashi: It seems like it would simplify things to find one fund company I could trust and do most of my investing through it.

Hash: I agree. Knowing the fund company – its investing philosophy and reputation – tells you a lot about how any individual fund will be run. If you believe in the company, then a change of managers for the fund might not be so dramatic.

For example, when a great fund manager decided to leave an investment company, one of the fund investors, a brokerage head in his own right, decided to take his money and leave as well. In his words:

> *"Graham-Newman can't continue because the only guy they have to run it is this kid named Warren Buffett. And who'd want to ride with him?"*[13]

So, maybe he should have trusted more in the philosophy and integrity of the company and given the new guy a try!

Start by looking into some of the largest and most respected, no load mutual funds companies. There are good reasons why so many people entrust their money to these guys. You can learn tons about investing and mutual funds simply by surfing around on their sites and reading their articles. You can also call them on their 1-800 numbers to ask about various funds. But companies change over time. See what companies are most often recommended by current, respected publications.

MINIMIZE TAXES WITH AN INDIVIDUAL RETIREMENT ACCOUNT (IRA)

If you're saving toward retirement, set up a total stock market index fund as an "Individual Retirement Account" (IRA) and put the maximum amount in it each year as allowed by law. You see, one of the biggest drains on a fund is taxes. In order to encourage us to save for retirement, the government allows IRA's to multiply tax free. It makes a killer difference in how much money you have in the end.

Akashi: This is incredible! All that magical multiplication stuff we talked about over the past weeks – we can actually get that working for us without a masters' degree in finance or tons of time studying companies and watching financial TV stations. It's really, really simple, like "Investing for Idiots."

Hash: It's true! But I *would* keep reading up on investing. As one successful investor said, his one constant through all his life experiences has been, "I never forgot to keep learning."[15]

Deferred Taxes Vs. Non-Deferred Taxes

Let's say you invest $5,000 per year in a taxable account and $5,000 per year in a tax-deferred account. Both average 10 percent interest, and you're in the 33 percent tax bracket. After 30 years, your taxable account could be worth $319,960, but your tax-deferred account would be worth $606,160. In this case, you end up with almost twice as much money by deferring your taxes!*

*Note: if your taxable account contained stocks that were never sold till the end of 30 years, there would be no taxable gains incurred until the sale.

Over time, you'll want to consider other investments as well. The more you know, the wiser your decisions.

So, let's imagine that you've got **step one** down: a four-month emergency fund in a money market account that you can get at easily when you need it.

Step two: you've got a total stock market index fund. This is the core of your long-term investment. With the magic of compounding interest, it could double in value every seven years or so.

Where do you go next?

3. Diversify Your Stocks Internationally.

Why do you think we'd want to own some stocks outside of the United States?

Antonio: Diversification! If the American economy starts sucking eggs, some other country might be doing great.

Hash: Exactly! I'd put about 15 percent into a good, low cost, no load international fund.[16] Don't confuse it with a global fund, which invests both nationally and internationally.

4. Diversify with Bonds.

James: But you said that bonds don't get the returns of stocks over time. I read the other day that if I'd invested $1 in the stock market in 1925, I'd have $1,775 by 2002, whereas I'd have only $59 if I'd put it in bonds.[17] That's a huge difference! Why would I want anything at all in bonds?

Define: Bond

An IOU from a corporation or government. You lend them money, and they promise to either make regular interest payments, or pay a lump sum at the end of the term.

Hash: I'm gonna keep saying this word until you're so sick of it that you'll want to barf up your grits: **DIVERSIFY!** You've worked hard for all those investment eggs. Don't put them all in a couple of baskets!

Also remember, **we can't determine future returns with any degree of certainty by looking at past returns.** Just because stocks beat bonds over the past 100 years doesn't mean they'll do it for the next 30 years.

Get this: although in an average decade (since 1926) stocks averaged slightly more than 10 percent, **two decades found stocks returning under zero percent. In nine decades they returned less than five percent.**[18] (Decades aren't necessarily consecutive here, so that two decades could be the years 1959-1969 and 1960-1970.)

Although bonds (20-year U.S. government bonds), have averaged a 4.8 percent return since 1926, they had one year of negative returns and one year achieved a stellar 15.6 percent return.[19]

My point? Over long periods of time, bonds just might clobber stocks. We don't know the future. You don't want to retire at age 65 and need to sell some of your stocks for living expenses only to find that Mr. Market decided it was time to go into a 10-year slump.[20]

Zweig puts it bluntly:

> *"Anyone who claims that the long term record 'proves' that stocks are guaranteed to outperform bonds or cash is an ignoramus."*[21]

How Much in Stocks? How Much in Bonds?

Antonio: So what percentage of my investment do I put into bonds?

Hash: Benjamin Graham recommended 50% stocks and 50% bonds.[22] Most of today's trusted financial advisers recommend that, since stocks are long term investments and tend to outperform bonds, we should start our younger years with a much higher percentage of our money in stocks. As we age, we should increase the percentage of our money in bonds. Now this isn't an exact science. Who knows what the percentage should be? Personally, I like Bogle's recommendation.[23] It makes sense and is easy to follow:

Let your age be the percentage of your investment made up of bonds.

Amy: So, since I'm 18 years old, I'd put 18 percent of my money into bonds and 82 percent into stocks. When I'm 70, I'll have 70 percent of my money in bonds.

Akashi: Great! Easy to understand and remember! But if I live to age 101, won't I have 101 percent of my money in bonds?

Hash: Smart aleck! When you're 101, you can do whatever the heck you want with your money! Go buy a *Formula 500* wheelchair for all I care!

How Bond Funds Behave

When you decide on a mutual fund company, read up on bond funds and how they behave. They can be a little confusing.

For example, when interest rates go up, your bond fund makes more interest, but it goes down in value. When interest rates go down, you get less interest, but your bonds go up in value. The longer term the bond, the more it fluctuates with interest rates. Call your mutual fund company and ask questions on their 1-800 number.

Amy: You're right. That's confusing. But if I'm following you, and long term bonds fluctuate the most, then they'd go up the most when interest rates go down. So I'd be wise to buy long-term bonds when interest rates are going down.

Hash: Sorry Amy, but if this were a football game, I'd throw a penalty flag. Okay gang, what is Amy trying to do?

James: Time the market by predicting the economy?

Hash: Touchdown! Investors get into trouble with it in bonds just like in stocks.

Just because interest rates have been dropping consistently over the past year doesn't mean they'll continue dropping. I don't care how many "expert economists" announce on CNN that they believe interest rates will continue to rise or fall, they really don't know for sure.

Once upon a time, a broker was buying a house and asked Buffett where he thought interest rates were going. Buffett replied that only two people know the future of interest rates – both live in Switzerland...and they disagree with each other![24]

James: Funny! So nobody knows the future of interest rates with certainty.

Hash: Precisely! For now, you don't have to know everything about bonds. I just don't want you to look at your fund report after a year of increasing interest rates and say, "My gosh! My bond fund lost money last year! I'm cashing out and getting into something better!"

Just know that if you're investing for the long term – what investors call a "long horizon" – long term bonds will always beat short term bonds. If you're investing for a medium term, go with medium term bonds; for the short haul, go with short term bonds. The shorter the term, the less they're affected by changes in interest rates.

Pulling It All Together

Akashi: Although I can tell that I've got much more to learn about stocks and bonds, the strategy – what I should do – seems simple enough.

After I've got my four month emergency fund in place, I keep "paying myself first." Only now I put it into my total stock market index funds, an international fund and my bond funds, keeping the percentage in bonds that roughly equals my age.

Amy: That's SO much simpler than short term trading or trying to pick the next Wal-Mart! This strategy frees me up so that I can play gigs with my band on weekends instead of watching tickers and following companies.

Hash: You've got it!

Akashi: So, do I watch the market and wait for the time each year when stocks are cheapest so that I can get more bang for my bucks?

Hash: I don't with my investing. That gets you back into trying to time the market, which usually doesn't pan out.

Dollar Cost Averaging

Buffett, Graham, Bogle, Zweig, Charles Schwab and hosts of others recommend "dollar cost averaging." It simply means: **invest every month or every payday, ignoring whether the market is going up or down.**[25]

I'll warn you that it's emotionally counterintuitive because, as you know, the herd gets whipped into an investing frenzy when stocks are going up and bails out when stocks are going down. You should be doing exactly the opposite. Dollar cost averaging helps you to do that.

Let's say that you make $4,000 per month. You pay yourself first, putting 10 percent ($400) into your mutual funds each month. Let's say the stock market's been going up for the last year, and you're afraid you should wait until it starts going down before investing. But what if you wait, and stocks keep going up for the next five years? You might have just missed one of the biggest booms in history!

Instead of trying to time the market, you dollar cost average by ignoring Mr. Market and investing the same amount each month. When the stock market is plummeting and everyone's getting out of stocks, you go counterculture, thinking "Wow! Stocks are a bargain these days! Look how many stocks I'm getting with my $400!"

Here's the cool thing about dollar cost averaging: your $400 purchases more stocks when they're cheap, less when they're expensive. And again, you don't have to spend all your valuable dating time worrying about the market.

Akashi: That **IS** cool. It cuts through all those emotional ups and downs that investors react to – the hopes and fears that make them buy and sell at the wrong times. **With dollar cost averaging, when the market goes up, I can say, "Wow! Those investments are really paying off! Look at them go!" When the market goes down, I can say, "Wow! What a great time to be buying bargain stocks!"**

How Often Do I Rebalance?

Amy: At the end of the year, if the stock market's going up much faster than bonds, I'll have a lower percentage in bonds than I should have.

Hash: True. Don't worry too much. Those percentages don't have to be exact. Just try to avoid selling off shares of one fund to give to another. Sales generate taxes. Instead, weight your giving more toward bonds that next year, until you achieve the percentage you want.

Retirement Through Your Company

By the way, if your company has a retirement plan, understand it thoroughly. Some companies may match what you invest, contributing $400 every time you invest $400. That's a killer investment!

Just make sure to understand how it's set up. What will happen to your retirement plan if the company goes under or is bought out? Are those investments yours no matter what happens to the company? Are they well diversified?

Make sure they don't overload you with company stock. If it's a great company, you might want to keep some of the stock. But don't keep too many eggs in that one basket. **Remember Enron.** The average employee thought it was a great stock to own, but then lost it all when Enron went under.

Beyond the Basics

James: But I'm seeing all kinds of funds out there. Example: some invest in real estate companies and others utilities. Shouldn't I consider them?

Hash: Remember, your total stock market index fund holds real estate companies and utilities as well. But different funds can serve different purposes, like minimizing taxes or maximizing interest income. Stick with the basics for now and explore other options over time.

Preview of Next Week's Breakfast (Next Week's Menu)

Akashi: This is great! Now I see how I can get multiplication working for me in a way that's easy to understand. But I've still got a question. Whenever we use 10 percent per year to estimate what our investment in stocks will bring in the future, we're basing our future expectation on past performance. Isn't that exactly what you've told us NOT to do? Past isn't prologue, right?

In other words, how can we know for sure that the stock market will perform for the next 100 years the way it has for the past 100 years?

Hash: You're sharp, Akashi! On the one hand, many would say that 100 years is a long time and surely gives us *some* indication of the future. As long as our economy stays healthy, we should continue to grow.

On the other hand, you're exactly right to question a guaranteed 10 percent increase in the future. I hope the return will be much more! But it may be much less. If America's economy starts going downhill for a long period of time, stocks won't do well. As Zweig has said,

> *"The only thing you can be confident of while forecasting future stock returns is that you will probably turn out to be wrong."*[26]

That's why it's good to diversify with international funds, bonds and other types of investments. Next week, Mrs. Kramer will bring in a guest to suggest other ways to diversify your investments - particularly real estate. Whatever the economy serves up in the future, your best protection is wise diversification.

Kramer: In addition to bringing Hash back, I've invited Travis, a successful investor who's still in his 20's. Wear blue jeans and t-shirts. He's kind of country. Think "Dukes of Hazzard." He's also cute and single.

Amy: I'll show up early!

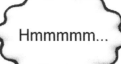

- Do you have an emergency fund? How much money do you think you should have in it?

- What are good places to keep emergency funds?

- What are some advantages to index funds?

- What are some ways to diversify your investments?

Assignment
Between Breakfasts

1. Write a list of questions about real estate investing.

2. Ask your parents or other relatives what they know about real estate investing.

3. Talk to a realtor you know about the ups and downs of investing in real estate. Ask her who she knows who invests successfully in real estate. List some questions, and give the investor a call.

4. Read a couple of articles on real estate investing.

Resources to Take You Deeper

For an overview of personal money management and summaries of a number of money management books, see www.enjoyyourmoney. org.

To Understand Mutual Funds

1. First, go to www.vanguard.com. Read their introductory articles on investing. Then, read up on index funds, exchange traded funds and other specific funds.

2. For a readable overview of personal investing, read Burton G. Malkiel's *The Random Walk Guide to Investing: Ten Rules for Financial Success*. As a Princeton professor of economics, he knows his stuff and offers sound advice.

3. For a more in depth understanding of mutual funds, read *Bogle on Mutual Funds: New Perspectives for the Intelligent Investor* by John C. Bogle (New York: Dell Publishing, 1994). Buffett calls it "definitive book on mutual funds," recommending that "any investor who owns or is thinking of owning shares in a fund should read this book from cover to cover."

To Understand Investing in Individual Stocks

1. Read *The Intelligent Investor: A Book of Practical Counsel, Revised Edition, Updated with Commentary by Jason Zweig* by Benjamin Graham (New York: HarperCollins Publishers, 2003). Buffett calls it "by far the best book on investing ever written." Having read it for the first time when he was 19, Buffett patterned most of his investing strategy after Graham's value approach. Get the edition with commentary by Jason Zweig, who updates Graham's wisdom with valuable research that's been done during the last 30 years since Graham wrote his final version. If you can't understand Zweig and Graham, or if they bore you to tears, you probably have neither the motivation nor the understanding to pursue individual stocks. In that case, stick to mutual funds.

2. Next, read *The Warren Buffett Way: Investment Strategies of the World's Greatest Investor* by Robert G. Hagstrom, Jr. (New York: John Wiley & Sons, Inc., 1994). Since Buffett has yet to write his own book, this book will give you the overview of his approach.

3. Read Buffett's shareholders' letters at www.berkshirehathaway. com. Both entertaining and informative, they reveal much of his thought processes in choosing winning companies.

Breakfast #5: Diversify with Real Estate and Prepare for Hard Times

Fast Forward to Reunion

Larry: This is amazing stuff. I've never had anyone take the time to explain how I can get my money working for me. It's almost like, once it's invested, it takes on a life of its own!

Kramer: Didn't you ever learn any of this in school or discuss it with your parents?

Larry: My mom died when I was 12. We were close. She watched me play baseball, even if it was just in the cul-de-sac. Was always there with a band-aid or a hug, whichever I needed.

Never hit it off with dad. He remarried when I was 14. Let's just say I didn't get along with the new family. I dropped out of school at 15, lied about my age to get a full-time job, moved into an apartment. Been working ever since. Not tryin' to get sympathy. Just letting you know why I don't know much about this stuff.

Antonio: Please don't feel stupid. I don't think any of us learned much about personal finance from either school or our parents. We sought out Mrs. Kramer because our parents were botching their finances.

Kramer: Our next guest, Travis, didn't have the best home life either. His dad was an alcoholic…and that was his *good* parent! His mom probably drove his dad to drinking.

James: I met her once. She was a real b-

Kramer: -we know. Since Travis didn't get much encouragement or stability at home, he became painfully shy, more secure around his car and his hound dogs than people. To this day, he has a hard time looking folks in the eye.

He couldn't put up with the constant conflict at home. I think he had that irrational feeling that plagues a lot of kids from unstable homes – like *they're* the cause of their parent's problems. Anyway, he moved out the day after high school graduation, trying hard to create a stable life for himself. I haven't seen Travis in the last couple of months. Have any of you?

(All eyes go to Amy.)

Amy: (Blushing) Okay…Okay! So we still see each other. He and his hound dogs and his car are doing fine. So, maybe I should tell about that breakfast.

Flashback

HASH BROWN'S, 9:00 AM

Kramer: (Calling from the entryway toward the parking lot) Good! I see you guys have already met Travis. See if you can break away from his car long enough for our breakfast meeting!

James: His '69 Dodge Charger rocks! It's fully restored and in mint condition!

Kramer: Believe me, I've heard plenty about that car.

Review

Hash and I are old folks. It's about time we introduced you to some financial wizards closer to your own age. Travis is twenty-eight-years-old, with no debt. Even his house is paid for. Beyond that, he's got some solid investments that are multiplying rapidly. Compare that to the average twenty-something who graduated college with over $20,000 in debt and little, if any assets. Twelve years ago, at age 16, Travis had nothing. I'll let him tell his story.

Travis' Story: Think Assets and Net Worth

Travis: I'm not much of a teacher. Just a country boy. Better at doin' than teachin'.

Anyways, I grew up lovin' cars.

James: Now you're talking!

Travis: As a kid, I was always hangin' out at the dirt tracks. The day I turned 16, I entered my first race, drivin' a friend's car. Got smoked big time, but loved every minute of it.

Point is, I loved cars. But race cars are a money pit. Knew I'd need a big stack of money to support that habit.

Fortunately, I'd met Mrs. Kramer in remedial English as a freshman. She talked me into stayin' in school and takin' her Financial Management course my sophomore year. She gave me some ideas for makin' money on cars. Here's how it went.

Vocational Training and Experience

Kramer knew I loved cars, so she encouraged me my senior year to take half days in high school and half days in auto mechanic classes at North Metro Tech.

Soaked up everything I could about cars from everybody I knew. After school and on weekends, I worked at my Uncle Bob's auto repair shop. It was less than a two mile walk from my house.

Those were my first two good moves: gettin' educated in a marketable skill and gettin' experience in the real work world.

Paying Cash

My third good move was steady work and savin' up my money 'til I could pay cash for my own car. Kramer'd warned me about credit cards and car payments. Didn't want any of that.

Buying Quality at a Bargain Price

My fourth good move was findin' quality for a bargain price. Kramer said that if it worked for Buffett with stocks, it'd work for me with vehicles. Sure 'nuff, I kept my eye out for a bargain and found some ignorant fellow sellin' his wrecked truck in his yard for $1,000. Wasn't drivable. His wife wanted it out of the front yard before a big shindig that weekend. He needed quick money so he could make a down payment on another truck to drive to work. Offered him $500 and settled on $750.

All I had to do was replace the front bumper, one panel and give it a tune-up. Found the parts at a local junk yard and put them on myself. Now I had $1,000 in a car that *Kelley Blue Book* told me was worth $4,000.

Now that got me to thinkin', "I just increased my **net worth** $3,000 in a couple of days of buyin' and fixin' that car. Hardly broke a sweat. That's more than Uncle Bob pays me in a couple of months. There's gold in them used cars."

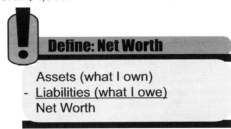

Define: Net Worth

Assets (what I own)
- Liabilities (what I owe)
Net Worth

Never got over that. For the first time I was financially worth somethin': $3,000. I owned an asset. That's the day I started keepin' score diff'rent from most folk. 'Stead of just countin' salary, I started countin' net worth. I put up a chart of my net worth inside my closet door to keep me motivated. It got really fun after that.

Flipping Cars

So, I kept right on savin' and keepin' my eye out for deals. I quickly discovered that lots of people out there need a reliable car for $3,000. If I could buy one for $1,500 that needed a little work and *Kelly Blue Book* said it was worth $3,500, I could sell it quickly for $3,000 and put the money into my next car.[1]

I'd buy a bargain car or truck, fix what needed fixin', clean it up nice, drive it to work and write the price on the windshield so that I could make at least $1,500 profit. Lots of people were in and out of that shop each day. I didn't have to pay a cent for that parkin' space that thousands of people drove by on Highway 92. No overhead. All profit.

Now just like Warren Buffett in high school, I didn't need that money at my age. I made enough from Uncle Bob to pay for my dates and insurance and races. **So all that money I made from sellin' cars − to the tune of fifteen grand a year, went into short term investments − like CD's and short term bonds.** Didn't put it into long term investments, 'cause I thought if I met my Daisy I just might need money to buy us a house or buy me a business.

I wasn't real happy at home, so I moved in with Uncle Bob after high school. Paid him a little rent to keep him happy. Two years later, Uncle Bob went back to drinkin' and lost his business. That cost me my job and that prime parking space. **But in that four years I'd saved a cool sixty grand.**

Amy: Wouldn't you have had sixty grand plus the interest from your CD's and Bonds?

Travis: (Sheepishly) Would have, but I dipped into the bonds for a few modifications on my race car.

I know it probably sounds easy, but it's hard for most folks to learn to think different, especially in how you keep score. Kramer told me back in high school that the motto of Apple Computer was "Think Different." Those two words have guided me ever since. It's part of what ya'll call "going counterculture."

Keeping Score

Antonio: I still don't understand. *You* keep score with net worth. How do *most* people keep score?

Travis: Let's talk football. It's great if the Falcons gain three hundred yards in a game, but yards alone don't get you on the scoreboard. You don't get points for yards gained. To win, you gotta turn those yards into touchdowns.

In managin' their money, people mistake gettin' yards for gettin' on the scoreboard.

Antonio: I'm still not following you.

Travis: People think they're successful when they have a large salary (yards gained), which allows them to borrow a lot to make payments on their expensive cars and expensive houses. Not talkin' down on them. They've gained some yards in life by workin' their way up in the world.

But if they tell ya they *own* a cool car and *own* a fancy house, don't believe 'em for a minute. Fact is, they own nothin'. They got no real wealth. They keep score by the *appearance* of wealth. Now that don't make sense to me. That big house and fancy car, they borrowed them from the bank, no diff'rent than if I'd borrowed my parents' car for a date. Wouldn't be right to tell my date it was *my* car if it were really my parents'. They may *say* they own their car and own their house. But they don't. They went and borrowed both of them from some lender.

They *look* like they got somethin', but really don't. As my cousin Billy in Texas puts it, they got a big hat, but no cattle. Billy and I keep financial score by net worth.[2]

The way *they* keep score*, they're* winnin'. Their house is bigger than mine, their car's more expensive. But they're a slave to their payments. While they're worryin' and workin' extra jobs, I'm out doin' stuff I like - huntin' with my hound dogs, racin' my car or helpin' needy folks with their car problems.

Most folks worry about missin' payments. I don't have any payments to miss. If they lose their job, they might lose it all. If they *do* lose it, they'll just have to deal with the fact that all that stuff was never theirs in the first place.

As far as I'm concerned, they got some yards, but nothin' on the scoreboard.

Now my car's not that expensive, but it's paid for. My house in the country's no Vanderbilt Estate, but it's mine. My net worth's decent. Theirs is close to zilch. I'm not braggin'. I'm just sayin' we don't see eye-to-eye on how to keep score. I love my car and my house in the country, and I don't have to lie awake nights worryin' about losing both of 'em.

Make Your Personal Residence into a Big Asset

Kramer: Tell them about how you ended up with a paid-off house.

Travis: Didn't start with a house. Kept $10,000 in an emergency fund. Bought a condo at age 22 with $50,000 cash. It was a **foreclosure**. Needed about $5,000 of work, which I did over the next year. Once it was fixed up, I could have sold it for $80,000. With that one fell swoop, my net worth increased $20,000.

After I was there 'bout five years, I missed bird huntin' and wanted a place in the country where I could keep hound dogs. Now each year, property values around that condo had risen between seven percent and nine percent, so that I sold the condo myself for $105,000.

Got a bargain on a **pre-foreclosure house** in the country for $100,000 and put $12,000 into it so that after a year of appreciation it was worth $130,000. That sweet deal increased my net worth by $16,000. And every year, the value of that house keeps goin' up at about seven percent.

Define: Foreclosure

A house offered at auction because the "owner" couldn't make the payments. A pre-foreclosure is sold in distress prior to the auction. Some are great investments. Some aren't.

Rehabbing Bargain Houses

Kramer: Tell them about your little house flipping business.

Travis: So back when I bought that bargain condo and found myself $10,000 richer, I got to thinkin' again – "There's some sweet money to be made in them houses." By that time I was makin' good money as a mechanic. Didn't have any house payments or car payments, so I started doin' some investin' on the side.

I studied up on buyin' and sellin' properties. Won't bore you with the details, but I got together with another investor and we threw our money in together, bought bargain properties, fixed 'em up, and sold 'em at a profit. It's not the crazy gains you hear about on the infomercials. But, we average making 10 percent on each house after taxes and expenses. We flip about two houses each year, reinvestin' our profits into each new house.

We always buy starter homes in family-friendly neighborhoods that look cute to women. Women usually choose houses, ya know. Husbands and boyfriends just go along for the ride and say "Yes dear" when their honey makes her decision.

Akashi: So staying with cheaper houses, you don't stretch yourselves, putting too many eggs in one basket.

Travis: True. But we also protect ourselves against a recession, or a bad housing market. In a recession, it would be near impossible to sell a $500,000 house, or to rent it out, at least without losin' a ton of money.

Way we see it, people got to have somewhere to live. Will always be a market for starter homes, unless you live in an area where the working class is leavin'. If we buy 'em cheap enough, we got a good margin of safety, no matter what happens. If the housing market gets bad and I get sick and need more than my emergency fund, we could always drop the price and sell it quickly, just to break even. In a severe depression, we could rent it out cheap, maybe to more than one family. We're always thinkin' of worst case scenarios. As Buffett says, the number one rule is…

Amy: Don't lose money!

Travis: And his second rule?

Amy: Refer back to rule number one!

Travis' Yearly Returns

Travis: Kramer's teaching you well!

Amy: By flippin' two houses a year, making a 10 percent return on each one, you're rakin' in over 20 percent on your investment each year! That's close to what Buffet averages in stocks![3]

Travis: Yeah. Pretty cool, huh? Since we do it all with our own cash and cash from home equity loans, it's easier to get the good deals. By reinvestin' our profits, we borrowed less and less with each house. Soon we won't have to borrow nothin'.

Amy: If you keep making over 20 percent per year, reinvesting that money, you'll double your investment every four years.

Travis: Yep. But I'm sure we'll lose money on one or two houses along the way. There's risk, you know. What if we find out too late that the county's plannin' to build a city dump across the street from a house we just bought?

The Education of a Real Estate Mogul

Akashi: I'm sure there's risk. But you make it look so easy.

Travis: Well, it may not be rocket science, but it ain't baggin' groceries either. I don't really like the phrase "flippin' houses". Sounds too easy, like flippin' pancakes. I think about as many people lose money at this game as make it.

I didn't jump into it. I joined the North Georgia Investor's Club, where I could talk to people who were doin' it locally. Learned from their mistakes. Learned from their successes. They recommended books that worked in the real world. I read them and thought about them.

I actually helped some investors rehabbing their houses, to see how it was done and to meet the handymen and realtors they worked with. You've got to get in with the people actually doin' this business to get past the hype and the bull. Doin' my research helped me separate fact from fiction, sense from nonsense.

Sure, we average over 20 percent per year. But it's an *active* investment. Takes time lookin' for properties. And I get dirty workin' on properties. Ya gotta like the process. It's not like an index fund where you can ignore it for years at a time.

Other real estate investors do it diff'rent ways. Some buy land and get it ready for a subdivision, so that they can make a killin' lot by lot. Others buy houses to rent them out. Some buy houses at the courthouse steps. Others put up signs that say, "Facing Foreclosure? We can help!"

Most work with a team.[4] We've got an experienced realtor who knows houses like I know my hound dogs. She'll bring us deals we could have never found on our own. She's got connections, you know. And she knows better than us how people want their houses to look. Our handyman can do a lot of things we can't do. Another on our team is really good at accountin' and money angles, keepin' our costs down and negotiatin' deals.

Akashi: Mrs. Kramer! You're a part of Travis' team! That's part of how you multiplied your money!

Kramer: Good detective work, Akashi. When Travis told me about what he was up to, I did my own research. You've got to know what you're doing in this business. But the relationships are equally as important. I didn't know anything about investing in real estate until Travis invited me to look into it with him. How could I know that this kid I was tutoring would eventually invite me to join him in a lucrative investment business? Get to know people. Help people out. Serve where you can. Make contacts. You never know where those relationships might lead.

(Hash pulls up a chair)

Akashi: Hash, is that your Harley for sale, parked in front of the restaurant?

Hash: Enjoy working on them in the evenings. When Travis told me years ago about flipping cars, I decided to flip motorcycles. I flip three or four a year. Plus, I get to ride them on nice weekends.

What About Stocks and Bonds?

Antonio: Travis, what you're doing is fantastic! But I'm trying to put this together with last week, when I'd decided to invest long term in stocks and bonds. Now you've got me thinking about real estate. Which do I do?

Travis: You probably don't have enough to invest in real estate right now. But think about it when you start to move into a place of your own. That's your first real estate investment. Don't bite off more than you can chew. Get a bargain and make sure your payments are way below your means. Start payin' that loan off as quickly as you can. If you do that, you're investing in real estate − your own home. That's an investment you can live in!

Investing for Hard Times

I also invest in conservative mutual funds, but there's somethin' else you need to know about me. I'm not so sure that America can keep on prosperin' like it's done in the past. That affects the way I save and invest.

In reading books by successful stock market investors, one of 'em said in passing, "I had to have a strong faith in the American economy."[5] Now that got me to thinkin' about three things.

First, We can't know for sure that the stock market's gonna keep goin' up 10 percent on average, even over large amounts of time. What if our economy doesn't do as well in this century as it did in the last?

Second, From the early 1800's to the early 1900's we went through about five depressions.[6] Add to that all the recessions. Shouldn't we prepare for more hard times, even if they don't last?

Amy: But I hear lots of people talking about how healthy the economy is. Inflation is low. Unemployment is low. The stock market is at record heights.

Travis: Which brings me to my **third point:** depressions and recessions have a way of sneakin' up on ya'.

People were pretty happy with things before the Great Depression. The economy was boomin'. Plenty of jobs. New technologies like broadcast radio and TV were up and comin'. Young industries like aviation and automobiles were taking off. The stock market was hittin' record highs.

Just two days before the stock market crashed, the chairman of National City Bank of New York told investors,

> *"The industrial situation of the United States is absolutely sound, and our credit situation is in no way critical.... The markets generally are now in a healthy condition.... I know of nothing wrong with the stock market or with the underlying business and credit structure."*[7]

Ya see, even the experts don't know what's comin' 'round the corner. Who knows? The stock market may keep goin' up forever. But I wouldn't bet on it. And I for sure wouldn't put all my eggs in the American stock basket.

Sure, I might miss out on some big time gains by not having more in the market. But I'm not tryin' to get rich quick. I just want to have somethin' left if everything falls apart.

Take this little sheet and think about it. I typed it up so I could hand it out to

---

PREPARING FOR HARD TIMES IN CASE OF ANOTHER DEPRESSION

Work

Jobs will be scarce, so **work hard and smart now. Make yourself indispensable by knowing more about your job than anyone else and getting along with everyone. I need to be the last mechanic my boss would ever want to let go.**

Lifestyle

1. **Get out of all debt; even pay off your house as fast as you can.**
    Even if you keep your job during a bad economy, you'll probably make less money because companies will be hurting. Ask yourself, "If my salary were cut in half, could I still make my payments?"

2. **Live way-y-y beneath your means.** People living too high will be in a mess. They'll lose tons of money if they have to sell their fancy cars and houses at a huge loss.

3. **Put more into your emergency fund.** In some areas, fifty percent of the people lost their jobs during the Great Depression. How long could you last without an income?

Investing

1. The stock market will crash, so **don't be caught with 90 percent of your money in stocks. I keep some world-class, blue chip companies, the least likely to go broke in a crisis.**

2. **Diversify globally. While some countries will be hit hard by an American depression, others may prosper.** For example, eighty percent of Coca-Cola's earnings come from outside the United States, making its profits safer than some businesses that operate only in America.[8]

3. **Invest in long term government bonds, like treasury bills.** They're as safe as our government. If a severe recession strikes, people will flock to these safer investments, fearing that less stable companies will default on their loans, driving up their value. Plus, the government will lower interest rates to almost nothing, which will also drive up the worth of the bonds.[9]

4. **Rent out a condo, starter home or a room in your house. But don't go borrowing lots of money to buy something.** You don't want to be stuck with payments that have to be covered by high rents. If families can't afford rent, maybe two families can afford it together. If inflation gets out of control, the worth of your own home will go right up with inflation.[10]

---

anybody who'll listen.

Amy: Sounds secure to me. Even if a deep recession *never* strikes, you're prepared for any personal crisis. In a depression, you'd have no house payments or car payments and will make killer money with those bonds. You'll be feasting on lobster while others are standing in soup lines!

Travis: Actually, I wouldn't want to flash my money around and write an article for the local paper sayin', "Message to Losers: I Told You So!" I just hope I'd have enough money to sponsor a soup kitchen and provide cheap housing to the down and out.

Amy: I was thinking that too, of course.

Antonio: Here's our pot of money for you, Travis. Your advice will save us much more in the future.

Travis' Scoreboard

Travis: (Uncomfortably) The money's not necessary, but thanks!

James: So Travis, what's your total net worth today?

Travis: I don't like to talk about it. But you seem like pretty nice folks and won't spread it around. If people think I'm rich, they'll start comin' 'round askin' for money. My truck's paid for. Could sell it for about $10,000. My house is paid for and worth

$130,000. Kramer and I each got $50,000 in a foreclosure home we're tryin' to sell. If we make our target 10 percent, I should get $5,000 profit after taxes. Got $10,000 in a money market fund (my emergency fund), $10,000 in a total stock market index fund and $10,000 in a long-term government bond fund. My hound dogs are worth about $200, but they're a liability. Eat too much and chew up the back seat of my truck.

Amy: Do hound dogs bark and keep you up at night?

Kramer: Amy…

Amy: What kind of movies do you like?

Kramer: Amy!

Amy: You're worth $205,000. And you're just 28? I like the way you keep score! Suddenly, I see the difference between men and boys. Hard to find anybody my age who can provide the security a woman wants. Now I may be no Daisy, but…. ya seein' anybody?

Takeaways from Travis

Kramer: (Saving Travis from a big time blush) I'm not providing a dating service this weekend. So, tell me what you've learned from Travis.

Amy: Like Buffett, he worked hard, lived way beneath his means and started saving early.

James: Until I pay off my car, I don't really own it. Never thought of it that way before. I'm gonna start paying more each month to pay it off early. Then, my car will be my first real asset.

Antonio: He didn't just jump into stuff, the way so many lose their money. He studied investments − reading books and talking to people.

James: He got a team so that he wasn't making decisions alone. I'm sure you guys bounce ideas off each other, keeping each other from making stupid mistakes.

Amy: Keep meeting new people. Be nice to people. You never know when a relationship might pay off.

Antonio: Adopt a lifestyle and investments that will weather the hard times. I think I'll combine some of Hash's recommendations with some of Travis'.[11]

Akashi: He changed the way he kept score. I think that was the huge transition that allowed him to make it big.

Kramer: Originally in science,[12] and later in the business world, people spoke of paradigm shifts − a radical move from one way of thinking to another. Most people can't break with the old paradigm – our culture's way of keeping score by appearances: expensive clothes, expensive cars and big houses. Research shows that people who successfully accumulate wealth have made the paradigm shift. They're more concerned with financial freedom and net worth than status or showing off.

If you want to accumulate wealth, start thinking net worth.

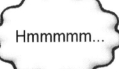

- What assets do you own? How much are they worth? Subtract your liabilities to discover your net worth.

- Ask your parents about their net worth. What would they change, if they could?

- How could you increase your net worth?

- Talk to your parents about their outlook for the future of our economy. Do you think a severe recession is in our future? Why or why not?

Assignment
Between Breakfasts

Most successful people give much credit to their wise friends and acquaintances who provide regular, candid advice. If you don't have such a group, think through how you could develop one.

Resources to Take You Deeper

For Specifics On Investing in Real Estate

On flipping properties, I recommend *Buy It, Fix It, Sell It...Profit* by Kevin Myers, 2nd Edition (Kaplan Business, 2003). Sanely and practically written by someone with plenty of experience.

On purchasing to rent, see *The Millionaire Real Estate Investor* by Gary Keller (New York: McGraw-Hill, 2005). Ideas from over 100 real estate investors.

On our personal experiences in both flipping and renting properties, see www.enjoyyourmoney.org.

Preparing for Difficult Times

Crisis Control in the New Millennium by Larry Burkett (Nashville: Thomas Nelson, Inc., 1999). Good lessons from the history of depressions and market speculation gone wild. Burkett believed that our economy was in bad shape - ripe for a deep recession. He gives practical hints to help us prepare for the possible hard knocks down the road.

Breakfast #6: The Breakfast that Almost Wasn't

Fast Forward to Reunion

Amy: Should we just skip Breakfast #6, since we didn't cover finances?

Akashi: For me, it was a pivotal point in my relationship with the group. And although *that* may not mean a lot to Larry, the story of the abductor came up more than once in later breakfasts, illustrating some pretty serious money issues.

In retrospect, that day seems almost surreal. You see it in movies but don't think it'll ever happen to you.

Larry: Okay, you can't leave me hanging. What in the world happened?

Akashi: Emotionally, I was ready to quit the group. Antonio and I still liked each other, but that take charge part of my personality kept him from committing to the relationship. I wanted the relationship to move forward, but he seemed reluctant, maybe scared.

Also, I was pretty jealous of Amy. She was such a flirt. So the breakfasts were getting awkward for me, to say the least.

Besides, Amy was so darn good at math, running all those calculations in her head, that I felt outclassed. It was like school all over again. My dominating personality hid a lot of insecurities, especially about academics.

But enough about me. Since our next topic was "Saving Money," we agreed to meet outside the entrance to Wal-Mart so that we could talk to the manager about retailing and pricing.

Hanging Out at Wal-Mart

The students were early. When we saw Mrs. Kramer walking toward us from her car, we started walking leisurely toward the front door. I halfway noticed a homeless fellow sleeping next to the building with a newspaper over his head.

It should have struck me as odd, since Wal-Mart doesn't allow that sort of thing. He must have positioned himself there shortly before we arrived. But my mind was busy figuring how to find out if Amy and Antonio had something going, without *acting* like I cared. You know how the game's played.

So, just as the automatic doors were closing behind us, we heard Mrs. Kramer scream and turned to see the homeless guy forcing her into his sports car.

James: It was a blue 2004 Mustang Mach 1, you know, the limited edition with the

310-horsepower twin-cam V8. Apparently, he'd stolen it the night before.

Akashi: So we all bolt out of Wal-Mart, just in time to see him shut the door and head toward Highway 41 with Mrs. Kramer in the car.

James: You're not doing this story justice. Can I do the chase scene?

Akashi: Go for it.

The Chase

James: So the abductor finds reverse, squealing out of his parking place, nicking the Blazer behind him before he shifts into first and burns rubber till he's out of our reach.

I took charge, shouting "Jump into my Camaro!" By this time, he'd secured quite a lead, heading south on Highway 41.

We fastened my regulation racing seatbelts for a rough ride and got major rubber in two gears before down-shifting for a fishtail merge into 41. Amy called 911 from the back seat, alerting the police.

"Put this in," I ordered Akashi, who was riding shotgun. "I drive better with music, especially Steppenwolf, particularly 'Born to be Wild.'"

Larry: I get it. Classic cars. Classic rock. Not a lot of mystery to you, James.

James: We hit the red light at the top of the hill, and as we waited for traffic to clear, I revved my engine. As fate would have it, the driver of the '68 Shelby Cobra next to me took my revving to mean I wanted to race. Besides, seeing the girls in my car made the challenge irresistible.

When the light turned green, we shot off the starting line, neck and neck up until 60 mph, when I hit third gear. I cut my blower in for extra horsepower, and apparently my challenger did the same.

Still side-by-side at 110 mph, Amy spotted the Mustang dashing into the industrial road to the right, sideswiping a diesel truck and then regaining control. I needed that right lane. I warned my riders, "I've got one more trick to shed this Cobra. Hold onto something."

I flicked the nitrous switch. When the spark ignited that nitrous, we sealed his demise in street racing history. I swerved in front of the Cobra, slammed the brakes for the intersection, ran the red light and took the sharp turn at about 35 mph, barely maintaining control as my friends kept their eyes glued to the rear end of that Mustang.

"We've got company," Antonio shouted from the back seat.

Sure enough, police lights were flashing, but they gained nothing on the vengeful Cobra, which seemed glued to our rear bumper.

Akashi saw the Mustang dash behind a gas station, and our newly-formed parade surrounded it. The policeman hopped out first, shouting on his intercom for everyone to remain seated. I yelled at the cop, pointing to the Mustang , "It's a kidnapping!"

After four more police cars and about 15 gawkers joined the party, things got sorted out.

From my car, I watched the policeman handcuff the kidnapper, read him his rights and haul him off. After a talk with Mrs. Kramer, he came our way, telling us that he understood our intentions and appreciated our help in apprehending the abductor. But he sternly warned us that if he EVER caught us racing for fun on public streets, we could kiss our drivers' licenses goodbye.

Then, he walked over to the guy in the Cobra, who asked all about Mrs. Kramer, explaining that she was a dear friend. When he saw her taken in the parking lot, he explained that he couldn't bear thinking that he might never see her again. The policeman let him off with a warning as well. We did the traditional hood-popping ceremony to compare engines.

When Mrs. Kramer walked over, she thanked us profusely. I said, "Do you know *everybody* in this town?" To which she responded, "I tutored that policeman through Social Studies. But who's the guy in the Cobra?"

"Somebody who just b.s.'d his way out of losing his license," said James.

Kramer: Great story, James! Can I take over now?

James: Sure! Especially since that's about all I remember from that day.

The Mystery Kidnapper Revealed

Kramer: I was too shaken to drive, so they squeezed me into the back seat between Antonio and Amy, leaving my car at Wal-Mart till after breakfast.

At Hash Brown's, I explained that the abductor was my brother Billy, who desperately needed money for a heroin fix. He knew I had savings and wanted to get me to an ATM.

Billy and I were inseparable through grade school. He was much more gifted at academics, landing scholarships to both Emory and Stanford. But amid the rigors of medical studies and internships, he turned to amphetamines one exam week to keep him going day and night. It worked! But after using it for several other exam weeks, he was hooked.

He carried on a successful practice for years, but finally the addiction caught up with him and led him to heroin. He lost his family, his practice and all his life savings. Now he lives with other addicts or on the streets.

When I hear of a drug-related shooting, I worry that he's dead. When I see a homeless person, I get nervous. When someone rings my doorbell, I fear that he may be there, desperate for money and as unreasonable as an animal.

James and Antonio pulled me aside and said that if I *ever* got spooked at home, to call their cells and they'd be there in a moment's notice. It meant a lot to me.

Akashi's Reflections

Akashi: That day changed my relationship with Mrs. Kramer.

After a previous breakfast, I had talked to her about my frustrations with Antonios' seeming lack of drive and inability to make decisions. She told me,

> *"Your strengths make you respectable; but, your weaknesses can make you loveable."*

She explained that, back in college, her husband gained her respect because of his skill and leadership on Georgia Tech's football team. But their relationship deepened when he revealed that he struggled with academics because of a learning disability. They fell in love as she tutored him in Math.

I didn't understand her statement till the breakfast after the kidnapping. To me, Mrs. Kramer was this gruff, no nonsense educator – resourceful and entertaining, but hardly friendship material. The day of the kidnapping, I saw her human side – her insecurities and weaknesses. Suddenly, she was fully human, with hopes and dreams and fears just like me. It wasn't just *us* who needed *her*. *She* needed *us*.

The day after the chase, I called her at home to check on her. After that, we began to talk and e-mail, especially about some problems I was facing. She became the mother I needed, the one who had time to first listen, then offer wise advice, and accept me whether I took the advice or not.

Final Thoughts from Amy

Amy: That day was a leap forward for the entire group. True, I had this deepening relationship with Antonio and saw Akashi as a threat. But a 15-minute episode involving a desperate drug addict, a life-threatening kidnapping and a daring high-speed chase has a way of stopping time and putting things into perspective.

From then on, it wasn't just money management that tied us together. There was something more. It's hard to explain, but that event unified us and got us through some difficult times. It also helped us to understand some of Mrs. Kramers' later sessions on the relationship between successful money management, life choices and teamwork.

- A large part of success involves knowing yourself - your strengths, your weaknesses, your interests. What are some of the strengths, weaknesses and interests of this story's characters? How could these characteristics lead to successful careers?

- Reflect on your own strengths and interests. In what types of careers could these characteristics flourish?

- Do you see your parents, bosses and colleagues only for the roles they play? If you saw them as real people with real dreams, real problems and real worries, how could that change your attitudes toward and relationships with them? How can deepening your relationships lead to greater success and fulfillment in life?

Assignment
Between Breakfasts

So far, we've talked about the excitement of multiplying your money through investing. But in order to invest, you've got to have money to invest. Since it takes money to make money, this next series of breakfasts will suggest scads of ways to save.

To make this more personal and practical, write down where your money goes in a typical month. The "Spending Worksheet" in the Appendix might help.

PART TWO

SAVING MONEY

Breakfast #7: Live WAY Beneath Your Means

OR, "A DOLLAR SAVED IS TWO DOLLARS EARNED"

Larry: That was quite a morning! But you didn't learn much about money management.

James: True, but that incident pulled us together as a group. I needed more than information. I needed the encouragement, understanding and accountability to make major changes in my spending habits. After that incident, I felt more comfortable with everyone, comfortable enough to do something that was pretty intimidating: to lay out my financial life in front of anybody. I acted cool about it, but inside I was pretty scared.

I'll tell about the next few meetings.

Flashback

Review

Kramer: Let's try to forget about last week. Any new thoughts about Travis' presentation?

Antonio: For a country boy, he sure knows his investing. He's got a good memory for all those things you taught him.

Kramer: For a country boy? For a *country* boy? Antonio! You're stereotyping! What if I said, "For a Mexican, that Antonio…."

Antonio: Sorry! It's so easy to do.

Kramer: To set things straight, most of the stuff Travis knows isn't from me. The auto mechanics course at North Metro Tech is rigorous. Over half the class drops it. Travis was one of the top in his class. And he's continued to take classes for special certifications, keeping him on top of his field.

After I helped him work around his reading disability, he began devouring information – sometimes reading, sometimes by listening to books on tape, sometimes by talking to wise people.

Amy: I paid him a visit last week…to ask more questions on investing, of course. His house is really nice, on a little knoll with a view of his acreage, surrounded by huge oak trees! Inside, he's got hundreds of books, organized on custom bookshelves. They range from history to philosophy to cars to investing.

Kramer: He's the most avid learner I've ever met. Maybe he's trying to escape his impoverished roots. Whatever the case, by coming across so country and so humble, he disarms people. They open up to him. That's one way he learns so much about real estate. Since he never brags about his own success, other local investors don't see him as a threat. He just looks up to them with his, "Golly! Gee whiz!" innocence and extracts every investing secret they know.[1]

James: I think Travis' greatest accomplishment was to save that much money when he was young. I'll bet that 99 out of 100 people would have *spent* that car flipping money instead of *investing* it.

Kramer: I agree. And that's a great introduction to this new series of breakfasts. **If you want to become financially free, it all starts with transforming from spenders to savers, from living beyond your means to living beneath your means.** Most never make the change. This lesson is critical.

James: That's my big sis Carmen standing in the entranceway. If it's okay, she wanted to sit in on this session. She's a single mom who's always looking for new ways to save.

Kramer: No problem at all! Carmen! Welcome to the group! How many kids do you have?

Introducing Carmen

Carmen: Two boys, ages six months and eight years.

Kramer: I'll bet they're a handful. You could really help us out in these saving sessions. Glad to have you on board!

Introduction

Kramer: I want to warn you about the next three weeks. If you buy what I'm selling, you'll be way out of step with today's culture. If you're not willing to be different, you'll never make it.

We're gonna talk about living beneath your means. Think about the successful people I've introduced you to – Oseola, Buffett, Hash, Travis. None of these could have made anything without massive saving. I'll give it to you straight: **if you can't save more than you spend, you'll never accumulate wealth. You'll always live in financial bondage.** And it's not just in your personal life. The same goes for your business. Jerry Goldress, president of Wherehouse Entertainment -

Akashi: - Is that the same as *Wherehouse Music*, where I buy music and games?

Kramer: Right. That's just one of their 111 stores scattered across the nation. So, Goldress was once asked to reflect on his success. One of a few big keys he mentioned was -

Akashi: - Let me guess, it's counterintuitive.

Kramer: Right. It's something you wouldn't ordinarily think. Did you drink too much coffee? If you interrupt me one more time… (pausing to make sure nobody breaks in). So Goldress said,

> *"Manage costs, not revenue. And remember that there is no such thing as a fixed cost."*[2]

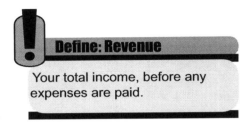

Define: Revenue

Your total income, before any expenses are paid.

What do you make of that statement?

Antonio: To make a football analogy, he's saying that defense is more important than offense. Your salary and investments are your offense. Your defense is controlling expenses.

It takes what most of us think about business and turns it upside down. We tend to think that the key to business success is selling more stuff than our competition. Goldress says that, from his experience, it's more important to cut your costs. And whatever costs you fail to cut will only grow.

Kramer: Sam Walton, when he was getting Wal-Mart off the ground, was a maniac about cutting costs. He always found the cheapest ways to get the best products. He'd fill up his car with women's underwear that he'd found cheap in some nowhere factory to sell at a discount at his store.

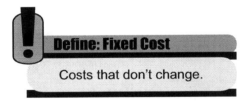

Define: Fixed Cost

Costs that don't change.

He refused to have fancy, expensive offices. His own home was nice, but modest. He drove his old truck around town and dressed plainly. When he took his staff on trips to find new products or open up a new store, they'd all pile into the same, cheap motel room to save money.

According to Sam's brother Bud,

> *"We had to keep expenses to a minimum. That is where it started, years ago. Our money was made by controlling expenses."*[3]

Wal-Mart wasn't the only discount retailer in those early years, and some had much better funding. But some of them were spending too much money and either fell behind or went under. Manage your costs! They may be more important than your income.

Amy, what's all the whispering about? If it's worth telling, it's worth telling the whole group.

Amy: I was just telling James that I don't like where this is going.

Kramer: Don't be afraid. Tell us. Candor and all that stuff. Right?

Amy: So, I've got a bad feeling about this session. Saving seems all about discipline, saying "no" to the things I want, cooking instead of eating out, sacrificing now so that I'll have something later.

When my parents nag me about budgets and saving, I think, "Just give me my fun today. Forget saving for the future; I might not even be alive then anyhow."

Kramer: Any of the rest of you agree?

James: I see the need to save for the future; but when it comes down to deciding whether to buy that spoiler for my car or put the money into savings, the car wins out every time.

Akashi: Same problem. Once I get my check, I want to eat out with my friends, go to a concert and buy the latest "Final Fantasy." I know I *should* save. I know that when I'm 60 I'll kick myself for not saving more. But, I fall for immediate pleasure over long term savings. Every time.

Kramer: I think you're seeing only two options:

> **Lifestyle #1:** The "**Sacrificial, Monastic Lifestyle**," where every time you look longingly at the gum machine at Wal-Mart, the logical part of your brain pitches a fit, screaming "*That 50 cents should be invested, with interest!*"
>
> All discipline. No fun.
>
> **Lifestyle #2:** The "**Spend Today, Tomorrow We Might Die**" **Lifestyle**. When you come to that same gum machine, you reason, "I'd hate to think that I'd skipped dessert on the Titanic, sacrificing today for a tomorrow that would never come. In fact, I'd rather order the appetizer, the chef's special and the dessert and max out my credit card just before we sink."
>
> You put the 50 cents in the machine and enjoy your gum.

But can't there be a third lifestyle that saves for the future while enjoying life today?

Amy: I think that both Warren and Oseola enjoyed life immensely. They just somehow enjoyed things that were within their budgets.

Antonio: Wouldn't the ideal be to find smart ways of getting at least the *main* things we want now, while saving enough for the future? Some of my past purchases were stupid. Avoiding *some* of my past spending wouldn't have hurt my present happiness at all.

Kramer: Sounds like a great place to start. Let's rid our minds forever of the notion that our lives have to suck today in order to save for tomorrow. **Our goal will be to**

have a purposeful, full life, both now *and* in the future. Here are a few ideas, which we'll expand upon over the next few weeks.

- **Realize that you *Can* Save.**
- **Learn to *Enjoy* Saving.**
- **Decide what you *Really* Want. (Question your wants.)**
- **Find Creative ways to Get What you Want Cheaper.**
- **Pay Yourself First.**

You Can Save

Most people say that they'd *like* to save, but they just don't make enough money to both meet today's needs and save for the future.

Amy: That's my parents. When I talk saving and investing, they say they don't make enough to save.

James: Mine too.

Antonio: Ditto.

Akashi: Yep.

Kramer: I think that at least three of your families, perhaps all four, make plenty to save. And I'll prove it.

Do all of your parents make the same salary?

Akashi: Very unlikely.

Kramer: I'll bet their salaries differ greatly. From what I know of your families, I'll estimate that one family makes $30,000 per year, another $45,000, the next $60,000 and the next $100,000. Yet, all of your parents claim that at the end of the month, their money's gone, with nothing left to save. Does anything about that strike you as odd?[4]

Akashi: If family #1 is paying their bills at $30,000 per year, then why doesn't the $45,000 per year family have $15,000 to invest, the $60,000 per year family have $30,000 to invest and the $100,000 per year family have $70,000 to invest?

More Income Becomes More Spending

Antonio: Maybe those who are making more have bigger needs, like taking care of elderly parents.

Kramer: Perhaps. But more likely, they've chosen to live a higher lifestyle – eat out more often and at nicer restaurants, drive nicer cars, live in nicer neighborhoods, take nicer vacations. When people get a significant raise, their first thought isn't,

"Great! Now I can start investing!"

Instead, they say,

"Great! Now we can qualify for a bigger loan and get that nicer house in that nicer neighborhood."

Antonio: So, no matter how much they make, they increase their "needs" so that there's still no money left over at the end of the month.

Kramer: Exactly. Dr. Thomas Stanley and Dr. William Danko discovered this when they studied the habits of millionaires. First, they needed to *find* the millionaires to interview them. Where would you look?

Ritzy Neighborhoods = Expensive Lifestyles

Antonio: I've seen *Lifestyles of the Rich and Famous*. I'd start by looking in the most expensive neighborhoods.

Akashi: Duh.

Kramer: Obviously. Or so they thought. But as they began talking to people, they made an interesting discovery. Many in those ritzy neighborhoods had no wealth. They were spending all their salaries on huge house payments and the lifestyle of those neighborhoods.[5]

Antonio: The neighborhood lifestyle?

Kramer: Think about it. To live in a high class neighborhood, you've got to landscape your yard professionally, have a certain kind of lawn mower, certain kind of car, take European vacations, send your kids to more expensive colleges, have a more expensive Christmas. And as that leader of Wherehouse Music said,

"... there is no such thing as a fixed cost."

Those costs go up every year.

Antonio: So, "keeping up with the Joneses" gets more expensive with each higher-priced neighborhood.

Kramer: Right. Stanley and Danko found that many of these folks in the most expensive neighborhoods had the *appearance* of wealth, but little or no *actual* wealth. As Travis' cousin in Texas says, "big hat, no cattle."

When Stanley and Danko finally found people who'd accumulated vast wealth, they tended to be in more modest neighborhoods, driving more modest cars, living a lifestyle far beneath their means.

Why do you think he named his book *The Millionaire Next Door*?

Akashi: Because if most of the truly wealthy don't flaunt their wealth, they may be living next door to any of us, driving normal cars like the rest of us.

Kramer: Warren Buffett and Sam Walton lived like that. But until Stanley and Danko did their research, I thought Buffett and Walton were a bit weird, the exception rather than the rule. Actually, they're pretty typical of millionaires.[6]

He also discovered that the millionaires weren't all lawyers and doctors and movie stars. They worked in an incredible variety of over 240 different vocations. There were antique dealers, auctioneers, beauty salon owners, builders, farmers, home repair/painters, janitorial services contractors. **Their distinguishing characteristic wasn't so much what they did for a living. Rather it was how far they lived beneath their means.** That's what allowed them to accumulate their wealth.[7]

Akashi: So, they took the saying, "A penny saved is a penny earned" seriously.

Kramer: Actually, they figured out that

$ \$ \$ \$ \$ \$ \$ \$ \$ \$ $

A dollar saved is two dollars earned.[8]

$ \$ \$ \$ \$ \$ \$ \$ \$ \$ $

Amy: What kind of math is that?

Kramer: Can't anyone figure it out?

(All fidget nervously with their food.)

Kramer: Let's say you make a pretty good salary, and you're paying out half of it for taxes and Social Security...

Akashi: Got it! If 50 percent of each earned dollar goes to Uncle Sam, and I work overtime to get more money, then I walk out with only one dollar of every two dollars I earn. But if I *save* a dollar, I keep the entire dollar. Savings aren't taxed. So, saving one dollar gives me the same amount of money as earning two dollars. Thus, "a dollar saved equals two dollars earned."

James: So if I were paying out half of my salary for taxes and stuff, and I needed $500 for my spoiler, I could either work overtime to earn an extra $1000 or save $500 and skip the work. Saving is looking a lot more fun than it did a few minutes ago!

Kramer: Let's take it even farther. Sure, a dollar saved is two dollars earned. But, if you invested that dollar…

Amy: (doing quick calculations in her head.) Using the laws of 10's and 7's, that dollar doubles every seven years at 10 percent interest. In 49 years, it becomes $128.

$ $ $ $ $ $

A dollar invested is $128 in future money.

$ $ $ $ $ $

Kramer: Let's call that $128 **"future money" – what your money *could* be if invested at 10 percent for fifty years.** Buffett could see that at an early age, very clearly. He couldn't see today's $20 as a mere $20. He saw it as a future $2,560. And no wonder he went ballistic when his wife redecorated the house! One thousand dollars spent on redecorating is a future $128,000!

James: Future money is cool, and I definitely want to start saving and investing toward my goal of a million dollars in my 40's. But for now, I just want to save up for that spoiler.

Kramer: OK, so let's dig into James' expenses sheet and start prospecting for gold. Maybe we can keep him from having to land a third job.

Enjoy Saving

Kramer: Look out! We're diving into the counterculture! We're gonna stop doing what we're doing just because everybody's doing it. This is where it gets fun!

- We're gonna decide what's *really* important to us and how to get it without ending up in financial bondage.
- We're gonna find cool ways to save tons.
- We're gonna *enjoy* beating the system.
- We're going prospecting for gold in those budgets!

See Where Your Money's Really Going

"How to Make a Million Dollars With Money You Can Probably Find Lying Around in Your Spending Sheet"

Kramer: Most people have no idea where their money goes each month. **Writing down everything you spend in a month is often the first step to finding big money.** James, hand us each a copy of your "Spending Sheet" so that we can try to find enough money in there for your spoiler.[9]
James' Monthly Spending Sheet

(He chose the categories relevant to his spending from the generic "Spending Sheet" in Appendix 1)

Income: $1,024 ($8 per hour for 128 hours per month)

Expenses (total of the below categories): $1,024

Eating Out: $340

> Meals: $8 per day = $240
> Snacks: $5 per day, 5 days per week = $100

Auto Expenses: $354

> Gas: $240
> Repairs: $34
> Insurance: $80
> Fix-Up: (No Money Left)

Hair Cuts: (My sister gives me free haircuts.)

Other Purchases: $110 (Tools, video games, movie rentals and stuff)

Clothes: $40

Taxes: $150

Recreation: $30

Charity: No Money Left

Saving: No Money Left

Investing: No Money Left

(The table is a blur of pencils scratching on napkins and the tap-tap-tap of calculator buttons.)

Saving with Meals Out

Finding Huge Money in Fast Food

Amy: $340 per month on meals. Break that down for us.

James: I get home from school at 4:30, drop my books and leave for work at 5:00. I'm dead tired and don't want to make supper, so I get fast food on the way. After work, on the way home, I get a banana split or maybe a barbeque sandwich, plus a large soft drink. On average, I eat out twice on weekends, usually with friends.

Amy: And an example meal is…

James: I don't eat at expensive places. A typical meal might be a fast food joint for a classic double burger with cheese, medium fries, apple turnover and a medium soft drink.

Amy: (click, click, click) So, that's an average of $8.00 per day for that evening meal. That comes to $240 per month. Plus, your late night snack is running about $5.00 each weeknight x 20 = $100 per month, **which brings you to a grand total of $340 per month eating out.**

Akashi: And you make $8.00 per hour?

James: Right.

EXPLORING DIFFERENT MONEY ANGLES

Akashi: Has it ever occurred to you that if you work four hours after school, one of those hours is thrown away on supper? Actually, more than one hour because part of that hour goes to pay Uncle Sam. That one, daily meal consumes *over one fourth* of your weekday salary!

James: (Swallowing hard) I've never thought of it that way!

A QUICK WAY TO THE SPOILER

Amy: So, if you really wanted that spoiler badly, you'd mooch off your parent's food from the fridge instead of eating out at all. In two months, you'd have $680 for your spoiler.

Akashi: (Finally getting comfortable with her calculator.) **That's $4,080 per year, the equivalent of $8,160 earned!**

Amy: Young Warren Buffett would have probably looked at those hamburgers and fries and thought, **"If I invested that $4,080 each year at 10 percent interest, it would become over $5 million in 50 years**

James: Those colas, burgers and fries are costing me millions! I'm scarfing down a fortune. How embarrassing!

Amy: (Hiding her spending sheet) Embarrassing to me too. I had no idea that eating out could add up to so much.

James: But all I do during the week is school and work. Can't I at least have the pleasure of getting something I like to eat?

Akashi: It's *your* decision what to do with your money. If fast food is more important to you than your spoiler, that's *your* decision to make.

A WORKABLE COMPROMISE

Amy: But what if James tries it one day but decides he hates stuff from the fridge. Then, he goes back to fast food and has accomplished nothing.

What about this compromise? Check out the value menus. You know, everything's 99 cents. Let's say James gets three of those 99-cent double cheeseburgers and the 99-cent fries. That's just $4.00. Order the complimentary water instead of the soft drink. It's better for you anyway. For your snack after work, reward yourself with something for 99 cents, and raid the fridge to finish filling your stomach when you get home.

Try it for a week. If you can do something similar at other restaurants, you've just saved half of your money.

You still get to eat out, yet you save $8.00 per day. **Just counting week days, you save $160 per month and can have your spoiler in four months. Then, you start putting that money in a 10 percent investment for 50 years, which gives you over $2 million, not bad for eating out a little more wisely.**

James: Nice trick, Amy! I get my food *and* my spoiler *and* my fortune!

Saving on Gas

THE COST OF DRIVING TO SCHOOL

Antonio: The next big money item I'm seeing is gas. Is there any way you can cut back?

James: School is a 20-mile round trip. Home to work is another 20-mile round trip, the opposite direction.

Akashi: Why don't you take the bus to school?

James: First, I'm a senior and don't want to ride the bus with all those noisy freshmen. I also LOVE my car and would rather be seen driving it to school. Besides, it saves me a little time.

Amy: What gas mileage does that manly muscle car get?

James: About 10 miles to the gallon, unless I kick in my Holley four-barrel carburetor a couple of times. If I do, I just make sure I'm pointed toward a gas station!

Amy: Impressive. (Pounding on her calculator) "So during the week, if you make no extra stops, you're driving 40 miles per day at 10 miles per gallon. You're burning four gallons per day, paying $12 per day (at $3.00 per gallon), $60 per week, for a grand total of $240 per month, or $2,880 per year (if you do summer school)."

THE QUICK WAY TO THE SPOILER

Antonio: So do you *really* have to drive to school? I mean, half of that money, $120 per month, is spent going back and forth to school. I say if you're the only senior who takes the bus, get comfortable with being different. Go counterculture! It's a no-brainer. Put up with the freshmen and go for that spoiler.

A Workable Compromise

James: But if I can't drive it to school, who gets to see my spoiler?

Amy: True. It's *not* a no-brainer for James. He loves that car. He doesn't want to keep fixing it up, having nobody to show it off to. I say take the bus Monday through Thursday. Thursday night late, you wash it really nice and drive it to school on Fridays, in time to impress girls for the upcoming weekend. You still save **$1,248** per year on gas. What do you think, James?

James: That's a HUGE return for a small sacrifice. I'll definitely consider it.

The Miracle of Cutting Costs

Kramer: James, congratulations for opening up your financial life to us. I know it's intimidating. But **do you see the miracle of how much money your friends have found for you? By slightly adjusting two habits, not even making a major life change, you save $1,248 per year on gas and $1,920 on food, giving you $3,168 every year. And that's from an income where you thought you had nothing to save!**

You're still eating out, and you still drive to school once a week. Putting your gas savings and food savings together, you get your spoiler in two months (your short term goal). After that, you start stashing that $3,168 every year into long term investments to save toward your million (your long-term goal).

Even with your present crappy salary, you could have over $1 million in 36 years. Once you get a job making more money, IF you continue controlling your costs, you could get your million in your 40's.

James: This is hard to believe! Something's got to be wrong. Before we ordered breakfast, I thought I had nothing to save. But now, halfway through my omelet, we've found enough gold in this friggin' "spending sheet" to get my spoiler *and* my million.

Kramer: It's proof of the wisdom of the *Wherehouse Music* guy. Our culture has programmed us to think, "I need more money, so I need more work." But **concentrating for twenty minutes on your expenses with some wise friends, you come out with a spoiler and your million dollars.**

The Incredible Potential of Saving While Young

James: But, it still doesn't make sense to me. I'm working only 28 hours a week, getting $8.00 per hour. How is it that I can make a fortune with that when adults may make $30.00 per hour but can't save a cent?

Carmen: Look at yourself. Your expenses are probably less than they'll ever be in your entire life. No kids to feed, no house payments. Food's free in the fridge, no health insurance. Whereas I'm having big trouble trying to save 10 percent of my salary, you guys might comfortably save 50 to 90 percent of your salary.

Akashi: It's how Buffett made all that early money, doing normal things like paper routes. It's not just that he worked hard and smart. He lived at home, had few expenses and refused to blow it on stuff he didn't need.

James: This is exciting…and…depressing!

Amy: Now you're sounding like Hash Brown.
James: *Exciting* in that I'm able to save so much. *Depressing* in that I didn't start it four years ago, when I started working after school.

Amy: (Surfing to an online calculator) Want to get *really* depressed? If you'd started saving that much four years ago, even at no interest at all, you'd have $12,672 today.

James: (Beating his head against the table) I could have bought my '77 Camaro, almost fully restored! If I'd just cared as much about my future self back then….

Older Spenders

Kramer: Enough with the whining. Just be excited that you learned about controlling expenses by age 18. I read an advice column in the *Atlanta Journal* just this week where a lady wrote in saying, "I'm 55 years old. I make $40,000 per year, and my husband makes $60,000. We don't have anything saved, but need to save toward retirement. Should I look for a better paying job?"

From what we've learned today, how would you advise her?

Akashi: I'd say, "Lady, you guys are making $100,000 per year and barely making ends meet!?! Control your friggin' costs! Live like a couple making $50,000, and you can save $50,000 per year! $50,000 saved is $100,000 earned. You don't even have to invest it. Just stick it under your mattress each year, and you'll have $500,000 in 10 years, when you're 65. "

Preview

Kramer: Easy to say, but hard to apply. These days, most people whine that they don't have enough money. For many, the answer lies in their fat budgets. We need to take another couple of weeks on this. Carmen, can you join us next week and give us some expert advice on saving on clothes and groceries? We want to know how to beat the system, save more and have more fun.

Carmen: If you allow part of the breakfast to be a field trip.

Kramer: It's a deal!

The Summary

To sum up this breakfast, what are your takeaways?

Akashi: *I need to occasionally track every dollar I spend. Otherwise, I have no idea where my money's going.*

Amy: *Find ways to save. A dollar saved is two dollars earned.*

Antonio: *Invest starting early, while my living expenses are low. A dollar invested is $128 in future money.*

James: *Little expenses, like eating out at cheap places or driving too much, adds up if you do it every day.*

Kramer*: A decent, but doable idea beats a perfect but passed-over idea. I think Amy came up with some great, workable compromises.*

- Why do you think most people can't save?

- Looking over your spending sheet, how could you save more? What are some relatively painless ways you can cut back? What would you like to do with that money?

Assignment
Between Breakfasts

1. Ask your parents for tips on purchasing clothes and groceries.

2. In whatever store you find yourself this week, imagine that a friend has asked you how to shop more wisely. Write down your own advice.

3. Find a couple of websites or articles to read about saving on clothes and groceries.

Resources to Take You Deeper

The Millionaire Next Door: The Surprising Secrets of America's Wealthy, by Thomas J. Stanley, Ph.D., and William D. Danko, Ph.D. (Pocket, 1998). Based on their interviews with millionaires. The "secrets" to accumulating wealth often involved ways they found to save and live way beneath their means.

Find many free ideas for saving at www.enjoyyourmoney.org.

Breakfast #8: Save on Food and Clothes

Review

Kramer: James, were you able to save any money last week?

James: Sure! I did revise some suggestions, however.

Kramer: Tell us about it.

Soft Drink Savings: Two Liter Name Brands Versus "By the Cup"

James: So, I tried substituting water for cola a couple of days. I admit it. I'm a wimp. Too Spartan for me. So I got this idea. I called Carmen to ask where to get cheap, name brand colas. She called me back in 15 minutes, telling me where they were selling five two-liter Cokes for $5. So I bought them and put one in the back seat of my car. When I did the drive through, I asked for a complimentary cup of ice and poured my own cola. **Instead of paying $1.29 for a small cup of cola, I got two whopping liters for a buck!**

More Soft Drink Savings through Generics

The next day, Carmen called with an even *better* idea. She challenged me to take a taste test − Big K Cola from Kroger versus the name brands. I'd tried cheaper brands before, but thought they didn't stand up to my favorite name brands. Maybe it was "The Power of Suggestion" − you know, people tell you the name brand is better. You just expect that the name brand will be better. Hot girls in ads tell you it's better. So you taste it and…Surprise! It tastes better.

I blindfolded myself and had my sister pour me several name brands and several store brands or generics.

Now this is important: I didn't ask myself, "Can I tell which is the name brand?" Instead, I asked, "Which do I like better or like just as well?" I actually found a couple of generics I liked better!

Next, I calculated my potential savings. I took my small soft drink cup left over from supper and filled it with ice. Then, I took my two liter generic and started filling up the cup. I got eight cups out of the two liter generic! **That's a cost of seven cents per cup, as opposed to $1.29 per cup! Since I was getting a drink both before and after work, I saved $1.22 per cup, or $2.44 per day.**

That's a savings of $890 per year, or $1,200,000 if invested at 10 percent interest for 50 years!

Now maybe it's just me, but $1,200,000 seems like an awfully high price to pay someone to pour my soft drink.

Kramer: By learning this little trick, you're telling me that:

- you sacrificed nothing

- you're having just as much fun

- it tastes just as well or better

- *and* you're saving a bundle

That's remarkable! It's unbelievable how many ways we can get rich, just by rethinking our little, daily habits. Count me in for a taste test this weekend!

Savings and Peer Pressure

Kramer: Great! Carmen's here!

Carmen: Sorry to be late. My babysitter…

Amy, Akashi, James and Antonio: (Interrupting and bowing repeatedly toward Carmen) We are not worthy! We are not worthy! Thou art the great saver!

Carmen: (Playing along, basking in her moment of glory) Finally! Some respect! (Sitting down) Usually people just laugh off my frugal ideas. I think it's fear − fear that people will look down on them for buying a generic cola or shopping at a cheap store.

Amy: My mom told me that she wouldn't be caught dead in a Save-A-Lot grocery or Big Lots. People might think she's poor. Nobody in her circle of friends would *ever* go there.

Antonio: Can you say "Peer Pressure?!?" It makes me want to say, "Mom, if every other parent jumped off a cliff, would you?"

Kramer: It's adult peer pressure, pure and simple. It keeps many an adult in perpetual financial bondage. As you know, I couldn't care less about what my peers think.

Billionaire Savers

I'd rather compare myself with peers like Warren Buffett and Sam Walton. Walton wasn't ashamed to drive an old truck. According to Sam's brother Bud, also one of the richest people in America,

> *"People don't understand why we're still so conservative. They make a big deal about Sam being a billionaire and driving an old pickup truck or buying his clothes at Wal-Mart or refusing to fly first class." "It's just the way we were brought up."*

> *"When a penny is lying out there on the street, how many people would go out there and pick it up? I'll bet I would. And I know Sam would."*[1]

To this day, although he's worth billions, Buffett buys his Cokes on sale.

Get this. When Warren Buffett and Bill Gates, the two wealthiest people in the world, were traveling together in China and stopped by McDonalds, Buffett pulled out his discount coupons![2]

But your parents can't stand for anyone to think they might not be wealthy. Largely due to peer pressure, your parents are living on the edge, borrowed to the limit, choosing the appearance of wealth over the real thing. In the event of a crisis, they have no reservoir. Here's the analogy.

Reservoir Analogy

Kramer: Solve this problem. Imagine that you've gone back to nature, living in the Blue Ridge Mountains. It's so far out in the sticks that there's no city water. You run a small farm, which is irrigated by a small stream.

The weather cooperates during your first few growing seasons. Plenty of rain. Plenty of sunshine. But midway through the next season, the rain stops, and the stream dries up. What do you do?

James: Dig a well.

Kramer: They tried, but couldn't find water.

Antonio: Put out barrels to catch rainwater.

Akashi: THERE IS NO RAIN. That's why the stream dried up, remember?

Antonio: Oh yeah.

James: There's nothing you can do. What you *should* have done was build a reservoir while the rains were coming in. You could have stored all those hundreds of gallons of water that went through your property, keeping it in a pond above your fields, so that you could use it during dry seasons.

Kramer: Exactly.

Amy: No fair. Trick question.

Kramer: True. But it made you think. Now what does this have to do with personal money management?

Amy: I've got to save up a reservoir of money for the dry seasons, like when I'm between jobs, or my car dies, or long term illness, or a major house repair, or a deep recession. Then I can pull from that reservoir.

Carmen: And don't forget that you need that reservoir to buy heavily discounted foods in bulk. People who live week to week can stock up on items while they're cheap.

James: Let's talk real life. My parents don't have a reservoir. There's just this stream of money coming into our family and flowing right through. They live paycheck to paycheck with no money reserves.

One day, Dad's car engine seized up. He'd already borrowed on the house for a vacation the year before, so there wasn't anything else to borrow on. He had to pay a taxi a huge daily fee to get to and from his 80 hour work weeks. It took about a year to get back to normal. But you know what? When he finally got his own car, instead of saving for the next catastrophe, he cut down his work to just meet expenses! Still, no reservoir.

Kramer: That's not rare. About one in four adults live paycheck to paycheck.[3] We live in a *spending* culture, not a *saving* culture. Every commercial tells us to spend. How many commercials urge us to save?

So, take the reservoir analogy further.

Antonio: Hmmm. To make a good reservoir…first, you've got to have a big enough stream of incoming water to both irrigate your current crop *and* to fill the reservoir. That's your salary. Or, I suppose you could have several streams of income. Whatever the case, you've got to land a good enough job and work enough hours to have a strong stream filling up that reservoir.

Kramer: Think Travis. He has multiple streams of income.

Antonio: Second, you've got to build a dam and stop any leaks.

Kramer: I think that's what most Americans fail to do. And, it just might be the most important. I like to identify three kinds of leaks:

- **Steady Drips.**
- **Major Gushes.**
- **Blowing up the Whole Dam.**

Let's save the major gushes and dynamite for next week. Today, we'll try to cork those drips. What kinds of drips do you think are draining people's reservoirs?

Steady Drips

James: I suppose drips are those expenses that seem small, but are so regular that they drain our budgets much more than we think. It's like my daily eating out. I had no idea that it was dripping out over ¼ of my entire salary. Maybe bleeding would be a better analogy. **Throwing out a five and couple of ones for a hamburger, fries and a Coke seemed like nothing. But it amounts to almost a quarter of a million dollars of future money.**

Akashi: Let me add **Cigarettes** to the dripping category. I was at a friend's house last night. She lit up a cig and I asked how much a pack costs these days. She said about $4.30 a pack. Now this is a girl who's always worried that she'll never make enough money to have anything. I told her that I thought I knew a way she could get rich, even with her meager salary.

I multiplied that $4.30 by 365 to find that her pack a day habit runs her $1,569 per year. Then, I went to her computer and surfed to one of those online calculators to discover that **if she invested that money each year at 10 percent interest, she'd have $2,163,211 in 50 years.** I said, "Do whatever it takes to break the habit, and start investing that money!"

James: Maybe I should act like a cig addict, but instead of lighting up after school, take my $4.30 and desperately deposit it into my savings account.

Kramer: Good thinking, Akashi and James! Let's let *Carmen the Great* give us some hints on stopping those pesky drips from draining our reservoir.

The Ramen Experience

Carmen: As a high school student, I had no clue about costs. My parents infuriated me by saying "no" to a lot of my requests for shoes and clothes. I thought, "It's just $50 here and there. They make lots of money. What's the big deal?"

So, when I landed my first full-time job and my own apartment, I remember cashing my first check and hitting the mall for some serious clothes shopping. I looked hard and found some great deals. Unfortunately, that spree caused me to run out of money a week before my next paycheck. I existed on Ramen noodles for an entire week!

My parents had set spending limits when I lived with them. Now I needed to set my own limits.[4]

The Envelope Method

Learn this from my Ramen experience: **Establish some limits.** You can't just go out and "get what you want" as if you've got an unlimited budget. I wasn't making a lot. It took almost everything I had just to pay utilities, rent and gas.[5]

I wrote out my budget and found ways to live within it. I didn't want to spend another week eating Ramen noodles. Fifty dollars a month was all I had for clothing. When I cashed my paycheck each month, I put $50 in an envelope and labeled it "clothing." Once that money was gone, I had to wait till next month to buy anything. That worked so well that I began doing an envelope for food and another for entertainment.

Soaking Up Wisdom

Next, I read everything I could find on getting the most out of my dollar. It's a science. I call it Cheapology. I'm always learning from new articles, websites and fellow Cheapologists. There's always some new angle I never thought of. Here are a few tips that I use the most. You'll have to read the books and sites I recommend to get more.

Amy: Fifty dollars on clothes? What can you possibly get for $50?

Clothing

Carmen: A good bit, depending on when and where you shop. I noticed on your expense sheet that you spend about $100 a month on clothes. If you could cut it down to $50 per month, you'd save $600 per year. That's $1,200 earned, or over $820,000 in future money.[6]

Write this stuff down, and you might just come out with ¾ of a million dollars from your clothes budget!

Hint #1: Never pay full price.

I buy clothes seasonally, when stores are getting rid of their summer stock to bring in their winter stock, or getting rid of the winter stock to bring in the summer stuff. Discounts are up to 80 percent. So, I save up my $50 for several months and rack up on $10 pants and $5 shirts.

Hint #2: Watch where you shop.

Find the cheapest places to buy quality clothes.

Hint #3: Get over the fads.

Pay $150 for a tennis shoe as a status symbol? I don't think so! Be good enough at your sport to get respect without the brand.

Hint #4: Go buying, not shopping.

"Shopping" is when you hang out at stores, just seeing if something catches your eye. Tip: Something **will** catch your eye. You'll buy it. You'll get home and say, "Did I really need another pair of pants? Bring on the Ramen Noodles."

"Buying" is what you do when your shoes wear through and you need a new pair. Go to the store that sells quality shoes at the cheapest price.

Hint #5: Hit the thrift stores

Akashi: I love thrift stores! I find the weirdest stuff there!

Carmen: You can go either weird or name brand. You see these cool designer jeans and name brand shirt I'm wearing? (She stands up to model her outfit.) $8 for the jeans, $5 for the shirt. I'm wearing $13 worth of clothes, compared to another person, wearing exactly the same quality, who paid $100 for it. Makes me feel pretty smart.

Know your thrift stores. Find which ones stock more of what you want.

Akashi: I've found some thrift stores closer into Atlanta that have more of the alternative stuff.

Amy: But it's all *used*, right? It seems kind of weird buying used clothes.

Carmen: Isn't everything in your closet used? I mean, after you wear a brand new shirt once, it's used. Are you gonna throw it away? The clothes you're wearing this morning, they're used. Right? So why would you have a problem *buying* used clothes, especially if you could save 90 percent off retail?

I have no problem at all buying used clothes. It's incredible fun beating the system by finding a $100 pair of name brand pants for $5.00. And someone else broke it in for me, free of charge, so that it's comfortable the first day.

Kramer: Great tips on clothes! I want to leave enough time for you to educate us on buying food, another big ticket item.

Food

Carmen: Can we take a field trip to the nearest grocery?

Kramer: Everyone finished with breakfast? Let's go!

Five Minutes Later...

Carmen: (Pointing to the walls) **For your health, spend most of your time shopping around the perimeter,** where they stock fresh fruit, meat and vegetables. Those aisles (pointing to the inner aisles) offer cookies, soft drinks, and other processed garbage that doesn't vaguely resemble anything on a farm. I especially avoid that "obesity aisle" with the chips.

Look at these vegetables. Which are the best buy? (Answering her own question) None of them. We're in the wrong store. **You can save by shopping the ghetto-looking, no frills store down the street**. I start there, then get what they don't have here. The plus of *this* store is variety.

Which of these ketchups do you buy? Answer: **always try the store brand or generic first.** The savings are significant.

What's a Twenty-Five Cent Savings?

James: I think my mom goes overboard with stuff like this. She'll rave about something costing a dollar at one store that she can get for 75 cents at another. I mean, what's a quarter these days?

Carmen: James, you're thinking the wrong angle. Don't think 25 cents. Think 25 *percent*.

Sure, if you get almost all your shopping done at one store, don't travel to another to get one item that's 25 cents less. It's a waste of time and gas.

But think this angle. Most of your cart is filled with low-cost items. A dollar here. Five dollars there. If you can average saving 25 percent on each item, a family may pay $750 per month on groceries rather than $1,000, saving $250 per month, or $3,000 per year. That's worth $6,000 earned, over $500,000 invested for 30 years at 10 percent interest.

I like to play a mental baseball game to make shopping more competitive.

- **Single = 10 percent off**
- **Double = 25 percent off**
- **Triple = 50 percent off**
- **Home Run = Over 50 percent off**

If I score well, I reward myself with a movie or something special. My hard work at saving has earned me a bonus!

James: So a quarter off a dollar item *is* a big deal. Baseball fans get excited about doubles.

Carmen: Remember the reservoir analogy. Small drips can drain your budget.

Sometimes generics taste different than the brand. Maybe better, maybe worse. But technology has advanced to where scientists can pretty well break down a brand name food to its exact components, allowing generics to copy them pretty well.[7]

Buying Quality

Akashi: Hey look how cheap this brand of juice is, compared to that brand.

Carmen: That ain't juice.

Akashi: Hello! It says right on the front, "Contains 100 percent fruit juice."

Carmen: Read the ingredients on the back. The first items listed are the primary ingredients.

Akashi: Hey, what's the deal?!? Sucrose, corn syrup, a bunch of chemicals and only five percent fruit juice?

Carmen: It's deceptive advertising. Studied it in Home Economics. Think about it

this way. Take a quart of water, add a cup of sugar (another name for sucrose), corn syrup and a bunch of artificial flavors. Is that good for you?
Akashi: No way!

Carmen: Now, add ¼ cup of 100 percent orange juice. Is it good for you now?

Akashi: Not really. Pour yourself a glass, and you're getting sugar water with a little juice splashed in.

Carmen: True, but it never said that it contained "*Only* 100 percent fruit juice." It said that it "Contains 100 percent fruit juice," a twist in wording that's technically accurate, but tricks the customer. That ¼ of a cup of 100 percent fruit juice means that it legitimately "contains 100 percent fruit juice."

So, when you're looking for the best prices, make sure that you're comparing apples with apples, not apples with Apple Jacks.

The best bread, the most natural, is 100 percent whole wheat. Not "contains 100 percent whole wheat." Not "wheat bread" with artificial coloring to make it *look* like whole wheat.

Look at the ingredients. You're not getting a better deal if you choose a product that's cheaper than a real food, disguised as a real food, but the ingredients show that it should be displayed in the candy section.

Dave Barry says that you don't need to weigh yourself or take a stress test to discover if you're out of shape. Just look out your back door. If that's American soil out there, you're out of shape. Much of the problem relates to the way our culture shops and eats.

Buying by the Ounce

Question: which is the better deal, the 24 oz. brand named Ketchup for $1.57 or the 46 oz. for $3.19?

Amy and James: (tap/tap/tap)

Carmen: Put up the calculators. It's right there on the price sticker. **Always go by the cost "per ounce" rather than total cost.** The larger is 6.93 per ounce, the smaller 6.54 per ounce. Usually, the larger quantities are cheaper per ounce, but not so in this case.

Someone check the price per pound on that whole chicken as compared with the cut up one.

Antonio: The whole chicken is much cheaper. Makes sense. **The less they've had to prepare something, the less the cost.** A block of cheese over shredded. A head of lettuce rather than cut and bagged for salad.

Go Generic

James: If we're talking about the same quality, I'm astounded at the differences in price. Look at these killer differences:

Baking Soda:

> Brand Name = 13.7 cents per oz.
> "For Maximum Value" Generic = 7.70 per oz.

Cooking Spray:

> Brand Name = 48.8 cents per oz.
> "For Maximum Value" Generic = 18.8 cents per oz.

That's over 50 percent savings on that cooking spray! A home run!

Carmen: Now some people won't touch value products. They live in mortal fear that if Mrs. Jones spots them checking out with a "For Maximum Value" product, she'll be labeled poor. For the self esteem challenged, it might help if we named the other products "For Mediocre Value" and "For Minimum Value." Then, perhaps the fear of being labeled stupid will overcome the fear of being labeled poor.

Akashi: But aren't some brand names superior in quality.

Carmen: True. Try both and research it. Often the products are exactly the same.

You think *those* are killer savings? Follow me to the pharmacy. This will *really* blow your minds.

Look at the ingredients of this brand name sinus/allergy medicine. Now, check out the generic.

Akashi: They're exactly the same thing, just in different wrappers!

Carmen: Now look at the price. You save over 40 percent with the generic! And check out this generic stool softener I was getting for my granddad: a 70 percent savings over the brand name!

James: (Whispering) Can you turn down the volume when you say "stool softener?"

Carmen: (Just as loudly) Get over it or I'll send you to the pharmacist to price Viagra.

James: So, about the stool softeners…

Carmen: The ingredients appear to be exactly the same.

James: Exactly!

Carmen: Let's double check with the pharmacist.

Antonio: (Whispering to James) Carmen and Akashi are embarrassingly fearless. They'll talk to anybody! I think they'd charge hell with a water pistol.

James: I know. Sometimes they scare me to death.

Carmen: (To the pharmacist) Excuse me! Are these two products exactly the same thing?

Pharmacist: Exactly the same, sold under two different names.

Carmen: So I don't get it. Why do people pay four times as much for that brand name?

Pharmacist: *They* don't get it. Or they've tried the brand name before and they swear it's better. More likely it's the power of suggestion. Some ad convinced them. Or, they're afraid to talk to the pharmacist about their stool softeners.

Carmen: Oh, it's not for me. It's for James over there.

Pharmacist: I see. (Looking at James) Hope this helps your constipation, son.

James: I'm out of here!

Carmen: Wait! Hang out just a minute. I want you to see something. Just act like you're looking for something and watch the people.

(Whispering) This is absolutely incredible! Person after person purchasing name brands, often paying four times as much, FOR EXACTLY THE SAME INGREDIENTS! And how many of them will go home moaning that they don't make enough money?

"Larger" Usually Means "Cheaper"

OK, so follow me a little farther. Compare the smaller and larger jars of spaghetti sauce. Notice a pattern?

Antonio: Larger sizes are usually cheaper per ounce.

Carmen: Don't always assume it. Occasionally you'll see quarts of milk on sale, cheaper per ounce than the gallon. But in general buy larger sizes. That goes for laundry detergent and tons of other stuff. **Always compare the price per ounce.**

Antonio: But our pantry's pretty small.

Carmen: Put long term food under your bed. Put a high shelf in your clothes closet. Put it in the attic. Making space for purchasing in bulk pays a killer wage.

Stock up on sale items. Look at this laundry detergent on sale for half price. Hey, sir, why is this so cheap?

Manager: We got a great deal on it and are selling 120 boxes at our cost as a promotion. There's no limit. Take what you want.

Carmen: I'll take 15 of those large boxes.

Antonio: Fifteen boxes?!? It would take *years* to use that much. Why 15 boxes?

Carmen: Because I don't have room to store any more. Come on, Antonio. The Math ain't that difficult. Imagine that over the next four years, I'd spend $300 paying full price for laundry detergent. Why would I save only $10 on one box when I could save $150 on 15? Why hit one home run when I could hit 15 home runs?

Antonio: But that's a lot of money to put down up front.

Carmen: True, another reason to keep money in savings. You can't take advantage of super buys if you don't have the money to buy quantity when something's cheap. Buy a freezer and you can stock up on frozen pizzas, chickens or steaks when they're marked down. It's a great investment.

This month, I'm paying hardly anything for food as I prepare items I stocked up on months ago. When you see a sale, don't choke, jump on it.

Ask the meat people when they tend to mark down meat. It might be certain days of the week, or during the night every day. If you're the first one there, you can get great deals. I just paid $18.00 for 18 lbs. of ground beef. That's half price. I'll freeze it and use it for the next two months. Eighteen dollars saved equals $36 earned, all because I was at the right store at the right time.

Amy: You just saved $168 in five minutes, the same as $336 earned. I don't know many people who can earn that much in five minutes.

"Loss Leaders"

James: But I still don't get why they're willing to sell something at their cost, or even less.

Carmen: Good question. For meat and other perishables, they've got to move it before the sell date. They can either drop the price to move it or risk throwing it away after the date. On other items, you've got to understand the concept of *"Loss Leaders."* Great bargainologists...

James: I thought you called them "cheapologists" earlier.

Carmen: Whatever. But the point is, great shoppers know the "Loss Leaders" for various stores. Here's how it works. Most stores have certain products that they make no money on. They may even lose money on them. Their strategy? Advertise your loss leaders. People will flock to the store for those cheap products, buying the pricier stuff while they're there.

Surely Wendy's can't make money off that .99 cent menu. From what I hear, it's a loss leader. But if you come for the value menu and wash it down with a large Coke, they've made a profit on the Coke. James beats the system when he orders the loss leader and brings his own cheap drink.

Movie theaters don't make money off ticket sales; they make money off popcorn and snacks.[8] Discount clubs like Sam's Club or Costco may sell you many products at just above their cost, making the bulk of their profits off membership fees.

James: But if everyone went to each store and bought only the loss leaders, wouldn't they go out of business?

Carmen: It'll never happen. Loss leaders have been around a long time, at least since Edison used the technique in the 1880's to sell incandescent lamps.[9] If people haven't figured it out in 125 years, I doubt they'll figure it out now.

Different Stores, Different Prices

James: Some stores get better bargains from distributors than others. One day, I compared auto parts stores for a new alternator. I was shocked at the price difference. It wasn't that one store was generally cheaper than another. It was just on this brand. I asked the manager, who said that they had an account with the distributor that handles that brand. I suppose each store works with different distributors.

Carmen: Good point! I'm often amazed at how an otherwise expensive store might have much better deals on select items. You're right; it's not just about loss leaders.

James: Earlier, you mentioned **discount clubs**.

Carmen: I'm a member of one. But since it's 30 minutes away, down in Kennesaw, I go only once a month to stock up on big items that they're cheaper on. But keep those receipts and compare product to product. Often, Kroger's FMV products (For Maximum Value) or Publix or Wal-Mart's brands beat the discount club prices. Learn what's cheaper at each store.

Coupons

Amy: So, I was in this checkout line and the lady in front of me got a cartload of food for about $10, using coupons.

Carmen: You can clip coupons yourself or pay a little to have someone else do the clipping, ordering them from a site like www.thecouponclippers.com. You'll find all kinds of testimonies on their forum of people sharing their shopping experiences where they bought $84 worth of goods for $6. No kidding. They're like Olympic shoppers. If you really get into it, you'll need a coupon organizer. According to "The Coupon Clippers,"

> *"You can easily save 20-30 percent of your grocery bill each week, and if you can double your coupons, you can wipe out 40-60 percent of that bill with carefully planned shopping trips."*

Check out the testimonials on their forum, where these extreme savers routinely share their latest store raid.

Coupons and "The Guy Thing"

James: OK, I suppose I'm too much a captive of my culture...but honestly...I can't see myself walking up to the cash register with my coupons in my wimpy organizer. What if a hot girl is in line behind me?

Amy: Glance up and say, "Finally, I've saved up enough for that spoiler!" *That* should empress her with your supreme manliness.

Akashi: If the hot girl happens to be *me*, just say you're saving for an extravagant date.

Kramer: Get over the macho thing. You're more likely to impress a girl with your personality and handle on life than the way you check out at the grocery store. Besides, the girl you want to marry probably brings her own coupons. Ask her if she wants to join you at Starbucks to trade ideas.

Blitzing and Finding Your Style

Kramer: Honestly, sometimes I fool with coupons, but other times they seem like too much of a hassle. Most coupons seem to be on name brands, which I avoid.

Carmen: You have to find your own style. Some make a killing with coupons. Others do a month of shopping at a time at a discount club. Others shop loss leaders and cheap products at several stores.

One technique I've found helpful is *blitzing*.

James: You mean, like in football where almost the entire defense runs in on the quarterback before he knows what hit him?

Carmen: Right. In shopping, it means that whenever I'm in a store to get an emergency item, like I'm out of milk or eggs, I pick up a sale paper at the entrance, do a quick read and blitz the store for unadvertised specials.

My theory is that almost every store keeps some spectacularly discounted items on hand to wow their customers and move old stock. Those change from day to day. If I shop once a month, I get only what's discounted that day. But if I blitz regularly and stock up, I get many more outrageously discounted items.

If there's nothing worth getting, I've wasted 10 lousy minutes. Big deal. But almost every time I blitz, I find several items at a steep discount.

Example: This morning, I discovered I was low on diapers. Emergency item. Poop happens, you know. So, I stopped by Eckerd's on the way here. As I walked into the store, I grabbed the sale paper, blitzed the store and found ½ price Tuna and ½ price batteries. I stocked up on both and walked out with two home runs. (I know I'm mixing football and baseball analogies, but nothing in baseball resembles a blitz.)

That five minutes of blitzing saved me $24. If I can make that kind of savings regularly, that's an hourly wage of $252.

Antonio: Correction: that's worth $504 per hour in salary, if a dollar saved equals two dollars earned. But even just thinking of that $24, you saved in five minutes what it would take me three hours to make at work at $8 per hour.

Carmen: Excellent angle. **We're talking major money for a small effort. Five and 10 minute blitzes, tearing through a store looking for deals, pays an outrageous salary.**

General Hints

Finally, a few **general hints:**

- Don't shop while you're hungry. You'll buy stuff you don't need.
- Make a list and stick to it, except when you see great discounts on things you'll eventually need.
- Plan on taking a little more time. Comparing costs and going to multiple stores takes time. Figure out how much you're saving per hour and you'll realize it's well worth it.
- Limit your eating out.

Well, I'd better go.

All: (standing and cheering): More! More! Encore! Encore!

Carmen: Sorry, but I've gotta relieve the baby sitter and get these diapers home.

James: I'll be quick, but here's a card and money from our collection, a small token of our appreciation for your wisdom. First, the card, which Akashi penned on her napkin during this session (clearing his throat):

Armed with loss leaders

She's the merchant's greatest fear

And since a dollar saved equals two dollars earned

She's a household engineer

And here's some cash. Each of us chipped in $4.00, giving you $20 to stock up on generic stool softeners, or whatever you need.

Carmen: You guys are too much! James, I'll pick up your stool softener and have it delivered to the front desk at your school. Hopefully they'll call you out of class, mentioning it over the intercom.

As I leave, don't you guys need to sum up your takeaways?

Action Points

Akashi: There's major gold in food and clothing savings.

James: Shop the cheap stores first, and look into thrift stores.

Amy: Do the major clothes shopping when they're closing out seasonal items.

James: Look into discount clubs.

Antonio: Limit my spending, perhaps using the envelope system for a category that's likely to get out of control, like clothing.

> **Kramer:** I want to study this more and talk to you further. Before this session, I thought I was frugal. But you've shown me some places I've been throwing money to the wind. You are indeed "The Great Saver." Also, I'll try blitzing. I just might get my quarter back. Quarterback. Get it?

All: Booo! Hissss! Corrrrny!

Preview

Kramer: So, you think you're saving a lot by corking these steady drips? Just wait till next week, where we concrete in a major gush with your cars. I think we can save you as much as half a million dollars on cars over a lifetime.

James, you're our car man. Can you surf the web for advice and consult some auto magazines to find tips for saving money on cars?

James: Sounds fun! Do I get paid?

Kramer: If your advice is valuable enough.

James: Works for me!

- If you were advising a friend on how to save on food and clothes, what would you tell her?

- What are the best places to shop for clothes and food in your area?

- Which of Carmen's ideas might work for you?

Assignment
Between Breakfasts

1. Come prepared to talk about your week's buying experiences.

2. Study up on ways to save on cars. Read articles. Talk to your parents, friends, car salesman and anyone who's willing to talk.

3. Solve this riddle about buying cars.

> *I'm 60 years old*
> *my money is gone.*
> *In a lifetime of spending*
> *something went wrong.*
>
> *Spent a half million dollars*
> *buying cars - quite a sum.*
> *But my rich twin spent nothing -*
> *zilch, nada - how come?*

Breakfast #9: Save on Cars

Review

James: I think I solved the riddle! Can I solve the riddle now?

Kramer: Try to stop bouncing so much and let's wait till after our food arrives. I hate to start this week's material until we review last week's.

Let's be candid with each other. Are you storing up water in your reservoir? Or is "The Counterculture Club" just a bunch of chitchat and grits?

Akashi: I used the envelope method to limit my spending on meals out. When the envelope was empty, I restricted myself to the fridge. I took the savings and put it in my money market fund at the bank.

Amy: I did an envelope on clothes. It worked! The money I saved is in a savings account.

Kramer: I tried some new generics and store brand foods and saved a ton. Did a blitz or two for some huge savings.

This is great! What we're doing is seldom done – breaking bad habits and forming new habits. Change isn't easy. Most get set in their ways, comfortable in their ruts. We resist innovation with everything. Change takes time. As Mark Twain put it,

> ***"Habit is habit and not to be flung out of the window by any man,***
> ***but coaxed downstairs a step at a time."***[1]

You can't put *everything* that we talk about each week into practice. But, at least question those old habits and start coaxing them down the stairs. One day, the new habits will seem as natural as the old ones once did.

Back to the Beginning

Let's think back to the very beginning. Our first weeks, we talked about the magic of multiplying our money through investing. We found that it's not just for old people, not just for people with huge salaries, but for normal people like us.

Next, we decided that it's no good to know about investing if we have nothing to invest. That means we've got to dam up a reservoir by living way beneath our means, saving up for big dollar items like spoilers and squirreling away an emergency fund in case of, well, emergencies. Only then are we ready to invest.

So how can we save? For the last two weeks, we talked about plugging up those steady drips - like food and clothes. This is our third week on saving. Saving is critical, since a dollar saved is two dollars earned, and people are letting millions slip through their fingers, one steady drip at a time.

Ron Blue got a Masters in business administration and spent most of his life writing, teaching and counseling people about personal finance. Once someone challenged him to sum up in a few words everything he knew about successful money management. Here's what he said,

"Spend less than you earn, and do it for a long time."[2]

Think about that statement. Write it down. Put it in your wallet or purse. It lets you know why we're spending so many weeks talking about saving. And overspending on cars is one of the biggest culprits that keep people from saving.

Field Trip

Before we eat, let's begin with a short field trip. Follow me.

(They step outside.)

We're here!

James: The parking lot?

Kramer: Right. Take a good look at the cars. Which owners do you think are wealthy?

James: Cars. Now *that's* my area of expertise. Wealthy owners? First, I vote for the owner of that *Jaguar XK8*. Suggested retail is over $70,000. And the insurance would have to be astronomical.[3]

Amy: I'd guess the *Hummer* next. I think that model runs over $50,000, besides eating lots of fuel. You'd have to make some serious dough to feed and insure that baby.

Hey, look at that old pickup. I doubt *that* owner's doing very well.

Akashi: But Kramer didn't ask, "Which owners have the highest income?" She asked, "Which do we think are wealthy?" Totally different questions. Someone might have a terrific salary, but spend it all on a lavish lifestyle.

Haven't we learned that most successful wealth builders are more concerned with saving and investing than spending and showing off? If the wealthy don't tend to live in extravagant neighborhoods, I doubt they drive extravagant cars. If a millionaire could be living next door to me, I suppose he or she could be driving that normal looking car parked next to mine.

Kramer: Good thinking, Akashi. The typical millionaire surveyed by Stanley and Danko paid $24,800 for his most recent car, ½ the cost of a new Hummer and 1/3 the cost of the Jag. That's pretty close to the average car purchase of non-millionaires. And remember, half of the millionaires paid less, some *far* less. Over one in three bought used cars.[4]

By the way, the old pickup's mine. I use it to work on our rehab houses. Sam Walton drove an old pickup, perfect for riding around with his bird dogs. Buffett was so disinterested in cars that he told his wife to pick him out something appropriate to meet people at the airport. Oseola didn't drive at all. I'm in good company.

Let's go back inside and see if our food's ready.

The Price of Extravagance

Cars. Why do you think most millionaires drive average cars?

Amy: (Surfing to the "True Cost to Own" calculator at www.edmunds.com) I suppose they value wealth more than appearance. They've thought through the expense of owning pricey cars. That Jaguar depreciates $22,538 the first year you own it. Once you consider five years of depreciation, financing, insurance, taxes, fees, fuel, maintenance and repairs, you've spent over $95,000.

Let's compare it to one of the most popular millionaire vehicles, a Ford F150 pick-up truck.[5] If somebody got it used, like many millionaires, her "True Cost to Own" over five years would be $29,238, or a savings of about $65,000 over the Jag.

Antonio: That five year fling with a Jag cost him over $9,000,000 in future money, if he invested that $65,000 at 10 percent for 50 years.

The Price of Being Known as Rich

Kramer: Another reason that many millionaires don't want showy cars is that they don't want the problems that come with the appearance of wealth.

Counterintuitive, I know. Most of us would love to be known as wealthy, to be famous, but we don't consider fame's drawbacks. Imagine for a moment that you win the lottery, have $5,000,000 and everyone knows it. What problems will you have?

Akashi. I couldn't tell who my real friends were anymore. I'd always be asking myself, "Do they like me for who I am, or just because I'm rich?"

Amy: Jealousy. I might lose some real friends.

James: People expecting me to give them money, especially friends and relatives. They'd think, "Hey, what's $500,000 to you? But to me, it could pay off my house and get my new business off the starting line."

Antonio: Lack of privacy. I hear that Michael Jordan can't even take his kids to McDonald's without reserving it entirely for himself. He's a prisoner of his fame, not able to go anywhere in public without being bombarded by fans looking for an autograph and a picture.

Kramer: You'd think that the high point in Sam and Helen Walton's lives was in October, 1985, when *Forbes* magazine declared Sam the richest man in America.

Instead, they consider it one of the *lowest* points of their lives. Photographers hounded them. Journalists wanted their story. From then on, innumerable people called and wrote to ask for a house, a car or support for their charity or business. In Helen's words,

"The whole thing still makes me mad when I think about it. I mean, I hate it."[6]

What To Do with a Free Rolls-Royce

Let me tell you a true story about a man named Mr. Allan. He's a self-made multimillionaire. One reason he's accumulated such wealth is that he lives way beneath his means. He lives in the same three-bedroom house in a middle class neighborhood that he's lived in for about 40 years. He's also a nice guy, helping struggling business owners with his counsel and money.

So one day Mr. Allan discovered that some of these grateful business owners had gone in together and ordered him a Rolls-Royce as a free gift of gratitude for all he had done for them. From what you know of Mr. Allan, how do you think he responded?

Akashi: I'll bet he was really grateful, but reluctant to accept it.

Kramer: Right. He turned them down.

James: But it was *free*!

Kramer: True, but here are the reasons he turned it down:

- It was not him. He stated, "There's nothing the Rolls-Royce represents that's important in my life."

- He loved fishing every weekend, driving his four-year-old non-luxury car to the lake and carrying home his bloody catch in the back seat. You just don't do that with a Rolls.

- If he drove it to work, his employees might get disgruntled, thinking that their hard work was fueling his lavish lifestyle.[7]

So much for the problems with the appearance of wealth. I'm not saying you can't go out and buy a luxury car or hot sports car. That's up to you. Just remember that the appearance of wealth brings both pleasure and pain.

Buying Cars, Just How Big a Gush?

James, you're our car expert. Educate us on how to drive quality cars for less.

James: Let me get out my notes. Cars are definitely a big gush item, draining our reservoir big time. **Before this research, I just thought in terms of my monthly car payments. Now, I'm looking at the total cost of the vehicle over time.**

Most Americans spend between $241,000 and $349,968 during their lifetimes on cars.[8]

The people who pay more aren't necessarily driving nicer cars. Many of them are getting ripped off because they don't know how to beat the system. Are you ready for some strategies for people who'd like to save enough on cars to have millions later in life?

Kramer: Bring it on!

James: But first, the riddle:

> *I'm 60 years old*
> *my money is gone.*
> *In a lifetime of spending*
> *something went wrong*
>
> *Spent a half million dollars*
> *buying cars – quite a sum.*
> *But my rich twin spent nothing –*
> *zilch, nada – how come?*

Amy: Paid nothing over 40 years of buying cars? I think he was a thief.

James: Perhaps. But Akashi and I found some other possibilities.

I brought Akashi with me, since she's as bold as a mongoose on steroids and won't take crap off anybody. We bled some used car salesmen and mechanics of their wisdom, starting with a bold, hairy, audacious question:

Buying a Lifetime of Cars, For Nothing

> *How can I get as close as possible to spending nothing over a lifetime of purchasing cars?*

We came up with several alternatives.

Free Strategy #1: The Albert Einstein Method

He never drove. He never spent a dime on a car all his life. Bottom line: if you can live near good public transportation, you may not *need* a car. More than half the households in New York City don't own a car, over 75 percent in Manhattan.[9]

If you save and invest the entire ¼ million dollars you would have spent on cars, you'd have a fortune!

Free Strategy #2: Drive a Company Car

Get jobs that provide company cars, free of charge.

Free Strategy #3: Buy Low, Sell High

Buy quality used cars cheap, and sell them at a premium. I thought of Travis, since he'd done that car flipping earlier in life. Turns out, he doesn't drive his muscle car to work. Too much wear, tear and gas. Instead, he drives a small, dependable car that gets good gas mileage.

So I said, "Travis, how much do you pay for your cars?"

Travis responded, "I don't pay for my cars. My cars pay me."

I said, "You mean to tell me that you *make* money every time you trade cars?"

"That's right," he said.

Here's how he does it:

STEP ONE: DO YOUR HOMEWORK

Define: Depreciation

The decline in value over time.

First, he consulted www.consumerreports. com to find the **most reliable** used cars with **great gas mileage**. Then, he consulted www.edmunds.com to find which models **cost the least to drive** and **depreciate the least** over time. He also asked other seasoned mechanics for recommendations, compiling a list of makes and models.

STEP TWO: LOOK FOR BARGAINS

He looked especially for **low mileage** cars with an **easy to fix problem** that made it hard to sell. Some bargain cars might have nothing wrong at all, just a motivated seller.

Each morning, he checked his list of models in www.autotrader.com, knowing that killer deals get snapped up quickly. He also checked local papers and cars being sold in parking lots and front yards.

One morning, he spotted a six-year-old Honda Accord for sale in a neighbor's front yard. Honda is known for reliable engines, which can easily run 300,000 miles. This car had 80,000 miles on it and was selling for $3,500, which was $1,950 below the *Kelley Blue Book* estimated selling price.[10]

The owner put it below market value for two reasons. First, he ran into a fire hydrant while trying to run over his neighbor's annoying dog, crunching his right front fender. Second, his wife wanted it out of the front yard before company arrived for the weekend.

STEP #3: GET AN INSPECTION AND ESTIMATE

Travis checked out the car himself. A non-mechanic would have paid $50 for a mechanic to do an inspection.

He found a fender at a local salvage yard, in the right color, for $100. If he paid someone to install it, add $50. He offered $3,000 cash and got it for $3,250.

Total cost for the purchase if you'd paid someone else for the inspection and repairs? You'd pay $3,450 for world-class, safe transportation, fixed up, that looks and runs great. It even came with an upgraded CD player.

STEP #4: ENJOY YOUR CAR FOR A FEW YEARS

Over the next three years, he drove the car 45,000 miles, changing the oil regularly and keeping it maintained. After the three years, he began looking for another bargain.

STEP #5: PURCHASE ANOTHER BARGAIN

Travis took his time and purchased another low mileage, reliable car for $3,250. He then advertised his old car for $4,000, selling it for $3800 - the *Kelley Blue Book* value for an excellent Accord of that year and mileage.

The bottom line? By purchasing a bargain and selling at a premium (like used car dealers do every day), Travis actually *made* $550 on a car that he drove 45,000 miles! His car paid him for the privilege of having Travis as its owner!

$ $ $ $ $

This strategy can work with any used car that's known for reliability and holds its value.

$ $ $ $ $

STEP #6: REPEAT STEPS 1 THROUGH 5

If Travis trades every three years, in 21 years he will have earned back more than the price he paid for that first car. After that 21 years, he'll continue driving attractive, world-class cars for the next 30 years, while *making* $5,500 in trades.[11]

Kramer: This is incredible! While the average person pays over a quarter of a million dollars over a lifetime of car buying, Travis will come out $5,500 ahead!

James: I couldn't believe it until I ran the numbers myself. I believe that anybody can do this, if they:

- save up the purchase price to pay cash
- learn which cars will last and depreciate little over time
- are willing to take their time buying (to find a reliable bargain) and selling

(to get a premium price). This means you must have enough saved to purchase your next car *before* selling your old car

Kramer: Give us some more hints! I'm writing as fast as I can!

Saving Tons Buying Cars

Strategy #1: Never Make Payments

James: Millionaires could easily make payments on their cars, saving the big cash to invest in their business or buy something else. Instead, the great majority of them buy their cars outright.[12] It's easy to see why when you run the numbers.

BOUGHT OUTRIGHT	"EASY" PAYMENTS
Original Purchase	**Original Purchase**
$20,000	$22,000
	(You don't get as good a deal when you finance)
	Payments (5 years at 8 percent) = $446 per month.
Total Paid over 5 years = $20,000	**Total Paid over 5 years** = $26,760.

Amy: With that $6,760, you could have bought a decent ski boat to take out on Lake Allatoona!

James: Or another car!

Akashi: Or a new computer, X-Box 360, a PlayStation III, Nintendo Wii and over 80 games to play on them! Payments are such a waste. That money could go for so many better, more fun things.

Kramer: Or two overseas vacations!

Antonio: Or sponsor three needy children in third-world countries for five years through Compassion International. They'd get nutrition, healthcare and education.

Akashi: (Embarrassed) I was gonna say that next.

Kramer: Me too....But remember, we're just talking about the money you'd pay in interest *over five years.* Most people will make payments on cars *for the rest of their lives.*

Amy: So, if they had to pay that $6,760 in interest over 10, five year periods, they'd pay $67,600 in interest over 50 years.

If they'd invested that $1,350 (amount paid each year in interest) each year at 10 percent interest, they'd have $1,728,404 at the end of that 50 years!

Kramer: That's astounding! If the average young person could simply save up enough to pay for his next car outright, and invest what he would have paid in interest, he'd be rich!

Because of purchasing with cash instead of making payments, the average millionaire spends significantly *less* on cars over a lifetime than the average non-millionaire who makes payments.

THE SAVER PLAN

If you're making payments, pay off the loan as quickly as possible. Once it's paid off, keep right on making payments, only this time into your savings account, until you've saved up enough to purchase your next car outright.

If you keep saving that $378 per month for a year, you'll have $4,536, plenty of money to purchase a good-looking, reliable used car when you need it.

Now you don't have to pay collision insurance, since you've got enough to pay cash for your next car. You're self-insured. That's more savings! Since you no longer need to save toward the next car, you begin putting that money into long term investments.

Amy: A perfect example of "it takes money to make money." Without the savings, you can't buy a car at a discount, self-insure or buy a bargain before selling your other car.

James: One more thing about car loans. If you have to get one, please don't get a six or eight year loan. You'll likely end up owing more than you can sell the car for. If regular loans are a bad idea, longer term loans are the pits.[13]

Strategy #2: Drive Less

Drive very little. Live close to your work or take public transportation. Warren Buffet lives five minutes from his office, on the same street. You won't be surprised to hear that his custom license plate reads "THRIFTY."

Strategy #3: Keep Your Car Longer

Some people think they have to get a new car every few years. Sam Walton drove his red 1979 Ford Pick-up truck forever.

Beyond Purchase Price

Akashi: I think the way you worded your question gave us only part of what we needed to know. You were asking only about getting by free in *purchasing* cars. But, the cost of a car is more than its purchase price.

You didn't take into account that by purchasing older cars, you'll probably spend more on maintenance than by purchasing newer cars. By purchasing used cars with 30,000 miles instead of 90,000 miles, your smaller maintenance costs just might pay for the added upfront cost of purchase.

James: Good point! In a minute, I'll talk about cutting the cost of owning and maintaining a car. But from the question we asked, we learned the incredible savings we get from **finding bargains on cars that are known to be reliable over time and depreciate slowly.**

Kramer: I can tell you've got lots more information. And, you can bet we'll be calling you for advice before our next purchase. Can you get us out of here in five minutes by listing some final hints?

James: Sure. But PLEASE keep learning about cars. There's a lot to know. The angles are fascinating! **I'm amazed at how much money people are throwing away in their ignorance. They could have much nicer cars if they weren't throwing so much money out the window.**

More Money Saving Strategies

PURCHASE QUALITY CARS.

Kramer has preached hard and heavy on long term thinking. To do this with cars, **you've got to think beyond your purchase price to "True Cost to Own."** Use this handy tool at www.edmunds.com. Go to "Tips and Advice" and "True Cost to Own." I wish it calculated for used cars further back than five years, but it's still a killer tool.

Simply choose the make and model, hit the button and **it tells you how much money you're likely to spend over the next five years. It takes into account depreciation, financing, insurance, taxes and fees, fuel, maintenance and repairs.** It's based on your driving 15,000 miles per year. If you drive more or less, take it into account.

Akashi: So, it would be much wiser to pay $1,000 more for a car upfront if it's gonna save me $5,000 over the next five years.

James: Exactly! With a high maintenance car, you might be able to afford to *buy* it, but not to *own* it.

Go for Great Gas Mileage.

Beyond being environmentally friendly, you save on a major steady drip. Use the U.S. government's fuel economy site (www.fueleconomy.gov) to estimate the gas mileage of various cars.

In general terms, think of it this way. Let's say gas costs $2.50 per gallon, and you drive 15,000 miles per year.

Money Angle #1: For every 10 mpg you cut down, you save $3,750 per year! In other words, buying a car that gives you 10 mpg better gas mileage could save you enough to buy another good, used vehicle every year!

Money Angle #2: If you were choosing between two cars of equal quality, it would be better to pay an extra $3,750 for the one getting the 10 mpg better gas mileage. In year one, your gas savings would pay off that extra amount. In each year following, you would save $3,750 per year!

Example: According to fueleconomy.gov, the top mpg this year is the 2006 Honda Insight, sipping 60 mpg in the city, versus the 2006 Bugatti Veyron, guzzling 8 mpg in the city.

The difference in cost, for those driving 15,000 miles annually, is $551 for the Insight versus $4,688 for the Veyron. Savings on gas? $3,244 per year. That's over $4,000,000 in future money (invested for 50 years at 10 percent interest)![14]

Get a Safe, Reliable Car.

Better to end up wealthy with all your bones in their right places, rather than broken and broke. Consult *Consumer Reports.*

Consider Repair Costs.

Parts for some cars can be very expensive. Again, consult *Consumer Reports.*

Find an Honest, Skilled, Seasoned Mechanic.

A mechanic once told me I needed a new transmission to the tune of $2,500. I got a second opinion from a transmission specialist, who fixed it with a cheap sensor.

Consider a Good, Used Car Over a New One.

Cars these days are running 200,000 miles or more quite easily. Consumer advocate Clark Howard says that, "New cars lose more than one third of their value in the first 12 months. In the first three years, they lose 60 percent of their value." If you purchase a new car, your drive off the car lot will likely be the most expensive fifty feet you'll ever travel.

Others will argue that you should purchase it new, since you could maintain it well from the start and get the maximum mileage. You can't usually know for certain that the used one was properly maintained.

But, with used cars a seasoned mechanic can tell you about how long big ticket items like the transmission or engine block will last. They can also tell you what tends to break in that model at so many miles.

Since pre-owned cars cost so much less, you're more likely to be able to self-insure, rather than pay for collision.

Clark Howard recommends purchasing quality used cars, since most have many more miles left in them.[15]

Another pointer. When buying used, always check the car's history using its VIN number at www.carfax.com.

Keep Your Car Maintained.

Above all else, change that oil regularly! Then, follow the standard recommendations for your car.

I'll say it again, keep learning about cars! There are many more ideas that I don't have time to tell you!

Buyer Beware!

Finally, after Akashi and I talked to numerous used car salesmen, we found this helpful list of definitions for the informed buyer. The quotes are how used car salesmen, and even private owners, describe their cars to potential buyers. The parentheses tell the rest of the story.

- "Owned by a Doctor" (And drag raced by his son.)

- "Never Been Raced" (Former owner too embarrassed.)

- "Low Mileage Car" (Odometer turned way back.)

- "Driven only 11,000 miles" (And towed the rest of the way.)

- "Rebuilt Engine" (We cleaned the spark plugs.)

- "One Owner Car" (Man by the name of Hertz [the rental company].)

- "Cream Puff" (Was in a head-on collision with a milk truck.)

- "Undercoated" (With rust.)

- "Second Car" (There were only two cars in the race.)

- "Doesn't Burn Oil" (It drips out before it has a chance to burn.)

- "I'll be Honest with You…" (Absolutely no meaning.)[16]

Kramer: When it comes to cars, many people will tell you anything to make the sale! Your takeaways?

Action Points

- **Akashi:** I don't think I want to take the time to flip cars every few years. Instead, I'll look for attractive, reliable, low-cost-to-own used cars at a discount and keep them as long as they stay reliable.

- **James:** I need to be more conscious of good gas mileage. My gas guzzler is eating me alive.

- **Amy:** Save enough to pay for my next car outright. Then, keep saving to self-insure and be able to pay for all future cars outright.

- **Kramer:** Get more advice from Travis, and read more about cars and trading. James has shown me some angles that should save me truckloads of money over time.

Thanks, James! Today, the money pot goes to you for your wisdom. Here is some food for thought.

Resources to Take You Deeper

www.consumerreports.org - objective (they accept no advertising) reports on the quality of used and new cars. Users must pay a small monthly fee to access many of their reports.

www.edmunds.com - auto prices, reviews, cost to own calculator, tips, advice, forums.

www.kbb.com - Kelley Blue Book allows you to find the value of both used and new cars of any make or model. Gives retail value, trade in value and private party values.

www.carfax.com - put in the VIN number of the used car you're looking at to get its history. Pay per download.

www.autotrader.com - find and compare used car prices in your area.

Hmmmmm...

- Which of these ideas sound most workable to you concerning saving on cars?

- Use the calculator at www.kbb.com to figure the difference in total cost over time between purchasing a car outright with cash and purchasing it with payments.

Assignment
Between Breakfasts

1. Next week, we'll talk about what will likely be the largest purchase of your lifetime: your house.

    I'll show you an amazing phenomenon, which I lay out in this riddle:

    > *Ralph and Becky*
    > *Live on the same lane*
    > *Neighbors in houses*
    > *Built exactly the same.*
    >
    > *But something's quite odd*
    > *I haven't a clue*
    > *Why Ralph pays one dollar*
    > *For Becky's every two.*

    Discuss the riddle with your parents.

2. Ask your parents' recommendations on buying a house. Ask them what their monthly payments are, the length of the loan and other specifics. Also, ask your grandparents or older relatives about the cost of their first house and their payments.

3. Read at least one article on hints for buying a house. Write down the best hints and bring them to next week's breakfast.

Breakfast #10: Save on Houses

Review

Kramer: James gave us a lot to think about last week. What are your thoughts after letting everything percolate?

Amy: Until last Saturday, I'd never once thought of the total I'm paying after all payments are made. My only thought in purchasing a car was, "Can I afford the monthly payments?" I certainly never thought how much those payments were costing me over a lifetime.

James: It's like the car dealers make their money by thinking long term, and we lose our money by thinking short term.

Akashi: The more I think about it, the more I kick myself for being so stupid. I never even asked the dealer how much I'd be paying for the car over the six year term. When I looked back at the contract, it was all there. Over time, I was paying twice what I could have paid with cash.

James: All this thought on saving is well and good, but I'll be candid about my percolations. Maybe I'm too materialistic, but I really, really want to get a Porsche. I think that by using the money techniques I've learned, I can get one by the time I'm 30.

Kramer: Nobody's telling you that you can't do that. All we're saying is, know the total cost. Besides wanting an expensive car, you told us you wanted to save a million dollars by the time you're 45. You might not be able to do both.

Think different angles. Run the numbers. Perhaps you can get a used one at a steep discount and sell it for a profit in a few years. Just make sure to figure in how much your total expenditures, including insurance, would have grown had they been invested in a mutual fund rather than in a car.

Amy: Here's a practical problem. If your main motive is to attract girls, you're likely to marry a high maintenance woman. If you *attract* her with a fancy car, you'll have to *keep* her with fancy cars. For the rest of your married life, be prepared to try to satisfy an insatiable appetite for fancy cars, fancy houses and fancy clothes. She'd be a major gusher in your dam.

Kramer: I should point out that different professions will require different kinds of cars. A traveling salesman needs a car that's nice enough to drive customers around, yet will take the wear and tear of a lot of miles. A realtor needs a large enough vehicle to take people to look at houses, plus nice enough to give the appearance of a successful realtor.

James: (Getting more animated) I still really, *really* want a Porsche. Don't you get it? IT'S NOT JUST THE GIRL THING. IT'S SIMPLY THE COOLEST CAR EVER MADE!

Kramer: Don't get defensive. We're not telling you to buy a Porsche or not buy a Porsche. Just don't do it because a commercial told you it was cool. As the Chinese philosopher Mencius once said,

> *"To act without clear understanding, to form habits without investigation, to follow a path all one's life without knowing where it really leads – such is the behavior of the multitude."*

If you know *why* you're doing it and how it fits into *your* life goals, then you're not following the multitude. We'll talk about life goals our final week.

Today, let's talk about what will probably be the largest purchase of your lifetime: your house.

Beating the System on Houses

ANSWER TO THE RIDDLE

Kramer: For homework, I asked you to try to solve this riddle about buying houses:

> *Ralph and Becky*
> *Live on the same lane*
> *Neighbors in houses*
> *built exactly the same.*
>
> *But something's quite odd,*
> *I haven't a clue*
> *Why Ralph pays one dollar*
> *For Becky's every two.*

Kramer: To keep our figures consistent, let's say that Becky bought her house for $150,000 and has a 30 year, 10 percent loan. How could someone get it for half her price?

Lower Interest Rates

Amy: I asked my parents. They suggested that even if the purchase price were the same on each house, if Ralph got a much better interest rate, like four percent, his monthly payments would be about ½ Becky's.

James: How could Ralph have gotten such a great rate?

Amy: That was my next question. Mom said that over the last few years, interest

Define: Credit Score

A number, roughly between 300 and 800, based on a credit report, predicting how likely it is for an individual to be able to repay a new loan. It's primarily determined by the timeliness of past loan payments, such as credit card payments and house payments.

rates have almost doubled. Ralph could have bought the house at four percent several years ago while Becky just bought hers at 10 percent.

Kramer: (Throwing Amy a breath mint) Congratulations! That's one solution to the riddle! Are there others?

Bigger Down Payment, Plus Lower Interest Rates

Akashi: Even if they bought their houses at the same time, if you make a bigger down payment or have a better **credit score**, you can get significantly better rates. Let's say Ralph had a better credit score and paid $50,000 down at seven percent whereas Becky paid down nothing at 10 percent. Again, Ralph makes ½ Becky's payment.

Kramer: Take your mint! Another winner!

Get a Shorter Term Loan

Antonio: You guys are just talking monthly payments. I took the riddle to mean that Ralph would pay one half of Becky's price *over a lifetime.* In that case, Dad suggested that Ralph has a 15 year loan and Becky a 40 year loan. By paying more each month, Ralph gets his house paid off in 15 years and pays ½ as much for the house as Becky over 40 years.

Kramer: Another winner! Take a mint!

James: How are you guys figuring all these mortgage rates and payments?

Antonio: Just Google the term "mortgage calculator." When you find one, put in $150,000 as the borrowed amount and play around with different interest rates and different years for the loan.

James: Got it! Wow! This is cool! Look at the difference in your total payments when you change the length of your loan:

Difference in Total Paid for a 10 Percent, $150,000 Loan

40 Year Loan: Total Paid = **$611,380**

30 Year Loan: Total Paid = **$473,883**

15 Year Loan: Total Paid = **$290,142**

Buy a Bargain

James: How about this angle? My dad got our house at a major discount when a bank threatened to foreclose on the owner. He bought it for $30,000 off the appraised value. Then, he did $5,000 worth of repairs. If Ralph got a bargain house, so that he borrowed $30,000 less than Becky, and got a 20 year loan, he would pay ½ what Becky would pay on a 40 year loan.

When you start playing with these calculators, you find lots of ways to get a house for ½ price and save $300,000 or more!

Why isn't everyone doing this?

Why People Lose Thousands in House Payments

Kramer: First, your mint! Congratulations!

To answer your question, some simply don't understand. Others can't think long term. Even if they know they can take advantage of a huge savings over time by paying a little more up front or monthly, they go for smaller payments.

But often, people simply can't take advantage of these incredible savings because they don't manage their money well. If you don't have savings, you can't put any money down. If your credit score stinks, you can't get the best interest rate. If you're making payments on cars and credit cards, you won't be able to afford the payments on a 15 year loan as opposed to a 30 or 40 year loan.

James: *But we're talking about saving hundreds of thousands of dollars!*

Kramer: Right. But most people don't even know what they're paying over the lifetime of a house. **People today think of "affordable monthly payments," period.** Americans think short term, not long term.

The same person who would be horrified at flushing $300,000 of today's money down the toilet thinks *nothing* of flushing $300,000 down the toilet over a period of 40 years. Another sad reason so many retire with nothing.

The Dangers and Benefits of Home Ownership

Amy: Something I don't understand. Why are money managers saying it's okay to make payments for a house, but not for a car. It seems hypocritical.

Kramer: Some money managers are leery of borrowing for anything, even a house. And I understand their concerns. If you fail to make your payments, you've broken the terms of the contract, and it becomes *the lender's* house. They'll auction it off on the courthouse steps to the highest bidder, and you'll go crying to mom and dad hoping to get your old bedroom back. That's why it's important to Travis to live in a paid-off house.

But most money managers look more favorably on house payments than credit card payments or car payments. Why? Well, you've got to understand the nature of assets.

A car (except for a restored classic) is an asset that goes DOWN in value over time – a *depreciating* asset. A house is generally an asset that goes UP in value over time – an *appreciating* asset.

The implications of this can be staggering.

Homes as Appreciating Assets

Inflation and rising home values will most likely cause your home to rise in value. My parents bought their house in Fayetteville for $51,000 in 1968. Since then, inflation has divided the purchasing power of the dollar over and over, making the house worth about seven times its original cost. Inflation is the enemy of stocks and bonds, eating into their growth. But inflation is the friend of a house, putting its arms around your home and making it rise in value as it rises. Plus, property values in some areas rise more than inflation, so that the house my parents paid $51,000 for in 1968 was appraised for $350,000 in 2005.

Comparing Houses and Cars

Compare a house, which is an *appreciating* asset, to a car, which is a *depreciating* asset. If you bought a brand new $20,000 car five years ago and financed it at seven percent interest for five years, you'd have paid $27,761 for a car that would be worth about $5,000 today. Each year, it would keep right on decreasing in value.[2]

Stocks or Houses: Which Pays Better?

Antonio: I read one article that recommended renting rather than buying a house. It was pretty persuasive. Once you figure in property tax, upkeep and other costs of home ownership, the way this guy figured it, putting what you saved into stocks would have paid more over time.

Kramer: In some cases, that might be true. For example, some people move every few years, spending lots of money in closing costs. The way loans work, your early payments go almost entirely to pay interest, so that a person who moves frequently never pays much into the house itself. In that case, he might have been better off renting.

But here are some reasons that I think, for the average person, home ownership is a great investment:

- **You get to live in your investment.** You can't live in a mutual fund.

- **You get to deduct your interest from your income tax.**

- When people compare the rise of house values to the rise of stocks, they don't tend to consider that **we can't know that the stock market will continue averaging returns of over 10 percent.** If our economy goes through a slump that takes 15 or more years to recover from, or if inflation were to soar, or if property values in your area rise enormously, your home investment would probably leave stocks in the dust. It's another way to diversify.

- **After my parents made their last payment in 1995, they no longer had to make another house payment as long as they lived.** Their payments were $168 a month on a house that, by 1995, would have rented for over $2,000 a month. If one of them lives thirty years after the loan was paid off, rent for that house just might be $6,000 per month! And they only have to pay upkeep and property taxes!

- A final consideration is huge for most people. **House payments are a forced investment.** If you slack on your monthly payments, you get kicked out onto the sidewalk. That's pretty motivating. Most people simply don't have the discipline to pay less for housing and put the extra money into an investment each month. Making a house payment takes less self-discipline.

Hints on Houses

1. As with cars, think long term. The poor tend to think only about the monthly payment. The wealthy think about the total paid.

2. Look for bargains. Few self-made millionaires pay the asking price for a house. They take their time. They bargain. They may pick out more than one house they like and see which offers the best deal.[3] It's funny how some people will run to a clothing store to save $15 on a shirt that's on sale, but not even look for a $15,000 discount on a house.

3. Pay it off as quickly as possible, unless you can invest that extra money conservatively at a much greater interest rate.[4] Consider the huge savings of a 15 or 20 year loan rather than a 30 year loan. Pay more than your required payments when you can.

4. Purchase within your means. Many people stretch themselves way too far and end up losing their homes when they get in a tight.

5. Buy quality. Some homes and neighborhoods go down in value. The three most important words in real estate are location, location, location.

6. Watch your credit score. It can save you tons on your house loan. You get a good credit rating by living way beneath your means, paying off credit cards each month and keeping a large emergency fund so that you don't get in a bind.

Think like a lender. A person with no savings and a bad credit rating is a much higher risk. You'll have to charge that person more interest to take on the higher risk.

7. If you can't handle credit cards, rebuild your habits by getting a one store card like a Home Depot or Lowes card, or any card you'd seldom use at your age. Purchase something every now and then for your parents to reimburse, and then pay it off promptly when the bill arrives.

8. Stay in a house as long as you can, unless you live in houses that you're planning to flip. Buying, selling and moving are costly. Consider adopting a lifestyle, house included, and keeping that lifestyle no matter how much your salary increases. Put your raises into investments, just like Buffett did.

9. Pay down as much as you can up front, without depleting your emergency fund.

Common Pitfalls

- **Buying beyond your means.** If you're stretched to the max, you can't enjoy life, even in a mansion. Especially don't believe the fable, "If I couldn't afford it with my salary, the mortgage company wouldn't lend it." Travis works with a realtor who, being a single woman, didn't want her name in the phonebook. Instead, she listed her dog's name: Rover. For years, even after Rover had died, she received notices from lenders that Rover had been pre-approved for a huge loan! If lenders will loan to a deceased dog, they'll lend you more than you can afford to pay off![5]

- **Getting a dangerous loan.** Don't just go for the lowest rate you can find. Thousands are losing their homes this year due to foreclosure because a few years ago, when interest rates were lower, they chose adjustable rate mortgages. When interest rates rose, their payments went right up with the interest rates, so much that they could no longer afford to pay.

  You'd think that we'd have learned something from all those who are suffering. Yet, almost 40 percent of the new loans in the first half of this year were non-traditional, high risk mortgages, compared to an average two percent over the last decade.[6]

- **Forgetting the cost of frequent moves.**

- **Purchasing at an inflated price.**

James: I worry that I'll never make enough in salary to afford a house.

Kramer: It takes a good bit to get by these days. To help you along, I'll warn you next week about how people lose their hard-earned money unnecessarily. In the following meetings, we'll talk about getting a good vocation and improving your salary.

So what are your main takeaway points?

Action Points

Akashi: If I want to buy a condo or a house in the next several years, I need to **start working on building a solid credit history now.** I've got a checking account. I've got a regular salary. I'm working on my savings. I think I need to get a credit card that's safe for me, like a Home Depot or Lowe's card. I'll go pick up something for my parents, charge it on my card and let them pay me back so that I can pay it off in full the first month.

Amy: Buy something I can afford. I don't want to be enslaved to huge monthly payments like my parents. I'd also like to do what Travis did, buying a bargain that he can afford, fixing it up and putting that money into another bargain a few years later. It seems like the quickest way to own a house outright.

James: Unless you *marry* someone who already owns a house outright.

Amy: Now that's a great idea!

James: Look long term, *not* just to monthly payments.

Antonio: Since houses are such a huge part of my lifetime expenditures, I need to **start talking to more people about houses and reading up on them.** By the time I'm ready to buy, I want to know what I'm doing.

- After determining what size house you want, would you prefer to be in a neighborhood where it is the largest house or the smallest house? Why?

- What strategies do you think would work best for you to save money on purchasing a quality house?

Assignment
Between Breakfasts

1. Ask your parents and friends, "What are some of the biggest ways people lose their money?"

2. Find and read an article on the same subject. Google such terms as "scams" or "lose money."

Resources to Take You Deeper

Clark Smart Real Estate **by Clark Howard and Mark Meltzer (Hyperion, 2007) - popular consumer advocate and radio personality Clark Howard educates us in everything from how to buy our first home to building wealth through real estate.**

www.clarkhoward.com - the site of Clark Howard, consumer advocate, author and popular talk show host. His tagline says it all: "save more, spend less, and avoid rip-offs." A section of his site deals specifically with real estate.

Breakfast #11: Ten Popular Ways to Lose Loads of Money

"Rule No. 1: Never lose money. Rule No. 2: Never forget Rule No. 1."
—**Warren Buffett**[1]

"Risk comes from not knowing what you are doing."
—**Warren Buffett**[2]

Fast Forward to Reunion

Larry: I've always dreamed of owning my own place, but I've never had a strategy for getting there. Now, I think I know, step-by-step, what I need to do. First, I've got to work my way out from under these credit cards.

Kramer: You're not alone. You probably need to start listening to Dave Ramsey's radio program and reading his book, *The Total Money Makeover*. I'll buy you a copy. In our next session, we talked more about ways people lose their money. Once you start getting out of debt and accumulating money, you'll find that everybody wants a piece of you. Here's how to keep from losing it all.

Flashback

Kramer: Remember the reservoir analogy?

James: Sure! First, you've got one or more adequate streams of income. Then, you build a dam by controlling your expenses and paying yourself first.

Amy: Then, you plug up those steady drips and major holes in the dam that threaten to drain it dry.

Kramer: While mishandling houses and cars can produce major gushes, I want to warn you about how people – often very smart people – blow up the entire dam, losing all of their hard-earned money.

Amy: Not sure where you're going with this one.

Kramer: Come on! This happens all the time. Think about it. What relatives or family friends, movie stars or athletes do you know who blew their entire fortune to shreds? If we don't learn from them, it could just as easily happen to us. What kind of explosives do you think they used?

James: Drugs did it to your brother. He had a great education, a lucrative business, plenty of savings and was headed for an early retirement. Then meth and heroin dried up his river and blew up his dam.

Akashi: Didn't Michael Jackson and boxer Mike Tyson get into financial trouble? Millions in income didn't save them from blowing up their dams.

Kramer: Now you're thinking! There are hundreds of others. It's easy to laugh these people off, thinking, "What idiots!" But my brother is brilliant.

My point? If so many smart, successful people can lose their hard-earned millions, we can lose our hard-earned thousands. During this breakfast we'll warn you of some of the most common ways people lose their fortunes. Hash, thanks for joining us for this discussion. Your success at losing money makes you quite an expert in this field.

Hash: Honor me with a trophy! But today I'll go beyond my own experience to pull in the experiences of many I've known and studied through the years.

Money Losing Tip #1: Do Drugs and Abuse Alcohol

Marijuana and Money

Hash: Marijuana is pretty popular these days. Was just as popular back in the 70's. I smoked it. And yes, I inhaled. Lots of misinformation on both sides of the debate. Sure, you probably won't end up in a gutter somewhere from just smoking marijuana.

But, no matter what lore you hear from your friends or read on the Internet, recent studies of the impact of marijuana on the brain convince me that it's addicting to a large set of users. People who don't believe it's addicting have to explain why over 200,000 people each year pay tons of money to rehab clinics to kick the habit.[3] Addicts lose money through buying marijuana, paying for rehab and missing work.

But it's not just potential addiction that scares me. The truly scary thing about marijuana is how it demotivates people. People who smoke marijuana tend to lose interest in their education and life goals. Marijuana smokers are much more likely to lose motivation for school and miss work.

Buffett says that one of the primary characteristics he looks for in successful business people is drive. In explaining their success, the number one characteristic that self-made millionaires pointed to was "being well-disciplined." Number four was "working harder than most people."[4]

Successful businessmen get their highs from succeeding at their business. When I smoked marijuana, I got my highs without going to all the trouble of succeeding at anything. It was a shortcut that kept me from achieving anything in those early years. It's probably why I dropped out of college my senior year. I was satisfied with chillin' with my buddies while others my age were getting ahead.

Successful businessman, celebrity and investor Ben Stein says,

"The men and women I know who have spent a lot of time smoking pot have, by and large, thrown their lives away in the pursuit of feeling

no pain. There are exceptions, but typically they can barely get out of bed, let alone pursue a career aggressively or save in a disciplined way. Basic, long-term sobriety seems to me a precondition for a successful life, and certainly a precondition – in most cases – for a life of prudence as far as money is concerned. The man or woman lost in marijuana-induced bliss cannot and will not be able to evaluate investment options and pick the best ones – it's that simple. One of the many blessings of sobriety is to be able to invest sensibly.[5]

Alcohol and Money

Alcohol is just as dangerous, if not more so. Don't fool yourself into thinking that because it's legal, it's harmless. The impact of alcohol abuse staggers the imagination. How many of you have an alcoholic friend or relative?

(All raise their hands.)

One day, when Warren Buffett was talking to an audience at Notre Dame, he implicated two of the biggest culprits he'd seen that rob managers of their success: "liquor and leverage - leverage being borrowed money." We'll talk about leverage in our next point.[6]

Alcohol Kills Led Zeppelin

Richard Cole managed Led Zeppelin from the very beginning till almost the end of their twelve-year run. Yet, in the end, he lost his money, his house and his job. Now how does a manager – someone who makes his business managing things – lose all his money managing one of the most successful bands in the world? Drugs and booze took over his life.[7]

When John "Bonzo" Bonham, Zeppelin's extraordinarily talented drummer, accidentally drank himself to death, guitarist Jimmy Page felt the band couldn't continue without him. The night that Bonzo died, one of the greatest rock bands ever died.[8]

Listen, if you're going to ruin your lives, at least find some new way to do it. It's embarrassing to ruin your life with things that we already know have ruined people's lives for thousands of years.

Other Artificial Highs

Do I even need to mention the hard stuff, like meth, heroin and cocaine? They can dynamite your dam in a hurry. If you want to have a successful, enjoyable life, don't get near that hard stuff. That should be obvious to anybody. But I singled out alcohol and marijuana because users often don't see how they can ruin their success.

Listen, there's an incredible amount of fun things to do in this world. Climb a mountain. Explore a cave. Visit weird and beautiful cities. Hang out with interesting people. Watch fun movies. Take an art class. Restore an old car. Don't substitute artificial highs for the real thing.

Money Losing Tip #2: Acquire Debt and Don't Take It Seriously

Kramer: It's often said that a fool and his money are soon separated. In my opinion, most smart people don't hang onto it much longer.

Thomas Jefferson: A Pretty Smart Guy

When President John F. Kennedy welcomed forty-nine Nobel Prize winners to the White House, he said,

> *"I think this is the most extraordinary collection of talent, of human knowledge, that has ever been gathered at the White House, with the possible exception of when Thomas Jefferson dined alone."*[9]

Just who was this Thomas Jefferson? He was both brilliant and accomplished -- the principle author of the *Declaration of Independence*, the third President of the United States and founder of the University of West Virginia. He was a political philosopher, horticulturist, architect, archaeologist, paleontologist, author, inventor and violinist.

But for all his brilliance in other matters, his personal finances were a disaster. He began his 20's with 1,000 acres of inherited land, including a plantation, a profitable grist mill and many other assets. He also inherited some debt, which he probably could have paid off early by selling some land at a decent price.

I suppose he assured himself that, if push came to shove, he could always sell some of his huge assets to pay off those lingering debts. But after his presidency, when he could have been enjoying the leisure life and basking in the fame of a well-lived life, Murphy's Law struck.

- Two years of drought were followed by the invasion of a fly, devastating his crops.
- He had to borrow more to pay interest on his debts.
- The Panic of 1819 caused banks to curtail his credit, so that he had to borrow more from others to cover these debts.
- Agricultural prices dropped.
- He tried to sell land, but money was tight and there were simply no buyers.
- He endorsed two loans of $10,000 each for a dear friend who was supposed to be worth $300,000. In the end, his friend couldn't pay, and the bank called Jefferson for repayment.

It was bad news all around, but he probably could have weathered the storm had he not been in debt. As one biographer said,

> **"But for his debts he might have trusted in God, husbandry, and the weather. Not until Jeff (his grandson) took a hand in the plantation business did Jefferson realize how far his estate was mortgaged to his creditors."**

It was Jefferson's retirement. He should have been enjoying himself. Instead, he lay awake nights trying to figure out how to keep his debts from burying him and his descendents. **In today's money, he was millions of dollars in debt**, and because of a depressed economy, people couldn't buy his land. At his death, his estate was sold in a lottery to pay some of his debts. His remaining debts burdened his descendents for years.[10]

Debriefing

Your thoughts?

Antonio: Just because you're smart and successful in one area, doesn't mean you're smart and successful with your finances. A lot of successful people probably think they're too smart to go bankrupt. They're more interested in their business than dealing with their personal debts. Before they know it, a crisis hits and they're sunk.

Akashi: Debt is sneaky. It's like a scorpion that slips into your shoe at night. You don't see the looming crisis. Your debt seems manageable, no big deal, until it gets out of control or you hit a series of unfortunate events. Then, it bites.

James: Cool analogy, Akashi. What strikes me is that there's no way any of us are as smart as Jefferson. **If debt could destroy his massive fortune, how much more easily could it steal our small assets?**

Hash: Over 120,000 people lost their homes to foreclosure last year.[11] I'm sure that most thought it could never happen to them. Behind those statistics are real people with real feelings. They lost whatever equity they had in those homes. Their credit is ruined, making it difficult to buy another house. If you were a bank, would you risk loaning $150,000 for a house to someone who couldn't make payments on their last house?

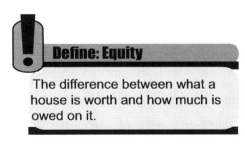

Define: Equity

The difference between what a house is worth and how much is owed on it.

Amy: Most of Jefferson's debt was tied up in land – what most of us would consider a stable, appreciating asset. But in a bad economy, people can't afford to pay what it's normally worth. I suppose any debt can be dangerous.

Antonio: He signed for that loan to a friend. It would be hard to turn down a friend in need.

Kramer: King Solomon, one of the wealthiest and wisest men ever, warned us about that 3000 years ago:

> *My son, if you have put up security for your neighbor,*
> *if you have struck hands in pledge for another,*
>
> *Free yourself, like a gazelle from the hand of the hunter,*
> *like a bird from the snare of the fowler.*[12]

Amy: I think **most of people don't plan for worst case scenarios**. Instead, they buy a house that stretches them to the max, then take on "easy payments" on a car and some furniture, assuming that their salary and expenses will be the same or better a year from now. But what if they lose their job and can't get another one for three months? They've just got to have that emergency fund in place, plus make sure that they've left a comfortable cushion between their house payments and their salary.

Antonio: Credit cards weren't even around during Jefferson's time. It's so much easier to get into debt these days.

Hash: According to consumer advocate and money expert Clark Howard,

> *"Debt is a disease and credit cards are one of the easiest ways to get sick. Nobody ever got wealthy borrowing money for gifts, clothes, restaurants, entertainment, or travel."*[13]

King Solomon warned borrowers that they were slaves to their lenders.[14] Today, borrowers seem to have neither fear nor shame concerning debt.

Prescription

Respect the awesome power of debt. If you don't have it, don't get it, except in rare cases where you're purchasing an appreciating asset (like a house) at a bargain price that can be easily sold to cover the debt. If you're in debt, take it seriously and work your way out of it as quickly as possible.

Kramer: Back when I found myself in debt, just after my husband's death, I needed more than information. I needed cheerleaders - people who'd faced debt, overcome it and could remind me over and over, "You can do it!" First, I started listening to Dave Ramsey on the radio. He'd overcome debt himself and took call-ins daily from people in more debt than me. Others called in who'd overcome debt and were building wealth. Ramsey was a lifesaver! Second, I read Ramsey's book, *The Total Money Makeover*. It gave practical how to's sprinkled with testimonies of people who'd beat debt. Again, exactly what I needed.

Third, I got involved with a small group studying money management through a local church. The instruction, camaraderie and accountability helped me to get on a budget and develop good financial habits. For me, it functioned as AA for the financially bound. I called it OSA - Over-Spenders Anonymous.

Money Losing Tip #3: Abuse Credit Cards

I could have dealt with credit cards under the last point, but I think they deserve a section of their own. For many, they are a disaster. While houses and cars may generate payments of eight to 10 percent, it's not unusual for credit cards to charge over 20 percent interest.

Hash: If you use credit cards, pay them off ENTIRELY each month. Never think of a credit card as a way to borrow money for something you can't afford outright.

If you're making payments on your credit card debt, put all your effort into paying it off and saving an emergency fund. Don't invest. Don't buy anything else. Just pay it off before it kills you.

Money management expert Larry Burkett used to recommend this recipe for managing your credit cards, to be used the first time you can't pay them off in full:

RECIPE FOR COPING WITH CREDIT CARDS

1. Set your oven for 375 degrees.

2. Line a cookie sheet with aluminum foil.

3. Arrange all your credit cards flat on the aluminum foil, touching each other.

4. Cook for 20 minutes, or until the cards meld into a smooth, colorful collage.

Money Losing Tip #4: Avoid Wise Counsel

Joe Gibbs is one of those rare people who found brilliant success in two extremely competitive fields – professional football and NASCAR. He coached the Washington Redskins to win three Super Bowls and was inducted into the NFL Hall of Fame. As head of Joe Gibbs Racing, his team brought home the coveted NASCAR Winston Cup.

But as with a lot of successful people, he got cocky about his personal finances.[15] In his own words:

> ***"Ironically, although I was never really arrogant about my success in sports, for some reason I had adopted an arrogance in my business dealings. When it came to money, I was overconfident for no apparent reason."[16]***

Three Royal Bungles

His finances unraveled in three huge losses. First, he lost $200,000 in a racquetball business. By his own admission, his motive was to "Make some easy money," with a "get-rich-quick scheme."[17] His other admitted weaknesses included lack of contentment[18], the desire to get richer[19] and lack of trust in God.[20]

His next fiasco involved investing in a home nursing care business. He knew nothing about nursing and again lost serious money.[21]

Finally, an acquaintance from college offered Gibbs the opportunity to join a partnership to build homes and apartments in Norman, Oklahoma. Gibbs would pay closing costs. Rental income would more than make the payments, giving them a tidy profit.

It seemed so perfect and risk-free. Oklahoma was booming due to the growing oil and gas industries. The need for oil and gas could only increase. New people would need new housing. His wife, Pat, was against it from the beginning, but what did *she* know about real estate investing? This was a no-brainer.

Things went smoothly until the oil-and-gas balloon burst, making Norman's economy burst, too. People left town in droves, and the ones who didn't leave had a hard time paying their rent.

The bottom line? His partners bailed out, leaving Gibbs responsible for millions of dollars of debt. A year after winning the Super Bowl, at the end of a stellar season that put his team in the playoffs, when he could have been basking in the glory of his success, he instead contemplated personally bankruptcy, owing millions with no means to pay.[22]

Digging Out of the Ashes

Unlike Jefferson, Gibbs didn't delay. First, he cried out for divine help. Then, he looked for wise human help.

Where did he find good advice? In addition to coaching, Gibbs had been helping troubled teens. While doing this, he found a kindred heart in Don Meredith, who had successfully started worthwhile initiatives from scratch. Meredith had integrity, heart, and the ability to get things done.[23] Meredith pulled together a team of accountants, attorneys and advisers who helped Gibbs meet with the bankers and work out terms of payment.

It wasn't easy. When Gibbs realized the extent of his debt, he and his family took it seriously. They cut the fluff out of their spending and applied "every bit of extra income beyond basic living expenses toward eliminating the debt."[24]

After Gibbs got out of debt, he kept his team of advisers, meeting with them monthly to keep him accountable and save him from creating yet another financial mess.[25]

His wife was the other essential part of his financial team. If he had listened to her advice from the beginning, he could have saved millions. Research shows that men tend to be more risky and women more conservative - one more reason for husbands and wives to listen to each other and balance each other. These days, Gibbs doesn't even carry a checkbook around. Instead, he asks his wife for cash when he needs it.[26]

Gibbs' advice? "Surround yourself with people who will hold you accountable."[27]

Debriefing

What could have protected Gibbs from his financial blunders?

Amy: Beware of "Get Rich Quick" schemes. He was making a good salary. If he'd dollar cost averaged it into stock index funds and bond funds, he could have saved and multiplied his millions much more safely.

Hash: As he said in his book, "The best way to get rich quickly is to get rich slowly."[28]

Akashi: None of the decisions were really dumb. He's obviously brilliant and had thought each investment through. **It shows me how easy it is to lose money in starting businesses.** In the future, I need to be super careful when a friend comes to me with a great business opportunity.

James: Even brilliant people need a group of wise, honest advisers. I've noticed that when I'm about to make a stupid decision, if I listen to my heart, I know that I should run it by my parents or someone else. I'm just afraid they'll tell me it's a stupid decision. Even if Gibbs had paid $1,000 to get their advice each time, those counselors might have saved him hundreds of thousands of dollars.

Kramer: Good point. Most of the millionaires that Stanley and Danko studied don't spend a lot on flashy stuff, but they *are* willing to spend money on wise counsel, such as from lawyers and accountants.[29]

Antonio: He needed more than advice; **he needed accountability**.[30] There's a difference. I can get great advice and fail to act on it. But, if I know I'm meeting with my accountability group next week, I know I'd better get my butt in gear. Sometimes that accountability can be found in a financial accountability group through a local faith community.

Hey, maybe "The Counterculture Club" should begin keeping each other accountable to manage our finances wisely. It's hard to do it on your own.

Amy: Be careful about going in with other people and signing your name as part owner, even if they are friends. Your partners may bail, leaving you holding the bills. Be very careful about who you partner with and what you sign your name to.[31]

The God Thing

Hash: I don't want to overlook the "humbled himself before God" part.[32] Gibbs spends a significant part of his book talking about it. Funny that people don't mention it more in financial books.

It might seem like an odd, unrelated step to those who aren't into God – maybe even a copout. But back during my drug rehab days, I was kind of shocked to find that God was mentioned in seven out of the 12 Steps in both *Narcotics Anonymous* and *Alcoholics Anonymous*. To beat addictive stuff like drugs and alcohol, most people have to admit their own helplessness and trust in God, or at least some higher power.

Not coming from a religious background, I assumed that NA and AA were sponsored by some church, or were started by some religious fellow who had a spiritual agenda and tacked God onto everything.

Kramer: Are you getting off track, or does this get back to finances?

Hash: Just follow me. My curiosity finally prevailed and I read up on AA's founders, Bill Wilson and Dr. Bob Smith. Alcohol was destroying both of their lives. Both had tried seemingly everything to quit. Neither were especially religious at the time. In fact, Bill Wilson was turned off to the whole God thing and wanted nothing less than to submit to Him.

But Wilson reluctantly discovered that many people couldn't kick the habit without encountering God. After trying everything else, he himself turned to God in an act of desperation. It worked! And the 12 steps have been central to dealing with addicts ever since.[33]

Makes me wonder if we should have a "Financial Idiots Anonymous" to help those of us who keep blundering. And here's something that really makes me go "Hmmm…." So many people who ruin their financial lives start their recovery on their knees. So why wait until you're on your back before you can look up? **If trusting God permeates our rehab efforts, why doesn't trusting God permeate our preventative programs?**[34]

For Joe Gibbs and a host of others, self-sufficiency and arrogance led them to financial ruin. Perhaps abandoning oneself to God cuts through those two character flaws, keeping us from getting into financial ruin in the first place. That's one reason I recommend organizations that not only teach financial wisdom, but also a trust in God. In fact, the leader of one such group personally helped Gibbs through his crisis.[35] Preventative programs could potentially save millions of people from the heartache that Mr. Gibbs struggled through.

Money Losing Tip #5: Trust the Wrong Counsel

Hash: Many people are scared to make their own investment decisions. Or, they just want outside advice on a decision they're thinking about making. Wise accumulators of wealth tend to pay regularly for wise counsel from either their CPA or lawyer, or both.

Antonio: Gibbs found some of his through his charity work.

Hash. Good point. If you remember my story about losing money in stocks, you'll know that I was taking counsel from the wrong crowd (people bragging about their stocks over breakfast) and reading the wrong books (the ones they recommended). I had no idea whether these people were either upright or informed. But you can run into the same problem with paying professionals for advice.

Funny Thing About Financial Planners...

Investment adviser and talk show host David Latko tells the joke about a busload of financial advisers, brokers and money managers who wrecked out in the country. A farmer found them and promptly buried them.

The police arrived just in time to find the farmer throwing dirt over the last grave. A startled officer exclaimed, "Were you absolutely sure they were dead?"

The farmer replied, "Well, some of 'em *said* they wasn't, but you know how them kind of people lie."[36]

I'm not saying that they're all scoundrels. Many financial counselors are sincere, wise, skilled people who truly have your best interests in mind. But choose carefully! Jason Zweig wrote that the investment world,

> **"...has enough liars, cheaters, and thieves to keep Satan's check-in clerks frantically busy for decades to come."[37]**

Understanding the Financial Planning Industry

Akashi: Why would these folks have a worse reputation than those in many other professions?

Hash: The problem comes with how some of them make their money. Many financial planners get more money upfront for recommending certain funds than others. Thus, their supervisors pressure them to recommend, not the funds that would bring the most profit to their clients, but the ones that would bring the most profit to their company. For those reimbursed this way, there's a huge conflict of interest between picking funds that benefit the customer and picking funds that benefit their business.

There's less conflict of interest in other professions, such as teaching. What if Suzie, your son's second grade teacher, had a profit motive in which reading curriculum to order? The "Fun and Effective" Curriculum has been proven to teach reading well in scores of documented studies. The "Students Love It" curriculum hasn't been tested anywhere. But since your school has a relationship with the publishing company, their teacher will get a $500 bonus if she orders "Students Love It." And since her principal gets a cut, she'll get in good with the administration, which is always a good idea.

Now it just happens that Suzie's out of money and her eight-year-old twins have a birthday next week. Does she give them each a minor league baseball cap from the thrift store, wrapped in an old newspaper, or take the $500 bonus and buy two shiny new bicycles? Easy to justify taking the bribe, I mean bonus, huh?

If this were the way our schools were run, wouldn't you question each teacher's choice of curriculum?

Akashi: So how can I find an honest, smart financial adviser?

Hash: You're risking tons of money, so plan on taking a little time.

Preliminaries

First, ask your parents and other trusted people you know, "Who are some local accountants that you respect?" Certified Public Accountants (CPAs) have to go through lots of training and get yearly updated certifications. They may do the taxes of hundreds of people who've either succeeded or crashed from the advice of a financial counselor. They probably personally know a number of financial counselors.[38]

Second, call the accountants and ask who they recommend and why. If several accountants recommend the same counselor, you may be on to something.

Third, find out what others are saying about them. Check your local *Better Business Bureau* to see if they've resolved any complaints that have been filed against them. Also, **Google the name of the company and the name of the financial counselor** (with the name of your city, to narrow the search) to see if any articles, blogs or forums are talking about them.

When you narrow down a counselor, set a twenty minute appointment to ask some questions.

Your Initial Meeting

YOUR OPENING STATEMENT:

> *"I want you to understand upfront that I can't make any commitment to your services today. It's not just my decision. I run all major decisions by my family and personal advisers."*

That one statement could keep people from innumerable financial blunders. After hearing an adviser's spiel about his impeccable credentials and all the wonderful things he will do to multiply your money, most of us feel obligated to sign the papers and turn over our money. If we don't, we feel like we're rejecting the poor soul or questioning his integrity.

That simple opening statement takes the pressure off. If at the end of the meeting he starts putting on the pressure (many are persuasive salesmen) and even offers financial incentives for deciding NOW, you can comfortably remind him that as much as you like him, you're committed to not making decisions without the input of those to whom you're accountable.

THE NEED FOR CREDENTIALS

You wouldn't seek medical help from an untrained doctor. But for some odd reason, people tend to entrust their hard-earned money to anyone who calls himself or herself a financial adviser, regardless of credentials.

So be prepared to ask some hard questions. This is difficult for most because it goes against human nature. Over a period of 25 years, thousands of people have come to David Latko's office for financial counsel, but *he's yet to have even one come armed with a list of questions about his credentials*. That suggests a strong aversion on the part of most humans to rattling people's cages by asking hard questions.[39]

To come across less like an interrogator, just tell the counselor that your advisers want you to get the answers to a few questions. If your personal advisers are worth anything, this should be true.

QUESTION #1: WHAT TRAINING AND CERTIFICATIONS DO YOU HAVE?

The minimal answer you're looking for is a CFP (Certified Financial Planner). (Under 6 percent of financial planners are certified as CFP's.)[40] Ask about other relevant degrees and training.

QUESTION #2: WHAT ARE THE TOTAL COSTS TO ME, AND ON WHAT BASIS ARE YOU PAID?

If he gets paid up front, how much? If he gets paid more to sell you one fund than another, there's a conflict of interest. Find another counselor.

A "fee only" planner is typically the way to go. He will charge you only for his time. (Don't confuse this with "fee-based" and "fee-oriented", which often pose as "fee-only", but may take commissions from sales of certain funds.) For larger accounts (over a few hundred thousand dollars), fees may be based on the amount of your assets. Those with millions may pay a retainer.[41]

If he recommends certain funds, **ask him how much it will cost you to buy them, hold them and sell them through him.** Do you pay something on the front end, extra to cash it out, so much for a withdrawal, a yearly fee, an early withdrawal penalty? This should all be put to you clearly and in writing because it's how many people get ripped off.

Here's how it unfolds. You give your financial counselor $500,000 to invest. Your first quarterly report comes in the mail, and you're shocked that although the stock market's neither gone up nor down, your $500,000 is down to $475,000. The $25,000 paid a five percent up front commission on the "load" mutual funds.

Then you find that there are yearly charges you didn't remember him mentioning. It was in the fine print that you never got around to reading. But if you get sick at your stomach and want to pull the money out, read that fine print again. You may have to pay another five percent or more as an early withdrawal fee.

Remember, if you contact a respected no load mutual fund that's known for low management expenses, you'll pay no upfront fee for the mutual fund, no fee to close it out and a minimal yearly fee. With the knowledge you have of investing from earlier breakfasts, you could be the primary decision-maker for your investments, paying a financial counselor for a second opinion. Read your mutual fund company's literature and newsletters. Call their toll free numbers to ask intelligent (and stupid) questions.

If your mutual fund company is top-notch, you'll find their client services department to be friendly, smart, and glad to answer questions. Also, when you've been with a mutual fund company for a long time or have a good bit of money with them, their professional staff might offer a free assessment of all your holdings, specific to your age bracket and goals, that will recommend how to allocate your investments.

From what we've already discussed about the basics of investing, you should be able to call a well-respected mutual fund company, tell them your objectives, read up on articles they recommend on their site, and start dealing directly with them.

If they can't answer questions to your satisfaction, or you want another opinion, consider paying a financial counselor for thirty minutes to an hour of her advice, rather than buying the funds through her. Why pay for something you don't need?

QUESTION #3: HOW LONG HAVE YOU BEEN IN THIS BUSINESS?

Newer advisers have a lot to learn. According to Latko,

> *"Seventy percent of all people who are licensed as financial advisers will end up out of the business within three years."*[42]

Get a beginning adviser, and odds are you won't have her for long.

QUESTION #4: WHAT SERVICES CAN I EXPECT FROM YOU?

"If I invest through you, how often will I get a statement on my investments? Do you offer tax and legal advice as well as financial? Will you evaluate my holdings on a regular basis?"

QUESTION #5: DO YOU RECOMMEND A LONG TERM APPROACH TO INVESTING, OR SHORT TERM TRADING?

If you agree with stock masters Buffett, Graham and Bogle, you know that, odds are, you'll lose money in short term trading. Don't deal with a broker who plans to call you with hot tips and lure you into regular trading. Remember the old saying: holding stocks makes *you* rich, trading makes your *broker* rich.[43]

Money Losing Tip #6: Gamble

Now, let's get to the sixth way to lose money. Some people seem to be able to handle playing an occasional hand of poker with friends for a few dollars or making the occasional bet on a baseball game. Others get a huge rush out of their betting that takes over.

Take baseball great Pete Rose. He loved baseball and had amazing talent. As the all time major league leader in hits (4,256), games played (3,562) and at bats (14,053), he won "three World Series rings, three batting titles, one Most Valuable Player Award, two Gold Gloves, the Rookie of the Year Award, and made 17 All-Star appearances at an unequalled five different positions."[44]

But the thrill of thousands of cheering fans wasn't enough. He developed the need to gamble, to the tune of $10,000 per day. And he wasn't just risking *his* money (he lost plenty). He risked his career. When the truth came out, he lost his life in baseball.[45]

"Why?" I ask myself. "Why would someone risk his money, reputation and entire career gambling for money he didn't even need?" For some, gambling becomes an irrational addiction that controls them. If you gamble, ask yourself, "Why?" If you gamble excessively, seek help. It's a fast way to financial suicide.

Akashi: I suppose the lottery is a form of gambling. My dad calls it "a tax on people who are bad at math."

Amy: Mom calls it "a tax on fools."

Hash: It's both. The odds of winning the lottery are astronomical. Let's say you're playing a typical lotto where you pick six numbers from 49. Your odds of winning the jackpot are about one in 14 million. But, those odds are good compared to the odds of winning Powerball.

So let's say you buy one lottery ticket per week. At those 1/14 million odds, how many years would it take before the odds would be in your favor to win?

Antonio: A thousand years?

Hash: Over a quarter of a million years (269,000 to be exact).[46]

Amy: If you count a lifetime as 100 years, **it would take 2,500 lifetimes of buying a lottery ticket every week to expect to win.** I think the odds of my arthritic grandmother getting miraculously healed, whipping herself into prime physical condition and winning a national racquetball competition would be better than that.

Hash: Yet, it makes sense to thousands of people to make that bet on a regular basis. Most who play are in the lower income brackets. Maybe they think that, as small as the odds are, it's their only chance at making a fortune.

Investing Lottery Money

Amy: Funny thing is, if they have enough money for lottery tickets, they've got at least *that* much to invest. What if they dollar cost averaged their money each month into a total stock market index fund instead of lottery tickets? If it increased in value at the historic average of 10 percent per year, how much would they have over a lifetime?

Hash: Let's run the numbers! I did this with one of my customers the other day. We were talking about stocks and he said, "I think I've got a better chance of winning the lottery than you do in making money off stocks." So I said, "I'll take the challenge! Let's do a little research and get back next week."

So the average lottery participant in Rhode Island spends over $100 per month on lottery tickets. If 50 years ago, they had started putting that $1,200 per year into a total stock market index fund, they'd each have over $1,300,000 today![47]

Yet in one survey, over one in five Americans stated that they felt their best chance of accumulating several hundred thousand dollars in their lifetime would be through winning the lottery![48]

Hash: The odds of the stock market getting 10 percent interest are pretty decent, given the performance of the market over the past 100 years.

James: It's certainly better than the odds of me living 250,000,000 years so I might win that jackpot!

Kramer: If you ever go to Las Vegas, take a serious look at those fabulous hotels. Where do they get the money to pay for those hotels? From people's gambling money! That should tell you who makes the money with gambling. The odds of the machines and games are set so that *they're* likely to win and *you're* likely to lose.

Money Losing Tip #7: Live Above Your Means

We've already covered this at other breakfasts. But, I'll take any excuse to mention it again.

> **You build wealth by living *beneath* your means. You lose money by living *above* your means.**

It's as simple as that. If you live *above* your means, spend your emergency fund and take on debt, when the first crisis hits, you're sunk. You lose your house and your credit and move back in with your parents. Only this time at home, you'll be responsible for *all* the chores and paying rent to mom and dad. Don't even *think* about asking for an allowance.

Money Losing Tip #8: Try to Get Rich Quick

Hash: So you've got some money to invest. You receive a letter from a local investment adviser. After some kind words and a rundown of his impeccable credentials, he writes,

> *"I'm sure you're hesitant to entrust your hard-earned money with someone you don't personally know, so I'll give you some proof of my skills in stock trading. I know some things happening at GFR (Get Filthy Rich Enterprises) that will make that stock go up over the next couple of weeks. Check the Atlanta Journal or your favorite financial website in two weeks on Saturday to see if I'm right."*

Out of curiosity, you check the AJC in two weeks, and sure enough, GFR stock has gone up. You're impressed, but still skeptical. Maybe it was a good guess.

Two days later, you receive a note from the investor saying,

> *"If you checked the stock market, you found that I was right about GFR. Had you invested $10,000, you would have made a quick $500, with no work on your part at all! Now THAT'S easy money!"*
>
> *Still not convinced? Watch GRQ (Get Rich Quick Schemes, Unlimited) for the next week. I'm not sure how much it will go up, but it will go up, and my clients will profit."*

Sure enough, in a week you check the financials and GRQ went up. Two days later, you receive another letter, urging you to invest in another stock.

Wouldn't you be tempted to invest with the guy? How do you think he predicted the short term direction of a stock so accurately?

Antonio: Perhaps he had inside information with the companies.

Akashi: Maybe he's an oracle.

Amy: I think he's a time traveler from the future.

Hash: Neither insider nor oracle nor time traveler, he's Hank the Huckster. Hank had no idea whether the stock would go up or down. Here's how he pulled it off:

Week 1: Hank buys a list of addresses in Acworth, Kennesaw, Marietta and Woodstock. He sends Acworth and Kennesaw letters predicting the GFR stock will go *up*. The same day, he sends a *different* letter to Marietta and Woodstock, predicting the stock will go *down*.

Week 3: Hank looks up the stock and finds that it went up, so he writes only Kennesaw and Acworth, where he sent the first winning letter. He gives them a second chance to observe his stock-picking skills, shooting off one letter to Kennesaw saying the GRQ stock will go down and one to Acworth saying it will go up.

Week 5: Hank discovers that the stock went up. So, he sends only the residents of Acworth a letter reminding them that he correctly predicted the two stocks, inviting them to invest with him.

Hank takes in lots of clients with hundreds of thousands of dollars, promptly cashes the checks, cleans out his office and heads out of town.[49]

Pretty slick.

But that's just one of many scams that rob people of their hard-earned money. Let's think up some tough questions that we could ask of people to keep us from falling for bad investments.

Amy: When I got that letter, my first thought would have been, **"If he's so good at picking stocks, why does he need my money?"** If he could make that much, he could invest his own $5,000 and multiply it to millions in a couple of years.

Hash: Exactly! But if you mentioned that to him, I'm sure he'd cough up some reasonable explanation, like that he enjoys helping others find the wealth that he's found. Or, he lost his wealth taking care of his terminally ill child and needs to build it back again.

Antonio: If a friend or relative came up to me with a hot prospect that seemed almost too good to be true, **I'd first of all assume that…it's probably too good to be true.**

James: I'd caution myself by remembering how much Joe Gibbs lost on hot prospects that looked like sure bets.

Amy: I'd want to take the pressure off by letting him know that I won't make any decision without running it by my family and personal advisers.

Akashi: I'd want to make sure I knew the field. Gibbs didn't know home nursing. Even if I knew the field, I'd want to get independent advice from others in the field.

Kramer: I'd check out the guy with the *Better Business Bureau* and look up his criminal record. I'd also want to know how long he'd lived here and how long he'd been in business.

Hash: I'd want to make sure that it fell in line with my long term investment strategy. If I checked out a new business venture thoroughly, and my wise counsel gave me the go-ahead, it might be worth it to risk an outside 10 percent of my investments, but not to risk the whole thing.

Money Losing Tip #9: Make Risky Investments

Mark Twain Loses His Fortune

Mark Twain was one of the greatest of all American authors, perhaps the most popular celebrity of his time.[50] His over 50 books, articles and short stories included *The Adventures of Huckleberry Finn* and the *Adventures of Tom Sawyer*.

Everybody knows Mark Twain the author; but few know Mark Twain the investor. He thrived as a writer, but sucked as an investor.

You see, when people know you have money, a steady stream of family, friends and strangers seek you out as either the savior of their struggling company or the lender to get their great idea off the ground. Twain was no exception.

He invested in a publishing house that went belly up. People would bring him inventions and convince him that they would become popular and pay off handsomely. For example, he invested in a "vastly more efficient steam engine" that had to be sold for scrap and an "improved" typesetting machine (to the tune of $200,000) that didn't work at all.

He finally learned his lesson about inventions, so that when an acquaintance came to him with some crazy idea about investing in a new invention called the "telephone," Twain turned him down flat. He felt sorry for the poor soul who invested a substantial amount, until Twain came home from a trip to find him rolling in cash!

But none of Twain's investments turned out that way. By his 50's he'd lost everything and found himself $144,000 in debt to over 101 creditors. He had to submit to the advice of wise counselors and launch a speaking tour to shore up his finances.[51]

OUR LESSONS FROM TWAIN?

Hash: Beware of "sure fire upstarts."

Akashi: He had plenty of money and plenty of smarts. What possessed him to risk anything at all? I think the "Get Rich Quick" thing must have a strong, almost irresistible appeal to many. We simply *must* put ourselves under wise, cautious counsel, like Buffett with Munger or Gibbs with his counselors. Otherwise, any of us could lose everything.

James: I think I'll put Buffett's quote on the back of my bedroom closet door:

"The first rule is: Don't lose money. The second rule is: Refer to rule one."

Money Losing Tip #10: Marry a Materialist

Kramer: Stanley and Danko discuss a mate's impact on finances in some depth. And no wonder. As you can imagine, you can make all the right decisions in the world, but if your mate's not a part of your team, you're sunk.

Antonio: I call it collateral damage.

Akashi: What?

Antonio: You know, like innocent victims in a war. If I marry a materialist, her lifestyle won't just affect *her* money and *her* lifestyle. She'll likely blow the entire family dam and drain both of our resources.

Kramer: Find a wise mate who shares your values. If you latch onto someone who's totally hung up on outward appearance – whose greatest thrill is a trip to the mall and whose greatest fear is a bad hair day – I don't care how great a body and face she's got. She'll go down from a hottie 10 to a mediocre 5 and a dreadful 2 in your eyes as she destroys the family finances.

James: But she's got to be hot, right?

Hash: Don't marry someone you're not attracted to, but as trite is it may sound, beauty *is* in the eye of the beholder. The more you behold a woman's wisdom and kindness, the more you'll see her beauty. The opposite is also true. A beauty who selfishly spends all your money will begin to look uglier and uglier.

Look for a life partner – a best friend – more than a trophy. If beauty would hold a marriage together, movie stars would marry once. But in Hollywood, beautiful people divorce all the time.

Akashi: So, I want someone who's deep as opposed to shallow?

Kramer: I don't think *deep* adequately describes the opposite of *shallow* in our culture. Someone can be deep in his knowledge of computer programming, but shallow in his knowledge of life and relationships. Concerning a great financial partner, you're not so much looking for someone who can explain $E=mc^2$ as much as someone who's wise in practical matters.

Buffett said that in choosing a business partner, he'd look for someone who has integrity and thought straight as opposed to brilliantly.[52] I think that's pretty good advice in looking for a mate.

James: Integrity...yeah. If she goes spending behind my back, or cheating on me...well, a relationship's got to be built on trust.

Kramer: Buffett says that integrity is like virginity, you only lose it once.

Antonio: If she cheats on me and divorces me for her latest fling, then I could lose half my assets overnight!

James: So where do we find mates who are wise, conservative in their spending, and have integrity?

Hash: Professor Stanley emphasized the importance of choosing the right mate. In fact, he devoted an entire chapter to "choice of spouse." He recommends two places to find a higher concentration of those with the qualities you want: colleges and church singles groups. Of course, you can also find shallow materialists in both places. But you'll likely do better there than hanging out at singles bars.[53]

Money Losing Tip #11: Keep Inadequate Insurance

Medical

Kramer: If I'd not had good medical insurance through the school system, I'd have been $250,000 in debt after my husband's long-term illness. A couple of suggestions:

First, make sure it's a reputable company. If you get an expensive, long term illness, some companies will raise your rates every year until you can no longer afford to pay. Your insurance should *insure* you against financial ruin in the event of an expensive, long-term illness. Check out the quality of your insurance company at www.ambest.com.[54]

Second, make sure you've got *enough* coverage. If you're with a reputable company, your agent should be able to advise you on a reasonable amount.

Life

Until you have dependants, you probably don't need life insurance. When you retire, you hopefully have enough saved up to provide for your mate if you were to die. You only need life insurance between those times. **Go for "Term" insurance with a reputable company.** It gives the best coverage for the money. Again, talk to a reputable agent for specifics.

Long-Term Disability

Hash: Disability insurance provides living expenses if you're no longer able to work. You're more likely to be disabled (for ninety days or longer during your working years) than to die. So, if it makes sense to carry life insurance, it might make sense to carry disability insurance as well. The government will provide some help if you get disabled, but might not provide enough for you to make ends meet. Check with your employer to see what they provide for disability. If they don't provide enough, talk to an insurance professional about your options.[55]

Summary

Kramer: Any thoughts to wrap up this breakfast?

James: Don't let people know that you have money. I could say "No" to strangers, but it would be hard to throw cold water on the great ideas of my family and friends. I think high profile people like Gibbs and Twain probably had people knocking at the door all the time with business "opportunities." It would be hard to keep turning those people down.

Amy: Just because you're smart and successful doesn't mean you can't fail at investing.

Akashi: Division is just as powerful as Multiplication. Maybe more so. Even Buffett, at his huge rate of increase, takes several years to double his money. But with bad investing, you can not only halve your fortune in a year – you can lose it all. We could work hard and smart for 30 years, get our million and then lose it virtually overnight.

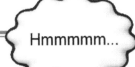

- Under which "Ways to Lose Money" would you most likely fall during your lifetime? What steps can you take to protect yourself?

- What decisions have you made concerning debt and the use of credit (particularly credit cards)? Why not set some personal standards before you're tempted to make your next purchase on credit? (Example: I'll never purchase clothes, toys or furniture with payments.")

- Who are some relatives, friends or acquaintances who could become your sounding board for financial decisions?

- What is your strategy for finding a mate with values similar to your own?

- Is your insurance company solid? Find their rating at www.ambest.com.

Assignment
Between Breakfasts

1. Ask your parents, teachers and friends about their advice on getting jobs and thriving at work.

2. Go to www.careerbuilder.com or www.monster.com and poke around, seeing what articles they offer and looking at all the types of jobs available. Find jobs that interest you.

Resources to Take You Deeper

If you find yourself in debt:

You need more than information; you need cheerleaders. That's what hosts like Dave Ramsey can provide. He'll give you a specific plan, then let you hear testimony after testimony of folks who've attacked extraordinary debt and found financial freedom on the other side. First, find him on the radio. If local stations don't carry him, find his radio show on the internet.

Second, get Ramsey's book, The Total Money Makeover: A Proven Plan for Financial Fitness (Nashville: Thomas Nelson, Inc., 2003). It's got just enough information, plus a host of testimonies from those who've escaped the debt trap.

To become more wary of scams:

www.clarkhoward.com - the site of Clark Howard, consumer advocate, author and popular talk show host. Listen to his popular radio show frequent his website to avoid today's money rip-offs.

Everybody Wants Your Money: The Straight Talking Guide to Protecting (and Growing) the Wealth You Worked So Hard to Earn by David Latko (Collins, 2006). Good guide to protecting your wealth, from another talk show host.

PART THREE

MAKING MONEY

Breakfast #12: Find Those Dream Jobs

"Choose a job you love, and you will never have to work a day in your life."
— **Confucius**

James: I'm glad we're finally talking about *making* money. I have a huge respect for Carmen and her ways to save. But I plan to make such a large salary that I won't have to worry too much about what I buy.

Akashi: Don't you get it? That's *precisely* why so many people with huge salaries have zero net worth. Every time they get a raise, their expenses rise to match their new salary. Remember what the *Wherehouse Music* guy said about controlling your expenses more than your revenues?

James: I suppose that's why guys like Buffett continue to buy their Cokes on sale. It's so difficult to get that through my thick head!

Kramer: *Extremely* difficult. *So* difficult that many Americans never get it in an entire lifetime. They're fifty years old, making huge salaries, and can't figure out why they have meager savings.

The Importance of Making Money

But as important as saving is, we *still* have to make enough in salary to cover our expenses and have enough to save. Most young people don't seem to understand how much it costs to live these days. They get stuck in low-paying, dead-end jobs that make it virtually impossible to get ahead, no matter how good they are at saving.

Making a Difference While Making a Living

Antonio: I'm not really that concerned about a great salary. I get more of a charge from hanging out with people and knowing that my life's making a difference.

Kramer: I like your spirit, Antonio! So you're thinking:

> *"How can I do the best possible with my finances, so that I can make the biggest life impact?"*

Antonio: Right. To me that means not spending all my time and effort chasing the almighty dollar. Some people are so caught up in "getting ahead" that they have no time for the bigger things – like their families, helping the needy and making a difference.

Amy: True. But others lose their impact by not paying *enough* attention to making money.

Antonio: How's that?

Amy: I know people who work two or three low-paying jobs just to feed their families and make ends meet. It takes all their time and energy. They have neither the time nor money to give. Land a job with a decent salary and you won't have to put in overtime or get a second job. You'll have more time to serve.

Kramer: Perhaps Antonio could find a job where he can make his impact *at* work, like going into religious ministry or the Peace Corp or another service organization. He probably won't make much money, but if he lives beneath his means, he can make his impact while earning a living.

Amy: Or, he could earn big bucks in his early career, and either retire early to make his life impact, or give that money away, like Warren Buffett. Didn't you say he's given away billions?

Kramer: Over 85 percent of his wealth so far. You can do a lot of good with that kind of money.

Ben Franklin Retires Early to Leave His Legacy

And good point on retiring early. Benjamin Franklin had a massive impact on the world with his inventions, community service and donations. He also thought long-term. He gave a little over $2,000 to the city of Boston and the same amount to Philadelphia, specifying that it be invested for 200 years before it could be used. Today, Philadelphia and Boston use Franklin's money (over $7,000,000) to help people finance their educations and homes.

But he made this impact largely because he worked hard at the printing business in his early years, lived frugally, saved and retired at age 42. That allowed him the time to start Philadelphia's library, experiment with electricity, invent useful gadgets, write important papers, get America started and all that good stuff. If he'd been stuck with no savings, working the check out line at a grocery store at age 45, he couldn't have left his mark.

The bottom line is, for many of us, if we can find jobs that pay a generous wage, we can spend more time with our families, have more money to save and invest and ultimately have more time to make our world a better place.

How can we land those dream jobs that not only pay well, but that we look forward to going to each day?

Can Work Really Be Fun?

Akashi: Is that really possible? I mean, my parents endure their jobs and live for the weekends and holidays. I don't know how many times they've warned me,

> *"You may **think** you've got it hard now, but just wait till you get a **real** job. **Then** you'll know what work **really** is."*

It's depressing. School's hard enough on me. They make it sound like I'm graduating from Purgatory to be welcomed into Hell.

Kramer: Actually, many people *love* their work! They can't wait to get to work in the morning. They get so caught up in their work that they lose all track of time. At the end of the day, when they glance at the clock, they're startled to realize it's time to go home, and they can't imagine where the time went.

Sam Walton loved retailing so much that even after he'd been diagnosed with an incurable disease, he spent much of his last two years flying to Wal-Marts and visiting his associates.[1] He described his career as "interesting, fun and exciting."[2] That's not unusual among successful people.

A 2003 study found 50.7 percent of the people surveyed indicating that they're satisfied with their current jobs.[3]

In fact, **if you look at the most successful people, one outstanding characteristic is that they love their work.** In Stanley and Danko's studies of the wealthy,

> *"The most successful business owners we have interviewed have one characteristic in common: They all enjoy what they do."[4]*

Don't you have any family members or friends who enjoy their work?

James: I have a friend who hated high school, but loved building websites. He did the one year web design track at North Metro Tech and started his own web design business. Last time I saw him, he was loving work and making a killer living.

Akashi: I have an uncle who sells cars at a Chevy dealership. He loves cars and the challenge of selling and interacting with people. He's always getting an award for top sales.

Kramer: I love teaching. It's not always easy, but it's incredibly rewarding. And there's always a new way to get across an old truth. I relish the challenge.

So work can either be fun and rewarding, or a boring chore. You'll be spending a large part of your life working. Let's talk about some ways to make the best of it.

Step #1: Know Yourself

Kramer: Please hold the "Duhs!"; but to find a job you love, you've got to know yourself pretty well. You see,

> *the perfect job is a perfect match between your personality/interests/ talents and a job environment where you can fully express those strengths.*

Amy: Surely I know myself pretty well. I've hung out with myself for 18 years!

Kramer's Path to Teaching

Kramer: You'd be surprised how little most of us know ourselves. It takes a wide variety of experience and a lot of reflection on it. In high school, I loved cheerleading. It's all I wanted to do. Hated academics. Figured I might teach PE and lead a cheerleader squad one day.

So, I volunteered one summer to help lead a cheerleader camp for middle schoolers. I *hated* it! I discovered that *being* a cheerleader and *leading* cheerleaders were two totally different things. **Reflecting on that experience** was invaluable for getting to know myself.

Amy: You hated academics? And you're a schoolteacher?

Kramer: Don't get me wrong. I loved to learn. I was intensely curious, always asking people questions about this or that. But I had some kind of disability that made it terribly difficult to memorize. That's why I always bring these notebooks to our breakfasts and refer to them when I need to pull out a quote or a statistic.

History was the worst. Other students could listen to the lecture without taking notes, not even read the text, and pass the final with a "B." I had to go over and over the text, painstakingly memorizing my notes with every memory trick in the book just to pull a "C."

But my junior year I took a business class that changed my life. My teacher told me that rote memory isn't that important in most fields. She pointed out that I had a knack for grasping deep concepts and expressing them simply. I was also able to take concepts from one subject area and apply them in another. She said I might be a great entrepreneur or a great teacher.

Can GPAs Predict Success?

So I began to look more at my strengths than my weaknesses. A loser memory doesn't make for a loser career. A "C" average doesn't make for a "C" life. **In fact, the average millionaire studied by Professor Stanley had a "C" average.**[5]

Amy: A "C" average?! I've been wasting my time pursuing the almighty 4.0?!?

Kramer: Not at all. Your ability to make "A's" points to some great strengths, including a good memory, concentration, discipline and organization. Those will serve you well in many careers. Also, your "A's" will help you get scholarships and secure your acceptance to your choice of colleges. And if you decide to go into certain fields, like law or medicine or engineering, you simply can't do it without strong academics.

But often the school experience gives us the impression that unless we're good at all subjects, we can't succeed in life. It's simply not true. Straight "A's" in high school is a good predictor of how well you will do in college, but not a great predictor of how well you will do in your career.[6]

A "C" or even "D" student may struggle with a disability or lack academic motivation. He's discovered a weakness – he stinks at academic learning in a traditional school environment. But let's imagine that he flunks Chemistry, but has a remarkable understanding of people. Let's say he bombs the SAT, but his emotional intelligence is off the charts. What kinds of jobs might he excel in?

James: Management. My manager attended a top college and is brilliant at academics. But he keeps losing workers because he doesn't know how to work with people. I think the owner will eventually fire him.

Akashi: Sales. You've got to understand people – their needs and motivations – to sell to them.

Kramer: Professor Stanley studied top people in sales and found that they were courageous and had outstanding social skills.[7] Unfortunately, neither of these highly valuable skills are either graded on report cards or measured by the SAT.

Akashi: I've gotten ISS for that combination of skills – courage and social skills. I talk out of turn, too long and too loud. Hey, maybe ISS would be a great place for businesses to recruit a sales force!

Kramer: Akashi, You've just *got* to become an entrepreneur to put your outside of the box thinking to good use!

The Best Salesman Ever

Professor Stanley says that the best salesman he ever met is Billy Gilmore, Jr. Stanley taught him at the University of Georgia. One day, Billy handed in a worse than pitiful midterm paper. After hours of allowed writing time, it contained only one paragraph. Stanley told him, in front of the entire class of 99 students, that it was the worst paper he'd ever read and suggested he drop the class.

But Billy wasn't about to quit. He visited the professor at his home – unannounced – and told him,

> *"You forgot one thing in your class. If you have courage, you can win. You don't have to be the fastest, the smartest. You have to have tenacity."*

Billy graduated with a 2.01 average – a low "C." But he honed his sales skills during his college years by working full time selling real estate. He polished his social skills by maintaining a full social life on campus.

After college, Billy Gilmore and Professor Stanley kept in touch, occasionally working together. Here's an example of how Billy's mind works.

A major corporation invited Professor Stanley to address a large gathering of professionals in Dallas. He calls Billy and asks him to help lead. Billy agrees. Now most people would have immediately sat down and started wording their talk. Not Billy. He calls the secretary of the national sales manager, who's putting the gig together. Billy asks if the boss's wife wears blue jeans, and then for her size. She tells him, "a tight ten or really a twelve."

You see, Billy sold ladies' wear, including blue jeans, to major retailers.

When Professor Stanley arrives at the conference, he knows nothing of Billy's behind the scenes scheming. So he's shocked when the conference coordinator rushes over to thank him profusely for the gift of blue jeans for his wife.

> *"...My wife loves the blue jeans. She can't thank you enough. She feels a lot better about me giving up my Saturday when there are blue jeans involved. They fit her perfectly."*

Unknown to Professor Stanley, Billy had ordered twelve pair of high quality blue jeans – tailor made in the wife's size – by a senior seamstress. And here's the kicker. Inside each pair was sewn a label stating "Size 8."

Billy intentionally didn't take credit, sending the jeans in Stanley's name.

It's no surprise that the national sales manager felt so positive about the conference. It's no surprise that he bought many of Professor Stanley's products. It's no surprise that Stanley's respect for Billy continued to skyrocket.

Billy Gilmore knows people. He cares about people. That strength of empathy made him tops in his field.[8]

Discovering Your Strengths

Kramer: So finding your strengths is incredibly important to landing a great job and succeeding at it. But it's not as easy as it seems. According to management guru Peter Drucker:

> *"Most Americans do not know what their strengths are. When you ask them, they look at you with a blank stare...." (Peter Drucker, leading authority on management and author of 35 books)[9]*

Imagine that a friend says, "I've got to get a job and have no idea what kind to look for. Give me some direction." How would you counsel him?

Antonio: Write down the things you enjoy and hate. Then, ask yourself *why* you enjoy or hate them. The more I think about it, some of the reasons I enjoy volunteering are that:

> 1) I get energized being around people.
>
> 2) I like helping people find their niche in making an event come off well.
>
> 3) I love the feeling that I've made a difference in someone's life.

That tells me a lot about what jobs I'd like...and what I'd hate.

Kramer: According to job coach Dan Miller,

> *"Looking inward is 85 percent of the process of finding proper direction; 15 percent is the application to career choices."*[10]

So don't get discouraged if you have to wade through some not-so-great jobs in your early years. Use the experiences to understand yourself. Mediocre jobs can be stepping stones to great jobs.

Akashi: Ask family and friends about your strengths and their ideas as to what vocation you should pursue. Others often see us in ways that we can't see ourselves.

James: Work or volunteer at many types of jobs. I've worked several jobs and learned something from each of them. I can't stand serving fast food. Something about the rushing around and people getting hot and bothered if their burger's not done immediately. Working with auto parts is a lot better. I feel I'm able to help people in an area I know something about.

The more life experiences you have, the more you have to reflect upon.

Amy: Didn't we take some kind of **personality inventory** at school?

Kramer: Good point! Try to set up an appointment with your school counselor to explain the results. Those inventories aren't perfect, but you'll probably come out with more than one flash of insight as to who you are and how you relate best to others. And take some inventories later in life, after you've had more life experiences.

Aren't There Only a Few Fun Jobs?

Another helpful insight came out of a vast study by the Gallup Organization. It blows to shreds a **popular misconception:**

> *There are very few cool and exciting jobs. Since not everyone can work at those jobs, most of us have to work at boring jobs.*

The Gallup organization surveyed over 2,000,000 people to understand how we can have the most rewarding, satisfying and productive work.[11]

They discovered that people differ greatly in their strengths and interests, and thus the kinds of work they enjoy. In other words, we're not all competing for a few jobs that everyone would love!

The problem is not that all the good jobs are taken, but that many workers feel that they've been miscast for their role, having to work at tasks they aren't good at and don't enjoy.

Marcus Buckingham, Sr. Vice President of Gallup, says that **to find the work you love, you've got to first discover your strengths, then find a job where you can use those strengths every day.**[12] The researchers identified over 34 strength themes, which could be combined in a myriad of ways to make each person unique.

That's great news! Not everyone *wants* to be the president of the company or the lead guitarist for a band. We're not hopelessly competing for a few cool jobs that anybody would enjoy. *You* may be incredibly fulfilled as a programmer, whereas another would be happier as a manager, another as a football coach, another as assistant to a company president.

Warren Buffett once said of his own career, "Money is a byproduct of doing something I like doing extremely well."[13]

Amy: So some accountants love running numbers and wouldn't enjoy playing professional baseball. Buffett loves studying companies and investing. Gates loves technology. Oseola loved washing clothes.

Kramer: Exactly! You're not out there hopelessly competing for the few cool jobs. "Cool job" is defined by the interests and strengths of the worker.

If you keep reflecting on your experiences, you'll get to know yourself better for the rest of your life, narrowing down more and more what you love.

Step #2: Know the Job Market

Kramer: After reflecting on your strengths, try to match your interests and strengths to jobs that pay enough to meet your life goals. It's fun to discover the almost infinite number of ways to make a living these days. Familiarize yourself with lots of jobs to see what's out there. It's an exciting time to live!

Amy: Which I assume leads us into our homework assignment.

Kramer: I almost forgot. What stood out to you from your surfing around on Monster.com and Careerbuilder.com?

Amy: Like you just said − the almost infinite ways of making a living. There's got to be tons of jobs out there that I would enjoy. I think I might actually enjoy accounting. But I'd want to do it for a firm I believed in, with workers I enjoyed hanging out with.

Antonio: I found lots of service organizations. Once I found a really cool one on Careerbuilder.com. Then, I found the organization's website to learn more about it. If possible, I'd like to either work near a vast wilderness or combine service with some type of wilderness adventures. I need to do more exploring on that site.

Akashi: I surfed around Monster for awhile, but then looked in my local yellow pages to find area businesses. I took to my car to go visit a few, asking people what they liked and hated about their jobs. I also asked my parents and relatives. I was surprised how much I learned just by snooping around and asking questions.

My parents showed me this cool, free tool at the New York Times: http://salary.

nytimes.com. A job's got to pay enough to provide a decent living. Find an interesting job on this web page and discover the salary range paid in your location.

But once I find a cool company, what's the best way to get hired?

Step #3: Become the Most Qualified for Your Job

Kramer: You've each worked a couple of jobs. What do you think?

Amy: First, do your best at your present job, even if it stinks. I've got friends who get tired of their job or mad at their boss and the next day they just don't show up! Unbelievable! What if they apply for their dream job, and the manager calls their old boss. I think your early jobs are your best references for your later jobs. Show up every day, do more than you're asked and get quotes from your managers as to how well you did. Include their quotes in your resume.

Antonio: I'd suggest finding some jobs you love on Monster and working backwards.

Akashi: Working backwards?

Antonio: Sure. Most people work forward in their preparation, guessing the qualifications an employer might want, then pursuing that education. Why not begin with the end in mind? Study the jobs you want; note the desired qualifications; then, plan your preparation to meet their qualifications.

Amy: Most of the best paying accounting jobs I see want me to have a five-year accounting degree, be certified as a CPA, have a couple of years experience in the field and be a nice person to work with. That means I need to not only pursue that degree, but I need to get some experience along the way and pick up quotes from managers and co-workers that I'm enjoyable to work with. Maybe I could co-op in college, working every other quarter to pick up experience. It doesn't look like they want a person who's got a degree with no experience.

James: In most of these jobs, I'm seeing experience as a main component. Even if I just worked for minimum wage or worked free somewhere to get my foot in the door, it might be just the experience to give me the edge in the future. Plus, I get some real life experience to discover if I like that field or not, just like Mrs. Kramer volunteering at the cheerleading camp.

Akashi: Once I find a company I like and have a good resume, do I just apply through Monster?

Step #4: Know How to Land a Job

Kramer: The way most people go after jobs is ineffective. Only about four percent of people who apply online get the job. Increase that to 10 percent for technical jobs. Only seven percent get jobs by mailing out resumes to employers.[14]

Amy: But I thought that's how everybody looked for jobs!

Kramer: Once again…

Everyone (in unison): You've got to go counterculture!

How to Beat the System

Kramer: Think like an employer. Anybody can look good on paper. And lots of creeps can turn on the charm during an interview.

Akashi: If I were an employer, I'd want a recommendation from somebody I knew, to make sure the applicant wasn't an ax murderer or had an irritating personality.

Kramer: Exactly! So if you discover a business you want to work in, talk to all your relatives, friends and schoolteachers to try to find some connection with somebody who works there. **A full 33 percent of people who get job leads from friends, family and acquaintances land jobs.**[15]

Here's another tip most don't think about. **Once you find a place you'd like to work, either show up at their office or call them on the phone, telling them of your desire to work there and asking if they need help.**

Akashi: But you don't even know if they're hiring or not.

Kramer: That's the point! Jobs that are advertised may get hundreds of applicants. You want to go for the ones that aren't yet advertised. Maybe someone just quit the day before, and the boss doesn't relish advertising for a new worker, taking endless phone calls and narrowing down scores of applicants. You stroll in with your pleasant personality, excellent resume and a passion to get started in their field. You're like the answer to their prayers! That's why **up to 69 percent of people seeking jobs this way actually land a job.**[16]

And make sure to follow up on your applications. I hear many employers say that when a person calls to follow-up on their resume, they put those applications on top of the pile. Calling and stopping by occasionally shows initiative and builds a relationship.

The future is so exciting! Ask people about their jobs. Try different jobs while you're young. Volunteer at not-for-profits. Meet new people and showcase your skills.[17] Keep learning and growing. It really is an exciting time to live!

Preview

It's one thing to land a job, quite another to excel in it. That's next week's critical topic. Amy, could you bring an inspiring story of a person you respect who worked hard in his or her field?

Amy: I think I already know the story! It's my favorite rock guitar maestro.

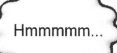

- What are your weaknesses? How can you either strengthen them or work around them?

- Look up some interesting professions on http://salary. nytimes.com. Which jobs would likely provide enough income to meet your financial goals?

- What are your strengths? How can you develop them?

- What new strategies would you like to adopt when looking for your next job?

Assignment
Between Breakfasts

1. Think through the jobs you've had. What sets apart the employees who last from the ones who get fired?

2. Go to a successful person you admire. Ask, "Why are you so successful at what you do?"

3. Read a couple of articles about successful people you admire. Write down some things they did that contributed to their success.

Resources to Take You Deeper

Richard N. Boles, ***What Color is Your Parachute? (A Practical Manual for Job-Hunters and Career-Changers)*** (Berkeley: The Ten Speed Press, updated each year). This is the bible of job seekers.

Marcus Buckingham and Donald O. Clifton, Now, Discover Your Strengths (New York: The Free Press, 2001). It will broaden your understanding of yourself, particularly if you take the free (with purchase of a new book) online "StrengthsFinder" profile. (Also on CD/Spoken Word).

www.careerbuilder.com - lots of great advice and resources to find jobs in various localities.

www.monster.com - another site with great job-seeking opportunities and information.

http://salary.nytimes.com - find the base salaries for vocations in your general location, provided by the New York Times.

Breakfast #13: Excel at Your Job

Review

Kramer: So, after having a week to reflect on last week's material, what stands out?

Akashi: Before that breakfast, I thought that my "C" performance in school pretty much sealed my fate to land a "C" job in the workforce. By concentrating on my strengths, I realize that I can look for jobs that cater to my strengths. VERY encouraging!

James: It's never occurred to me that so many people could actually *enjoy* their work. Sounds a lot better than enduring the eight to five, while living for weekends and vacations.

Amy: I've learned a lot just browsing through jobs on www.careerbuilder.com and www.monster.com. I've also run many vocations through http://salary.nytimes.com to see what they pay in metro Atlanta.

Transition

Kramer: Once you *get* a good job, you want to *thrive* there, becoming an asset to the company and indispensable to your employer. As a result, you feel good about yourself, get along better with the management, receive better raises and have more fun. Here are some ways to thrive.

1. Learn the Traits That Make People Successful

"If I have seen further, it is by standing on the shoulders of giants." (Isaac Newton, hero to Einstein)

Kramer: To prepare ourselves for success, let's concentrate on developing habits and traits that make for success in vocations and money management. What characteristics do you think are most important?

James: Luck? I've got to wonder if most millionaires were either born into wealthy families or lucked into a great job.

Kramer: Actually, very few were lottery winners, and most didn't inherit their money. Most of the millionaires interviewed by Dr. Stanley ran their own businesses.

Amy: I'd guess hard work and marketable skills.

Antonio: I think they love their work.

Kramer: You're on the right track! Here's a handout of what Professor Stanley discovered by asking over 700 multimillionaires – super-successful at both business and accumulating wealth – what factors were most important to their success.

I listed only those items deemed important by over half of them.[1]

Here's how they responded:

SUCCESS FACTOR	TOTAL RESPONDING EITHER "VERY IMPORTANT" OR "IMPORTANT"
Being well disciplined	95 percent
Getting along with people	94 percent
Being honest with all people	90 percent
Working harder than most people	88 percent
Loving my career/business	86 percent
Being very well organized	85 percent
Having strong leadership qualities	84 percent
Having an ability to sell my ideas/products	82 percent
Having a supportive spouse	81 percent
Having a very competitive spirit/personality	81 percent
Making wise investments	76 percent
Willing to take financial risk given the right return	74 percent
Having good mentors	73 percent
Seeing opportunities others do not see	72 percent
Having extraordinary energy	71 percent
Having an urge to be well respected	69 percent
Finding a profitable niche	69 percent
Having a high IQ/superior intellect	67 percent (only 20 percent of these said "very important")
Being my own boss	65 percent
Being physically fit	65 percent
Investing in my own business	54 percent
Specializing	53 percent
Ignoring the criticism of detractors	51 percent

Kramer: What strikes you about this list?

Amy: "High IQ" and "Superior Intellect" didn't make the top 15, and only 20 percent of them considered it "very important." I'm sure they're not dumb, but I'm shocked that **most of the characteristics are character traits and life skills**. Just working down the list I see discipline, people skills, honesty and diligence as the top four.

If schools are supposed to prepare us for the job market, I'm surprised that they're not putting more effort into instilling those traits.

Antonio: It makes sense when I put myself in the boss's shoes. If I were choosing between two engineers with the same set of skills, wouldn't I look for someone who showed evidence of being a hard, honest worker who I might enjoy working with?

Kramer: Right. Good businesses look for good people. Warren Buffet can spot a good business better than anyone. He once said this about finding a business partner. Raise your hand when you hear a character quality.

> "I think you'll probably start looking for the person that **you can always depend on**; the person **whose ego does not get in his way,** the person **who's perfectly willing to let someone else take the credit** for an idea as long as it worked; the person who essentially **won't let you down, who thought straight** as opposed to brilliantly."[2]

Akashi: So, although a high school diploma and college degree might be important to my next employer, they're going to look long and hard for evidence that I'm an honest, hard worker who's easy to get along with.

Amy: This cuts against the popular opinion that people get ahead by being ruthless: either running over people or using them to further their greedy purposes. Even the word "boss," sounds cold and...you know...bossy.

Kramer: For sure there are plenty of uncaring bosses out there. But the great ones care about their employees and their customers. Jack Welch, considered one of the greatest business leaders of all time, speaks of the role of great managers as "pastoral" and "parental." They must listen, love, nurture, and help those off-track to get back on track.[3]

Amy: I'm kind of surprised to see the word "honesty." To get ahead at school, it's almost a part of the student culture to lie and cheat.

Kramer: But think of it in the context of a business. As Buffett has said,

> *"Somebody once said that in looking for people to hire, you look for three qualities: integrity, intelligence, and energy. And if they don't have the first, the other two will kill you."*[4]

Paul Orfalea, the founder of Kinkos, quoted a 2003 study of 1,500 companies, which found that:

> *"Firms with strong ethics had higher firm value, higher profits, higher sales growth, and lower capital expenditures. "*[5]

Then, he says:

> *"People need to understand that they will make a lot more money in the long run if they conduct themselves with integrity."*[6]

Antonio: If this list of qualities is what's most important to employers, my resume needs to bring this out. It's not just my degrees and places I've worked. To land a dream job, I need to demonstrate those qualities in school and in my present job. Then, I need to get statements or reference letters from my teachers and coworkers and supervisors saying that I demonstrate these qualities.

Kramer: Great ideas! Listen, Stanley's list is powerful advice from 700 highly successful money-makers and money managers. It bears a lot of reflection. Put it on your refrigerator or your bedroom bulletin board. Put checks by characteristics you need to work on.

Here's how Benjamin Franklin worked on his character. As a young person, he wrote a list of thirteen character qualities that he thought were critical for his success. He would concentrate on one each week, noting when he failed at that virtue.[7]

2. Build a Team to Round Out Your Weaknesses

Kramer: **"Having Strong Leadership Qualities"** ranked high on Stanley's list. It implies that you're leading a team of people, with each having the necessary strengths to perform needed tasks.

Jack Welch begins his autobiography by saying that, "Nearly everything I've done in my life has been accomplished with other people." He explains that whenever he writes, "I did this" or "I accomplished that," we should understand "I" to include many of his colleagues and friends.[8]

As we said last week, we all have strengths. But we also have weaknesses. None of us are perfect. None of us can "do it all." **The successful try to work on their critical weaknesses and work around those they can't eliminate.**

Akashi: Several weeks ago, Mrs. Kramer lent me a set of CD's by Paul Orfalea, the super-successful founder of Kinkos, the copy store. I think his stores make about $2 billion each year. Orfalea suffered from Dyslexia and ADHD to such an extent that he never learned to read. He couldn't even run the copiers at his stores.

So how did he complete school and start a successful business? He used his deficits to his advantage. In the fourth grade, he met Danny, whose entire family helped him with his academics. Here's a quote I wrote down from Orfalea:

> *"Every major success I've had in my life has come about because I knew that somebody, often anybody, whether it was my wife, friend, or business partner, could do something better than I could."*[9]

He learned to depend on others to offset his weaknesses and specialize in what *he* could do best – getting ideas from his stores and his competitors and passing them on to his partners and employees. As one associate said, "Paul is a walking brainstorm." That was his strength. He offset his weaknesses by depending on his team.[10]

Kramer: All the greats have weaknesses:

- **Leonardo DaVinci** had incredible talent, but had terrible problems completing tasks.[11]

- **Jack Welch,** respected business leader, struggled with a stutter.[12]

- **George Lucas**, producer and writer of *Star Wars*, is a great story-teller, but can't spell worth anything.[13]

- **Steven Spielberg** is one of the most successful movie directors of all time, but couldn't memorize lines well enough to be in his high school plays.[14]

- **Albert Einstein** had trouble with memorization and languages, and was told by a teacher that he'd never amount to anything.[15]

- **C.S. Lewis**, Cambridge professor and wildly successful author of *The Chronicles of Narnia*, suffered from what he described as "extreme manual clumsiness." Because of this, and a thumb with only one joint, attempts at making anything ended in frustrating failure. Math was equally elusive.[16]

We all have weaknesses. We just need to learn how to work around them. Management guru Peter Drucker says,

> ***"The specific job of the manager is to make the strengths of people productive and their weaknesses irrelevant."***[17]

James: So if I land the right job, with the right team, my weaknesses won't matter as much because the strengths of others will make up for my weaknesses.

Kramer: Right. I always thought of small-time real estate investing as an individual sport. You find a bargain property, buy it, fix it and sell it. Sounds like a job one person can handle.

But when Gary Keller interviewed 100 successful real estate investors, he was surprised by an unexpected insight:

> ***"Again and again, throughout our research, investors referred to all the people who helped them succeed. They had relationships with people who sent them opportunities, mentored them, helped them buy and maintain their properties, and in many cases provided services that enabled them to do more while spending less and less effort."***[18]

Keller concluded that building a quality team is one of the big secrets to successful real estate investing.

Antonio: That seems to apply to most fields. **In sports,** coaches preach "the team" over "the individual." **Musicians** need other instrumentalists, travel specialists, a reliable stage crew and a talented recording company with an effective sales team. **In movie making**...well...whenever I watch a movie, I like to sit through the credits. It takes much more than directors and actors to make great movies. The credits tell the story of caterers, writers, editors, travel agents, assistants, grips (whatever a grip is!) and a host of others.

Kramer: The bottom line?

Antonio: It takes a winning team to make you successful. Find that winning team.

Akashi's Weaknesses

Akashi: It's hard for me to admit my academic weaknesses, but I think I should let down my guard a bit. In Kindergarten and the first grade, some could look at the abc's once or twice and know them. It took me forever. And those multiplication facts – I'll bet Amy looked over those flash cards a few times and knew them cold. I flipped them hundreds of times. It was torture for me, and I never mastered those basics.

Later in school, with grammar and algebra, things got even more complex. I decided that I had two choices: (1) decide that my teachers and fellow students were smart and I was dumb or (2) decide that the entire system was stupid and I'd just act like I didn't care. I chose the latter.

My parents made a bad situation even worse. My big sis made straight "A's" and got into Georgia Tech. My brother was valedictorian of his class and attended Massachusetts Institute of Technology. My parents thought I should be able to do the same, but I couldn't. They thought I just needed more motivation, so they continually preached to me that I'd never be able to compete in the real world with my bad grades. I became the black sheep of the family, the slacker, the loser.

My experiences at school affected my attitude toward this group. Every time Amy calculated investments in her head or showed her almost total recall for facts, I'd just die inside. I felt so outclassed. It was school all over again. I wanted to quit The Counterculture Club.

In school, if teachers covered something I couldn't understand, I'd put my head on my desk and act disinterested. If they called on me to read, I'd refuse and say I didn't feel like participating.

Mrs. Kramer called my bluff. When she announced we were going to read aloud at one breakfast, I said I was tired and put my head down on the table. She put two and two together from other comments I'd made. When I called her after the car chase, she asked if I'd ever been tested for disabilities.

To make a long story short, I got tested and found I'm dyslexic. Now I'm getting special help at school. Mrs. Kramer's been feeding me some CD biographies of successful people, especially those with learning disabilities. For my entire life, I've only concentrated on my weaknesses. For the first time, I'm beginning to focus on my strengths.

I've had to redefine "smart," which is used in school almost exclusively to describe people who pick up things quickly in a classroom setting. When someone aces a Math test and a teacher says, "She's really smart," I wish she'd learn to say, "She's really smart *at Math*." She may be dumb at relationships or languages or leadership.

I learned that, according to our current understanding of the brain, there are many intelligences, and that I was smart in my own way.[19]

Unfortunately, the *language* of smart hasn't kept up with the *science* of smart. So I've never heard anyone refer to me as smart, either at home or at school.

Other Weaknesses

Amy: (Laughing) That's just *too* funny.

Akashi: (Getting defensive) What's so funny about it?

Amy: *I've* always been so intimidated by *you*! Sure, I can crunch numbers in my head all day long. But you can take those numbers and apply them to real life. Think back to our breakfasts. Almost every time Mrs. Kramer asks us to respond to a thoughty question that doesn't involve computing numbers, either you or Antonio leave me in the dust. It's sooo embarrassing!

Antonio: (To James) Is it just me, or is this a girl thing? Did you know any of this ego warfare was going on?

James: Not a clue.

Kramer: Don't you see what we're learning here?

Antonio: Never underestimate the ability of girls to get jealous about stuff?

Kramer: Apparently James and Antonio are weak in "Emotional Intelligence." And PLEASE stop stereotyping us girls.

Akashi, thanks for letting the rest of the group in on your struggles. I'll bet everyone here has struggled with one personal weakness or another.

Amy: As I was saying, I'm great at Math and rote memory, but have a hard time discussing how an article might apply to real life. I also have difficulty reading people – their character and intentions. Makes me kind of gullible.

James: Memorizing names and numbers – that's what I hate. Classes like history kill me – they're all about memorizing names and dates. I'm also embarrassed when I can't remember people's names at school and at work.

Antonio: I have problems making decisions and motivating myself to complete tasks. I'm also disorganized, which makes it hard to get places on time. I often have difficulty concentrating. Because of this, school is a bear. I'm being treated for ADD, which helps some.

Putting Together an Imaginary Team

Kramer: So much for our weaknesses. Let's concentrate on our strengths. Imagine we're starting a business. What strengths do we have in our little club that might prove useful?

James: Amy's math skills *are* awesome! I'd want her running our numbers. Also, with her memory, I think she'd be great at studying the competition to find what they're doing right and wrong, how they price their products and reporting back. Her organizational skills would also come in handy.

Antonio: James is a leader. I'll never forget his taking charge during the car chase. He's also got awesome drive and vision. I'd want him to keep us on track accomplishing our goals. He's a work horse and would make sure that what needed to get done would get done.

Akashi: Antonio has a great heart and strong relational skills. If I had a boss or manager over me, I'd want it to be Antonio. He'd treat us all fairly and help us to work through our conflicts.

Amy: Akashi can see outside of the box and apply wisdom to any real life situation. She's also fearless. I think she'd chase Moby Dick with a row boat, a pocket knife… and a jar of Tarter Sauce. Remember when she asked the hard questions of all those used car salesmen? Those are great traits for entrepreneurs or any job in sales.

Kramer: So we all have strengths and weaknesses. None of us are perfect. To be successful in life, we've got to find a team, so that we can spend our time doing what we're good at, leaving the tasks we hate to others who love those tasks.

3. Work on Your Relational Skills

Kramer: I learned to put relationships first the hard way. Fresh out of college, I loved students and had a passion to teach them. I thought my ideas were great and didn't see any need to learn from the older teachers. I pretty much isolated myself with the students.

I'd talk openly about what other teachers did wrong. Among teachers, I badmouthed the administration. I soon discovered that gossip has a much more effective circulation than the school newspaper. I took our school counselor out for lunch and asked her to be candid with me. She said that I was winning with my students, but flunking with my colleagues. They hated me and made life hard on me as a teacher.

She recommended that I read Carnegie's perennial best-seller, *How to Win Friends and Influence People.* I read it through once, and then took a chapter at a time to try to apply it to life.

Antonio: So it turned things around?

Kramer: Actually, I'd alienated people so badly that I started over at a new school. **I don't care how great your skills are, if you blow your relationships, you'll blow your job.** I continue to read the book once every five years or so.

If you haven't already found it out, three of the biggest words in success are: relationships, relationships, relationships. The 400 multimillionaires put it number two on their list.

Here are a couple of quotes from Carnegie's book:

> *"Even in technical lines such as engineering, about 15 percent of one's financial success is due to one's technical knowledge, and about 85 percent is due to skill in human engineering – to personality and the ability to lead people."*[20]

> *"The ability to deal with people is as purchasable a commodity as sugar or coffee. And I will pay more for that ability than for any other under the sun." (John D. Rockefeller, famous American businessman and philanthropist.)*[21]

Relationships are so important that we could easily spend a year studying them. But what application do you see this having in your lives?

Application to Life

Amy: This week, I'm gonna get to know at least one new person. Sometimes I'm so intent on getting grades that I don't even think about the people sitting beside me in class. I need to break out of my shell and at least meet some of them.

Antonio: I suppose that high school is one of the best times to get to know people, since we rub shoulders with so many each day. And many of those relationships might prove critical to getting me a great job. I heard that, in school, Sam Walton made it a point to always say "Hi" to other people before they said "Hi" to him. He carried that habit with him as he ran his stores.[22]

James: If that book by Carnegie is so good, I think we all should read it and help each other to apply it.

Amy: I'm all for that!

Kramer: Here's one of my favorite tips from Carnegie that I'll leave with you:

> *"You can make more friends in two months of becoming interested in other people, than in two years of trying to get other people interested in you."*[23]

4. Demonstrate a Servant's Heart

If your bosses and your customers know that you have their best interests at heart, you'll likely become the best paid and will be the last to be let go during layoffs.[24]

5. Work Hard

"Everything comes to him who hustles while he waits."

— Thomas Edison, "The Wizard of Menlo Park," who is considered the world's most prolific inventor, with 1,093 inventions, an average of one invention every 12 days of his adult life!

Kramer: "Being well disciplined" and "working harder than most people" came in at number one and number four in Stanley's survey.

Antonio: I didn't really want to hear the "work hard" thing.

Kramer: I know. Many wish they could win the lottery and not have to hear the word "work" – ever again. But oddly, getting out of work might not be much fun. The leisure life is highly overrated. Lots of people retire each year with plenty of money, only to go back to work to have something to do – something bigger to live for than TV, video games and popcorn.

If plenty of money and a life of leisure would make everyone happy, why do you think that **Bill Gates** (net worth as I write of $51 Billion) and **Warren Buffett** (75 years old and worth $40 Billion), the first and second wealthiest people in America, don't just retire with their billions? Apparently, they love their work.

The great Russian novelist **Leo Tolstoy** grew up in a wealthy class of Russians, while the poorer people did most of the work. But he observed something strange: the people who worked seemed happier than the privileged class. He renounced his class to work among the peasants and decided that "work, and not idleness, is the indispensable condition of happiness for every human being."[25]

Akashi: Hmmm. So maybe work isn't so bad, especially if we can find work that we like. The super-successful people I know of seem to love working hard at what they do. When it's tough, they relish the challenge. There must be something intoxicating and addicting about looking back and seeing a job well-done.

Kramer: According to Pulitzer Prize Winning Novelist James Michener,

> *"The master in the art of living makes little distinction between his work and his play, his labor and his leisure, his mind and his body, his information and his recreation, his love and his religion. He hardly knows which is which. He simply pursues his vision of excellence at whatever he does, leaving others to decide whether he is working or playing. To him he is always doing both."*[26]

Here's what some successful people say about hard work:

Kemmons Wilson, Sr., founder of Holiday Inns, at a high school commencement: *"I really don't know why I'm here. I never got a degree, and I've only worked half days my entire life. I guess my advice to you is to do the same. Work half days every day. And it doesn't matter which half. The first twelve hours or the second twelve hours."*[27]

Steve Vai and Yngwie Malmsteen, Rock Guitar Maestros:

> **Malmsteen:** *"Steve, on average how long did you practice in your teens?"*
>
> **Vai:** *"It varied. I enjoyed a social life with my friends **but I had a schedule that was no less than nine hours a day** and tried to stick to it. I was anal. It helped me stay on target."*
>
> **Malmsteen:** *"That's why you're good. There's no shortcut.... **I sacrificed everything.**"*
>
> **Vai: *"To be either a shredder or virtuoso you have to practice a lot and perfectly."*[28]**

Pat Riley, one of the greatest basketball coaches of all time: *"The most profound basic of all is **simple hard work**."*[29]

Former U.S. President Harry S. Truman: *"I studied the lives of great men and famous women, and I found that **the men and women who got to the top were those who did the jobs they had in hand, with everything they had of energy and enthusiasm and hard work.**"*[30]

P.T. Barnum, of Barnum and Bailey's Circus: *"Whatever you do, do it with all your might. Work at it, early and late, in season and out of season, not leaving a stone unturned, and **never deferring for a single hour that which can be done just as well now.**"*[31]

Andrew Carnegie of Bethlehem Steel: *"The average person puts only 25 percent of his energy and ability into his work. The world takes off its hat to those who put in more than 50 percent of their capacity, and **stands on its head for those few and far between souls who devote 100 percent.**"*

Application to Life

Kramer: Give me your thoughts on working hard.

Amy: I think you've got to balance work, relationships and service. Those quotes on working 12-hour days and devoting 100 percent to your work are scary. One hundred percent doesn't leave room for anything else. Sure, we need to work hard, but there's more to life than work. Sometimes I'm so focused on making "A's" that I ignore my little sister's problems and hurt my other friendships.

Kramer: Agreed. I know star teachers who ignore their families.

Akashi: I, for one, need all the motivation to work that I can get. I play way too many video games. I think I'll set an alarm clock to remind me to turn off the games and find more productive things to do.

6. Never Give Up

Kramer: One aspect of hard work is overcoming difficulties. Amy, do you have a story for us?

Amy: Sure. Have any of you heard of Jason Becker?

Antonio: The guitar player?

Amy: Yes! He's a hero among rock guitarists, but not as well known outside guitar circles. You've just got to watch some of the documentaries and clips of him on www.youtube.com.

If you watch some of those films, you'll see this young guitar player yo-yoing with one hand as he plays an outrageous guitar part with the other. Well, Becker blows me away with his skill. But his *story* is even more remarkable than his ability.

The Jason Becker Story

His parents gave him his first guitar at the age of five, and he never put it down. He was fortunate to find his passion early, and he pursued it relentlessly. By the age of 13, he could play virtually anything that he'd heard. He landed his first record deal at age 17.

But it's one thing to be an incredible player, another thing to get a break into the big time. His big break came at the age of 21, when he was asked to play with singer David Lee Roth, formerly of Van Halen.

But four months later, tragedy struck. His fingers didn't seem to cooperate the way they used to. Doctors ran some tests and came back with bad news – he had ALS, better known as Lou Gehrig's Disease. They said that his muscles would slowly shut down and he'd die within five years.

At that point, most of us would have checked out of our ambitions and gone to live our last years at the beach. But not Becker. He kept on touring like nobody's business. You see, Becker loved music. Nothing like a little incurable disease was going to stop him.

Eventually the disease took such a hold on his fingers that he could no longer play those intricate guitar solos. So what do you think he did? Quit?

No. He just concentrated on *composing* with his guitar, letting others play his music. But later he could no longer play guitar at all. Did that stop him?

No. He continued composing on keyboards, even when it got to the point that he could play with only one finger. But then his last finger quit working. Did that stop him?

No. Someone set him up with a sensor on a head set, communicating his head and facial movements to his computer. Move your mouth this way to choose a higher note, that way for a lower note. He could click the mouse with his chin. In this tedious way, he kept writing music, until all he could do was move his eyeballs.

(Amy begins to choke up) But even that didn't stop him.

The last I heard, he discovered a way to communicate with people and a computer via his eyes. Eye to the left top quadrant might be "A," far left quadrant "B." And he continued to compose.

He should have died years ago, but he still hears the music in his head, getting it out to the world through his eyes. His latest songs came to us from inside his brilliant mind through his eyes, composed painstakingly over a period of years. An acclaimed ballet recently performed to his music.

Becker's dad once said of him,

> ***"He's the ultimate optimist. Nothing stops him."***[32]

The Point

How does Becker motivate me? When I'm discouraged because an assignment is taking a whole weekend, or if people aren't nice to me at work or if I try for weeks to get down a bass part that seems beyond me, I play his *Perspective* album on my I-Pod and realize that if Becker can compose with his eyes, surely I can gut it out with a fully functioning body and brain.

Kramer: And the next time I'm ready to strangle my students, sick and tired of preparing one more lesson plan, ready to throw in the towel and take early retirement, I think I'll throw in a CD of Becker and realize all over again what an aging widow can accomplish.

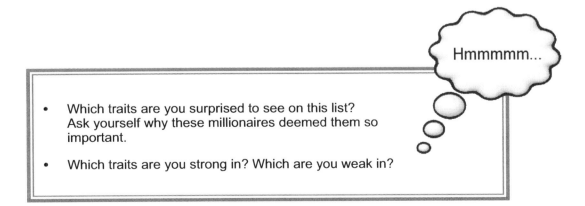

- Which traits are you surprised to see on this list? Ask yourself why these millionaires deemed them so important.

- Which traits are you strong in? Which are you weak in?

Assignment
Between Breakfasts

1. Tape Professor Stanley's list of traits to your closet door, and reflect on it for a month. How could you continue to grow in your strengths and work on your weaknesses?

2. Put an asterisk by each trait that you feel is important to develop. Take a week to work on each one of these.

Resources to Take You Deeper

How to Win Friends and Influence People by Dale Carnegie (Pocket, Reprint Edition, 1998). If you can read only one self-help book in your lifetime, let it be this one.

Life's Greatest Lessons: 20 Things That Matter by Hal Urban (Fireside, 2002). Great book on growing in character. Not preachy. Learned it from the school of adversity and mistakes.

Copy This! Lessons from a Hyperactive Dyslexic Who Turned a Bright Idea Into One of America's Best Companies by Paula Orfalea (Workman Publishing, 2007). If you've got learning disabilities or teach those with LD's, get this book (or listen to the audio CD).

Winning by Jack Welch (Collins, 2005). Great principles for winning at business.

Autobiography of Benjamin Franklin (reprinted by Buccaneer Books). A classic on how one of the greatest Americans accomplished so much in a lifetime.

Breakfast #14: Invest in Your Mind

In times of profound change, the learners inherit the earth, while the learned find themselves beautifully equipped to deal with a world that no longer exists.

— Al Rogers, Global Schoolhouse Network

Review

Kramer: So, what stands out to you from last week's session on thriving in your jobs?

Antonio: I always thought I needed to be able to do *everything* well. Knowing I'll have a team is pretty comforting. I want to keep my eyes out for that team.

Akashi: I was really inspired by Jason Becker's story. Thanks for putting it together for us, Amy. I watched his interviews and clips of his playing on www.youtube.com. Now, when I'm struggling in a class, instead of giving up and putting my head down on my desk, I think of how Becker keeps plugging away at his music, taking years to write an album without the use of his hands.

Then I ask myself, "Akashi, *so what* if I have to take this class three times before I pass it? If Becker can gut it out, so can I."

Kramer: That story motivated me as well. I put more time into my lesson preparations last week, being grateful for the full use of my hands and ability to use my computer.

Introduction

Today, I want to leave you with my main point about how to succeed with your money. I'll put it simply. If you get nothing else from our breakfasts, don't miss this: **invest in your mind.** All your other investments can be lost overnight in a tragedy, severe recession or government breakdown. But nobody can take away the investment you put into your mind.[1]

The more you learn about your job and your business, the more indispensable you become. The wiser you become, the more desirable you become to other employers. The more you learn about saving and investing, the better decisions you make and the more successful you become with your money.

But rather than lecture you, let me tell you a story of a life-long learner. Jot down hints that might help you to become an avid wisdom-seeker.

Sam Walton: A Passion to Learn

Wal-Mart is the largest retailer in the world and the second largest corporation in the world, with a 2007 net income of over $12 billion. It's the largest employer in both the United States and Mexico.[2]

It was started by a country boy who, for his entire life, loved calling his bird dogs into his old pick-up truck to go tramping through the woods quail hunting. The story of how he became the best merchant who ever walked the planet can tell us a lot about achieving our own success.

Work Around Your Weaknesses

Sam Walton wasn't all strengths. Academically, he didn't consider himself a gifted student in high school, but he worked hard and made good grades.[3] He also made it through college, although he wasn't that great at accounting.[4]

According to Sam, he "never learned handwriting all that well." Nobody could read it. Also, he'd foul up organizational details, like sales slips and cash register transactions. At Penney's, his first full time job out of college, his boss told him,

> *"Walton, I'd fire you if you weren't such a good salesman. Maybe you're just not cut out for retail."*[5]

His boss must have lacked a strength called "discernment." Walton would become the best retailer ever.

He was a terrible driver[6] and admitted to being hopelessly disorganized.[7] People would show up for scheduled appointments from out of town, and Walton would be out of town visiting a store. His personal secretary finally refused to make appointments for him, knowing he might not show.

Build on Your Strengths

But Walton also had strengths, which he developed tirelessly. He was a great leader and team builder.[8]

He set extremely high personal goals[9], which he accomplished with his team through his competitive spirit and intense drive. His entire life, much of that drive was focused on **learning**.

Learn by Doing

He **learned a lot about hard work and sales from his early work experiences.** At age seven or eight he sold magazine subscriptions. Later, he raised and sold rabbits and pigeons.[10] From seventh grade through high school[11] he ran paper routes.

In college, he added more routes and hired helpers, making some serious money.[12] He needed it, since he was paying his own way.[13] He did whatever it took to make ends meet, waiting tables in exchange for meals[14] and life guarding on the side.[15]

Besides learning hard work, **he learned people skills**. In college, he aspired to become the student body president. Here's a trick he learned that he'd use the rest of his life:

> *"I learned early on that one of the secrets to campus leadership was the simplest thing of all: speak to people coming down the sidewalk before they speak to you. I did that in college. I did it when I carried my papers. I would always look ahead and speak to the person coming toward me. If I knew them, I would call them by name, but even if I didn't I would still speak to them. Before long, I probably knew more students than anybody in the university, and they recognized me and considered me their friend."[16]*

Get Formal Education

He majored in business at the University of Missouri.[17] Later in life, he'd take formal classes as needed. But the most striking thing to me about Sam was that he **never stopped learning. In fact, he became a learning machine.**

Way before personal computers came along, he felt that Wal-Mart needed to move toward computerization:

> *"I was curious. I made up my mind I was going to learn something about IBM computers. So I enrolled in an IBM school for retailers in Poughkeepsie, New York."[18]*

He wasn't your typical, passive student. He knew how to get the most out of the learning environment.

Abe Marks was one of the speakers in Walton's class. So Abe's sitting there innocently reading a newspaper, when he gets this feeling that somebody's standing over him. It was Walton, who introduced himself, saying that he came to the conference to talk with Abe. In Abe's words,

> *"So he opens up this attaché case, and, I swear, he had every article I had ever written and every speech I had ever given in there."[19]*

He goes on to pull out his accounting sheets and asks Abe to look them over.

He was about 10 years ahead of the computer revolution. But because he caught the vision early, he was ready for it when it came. Walton

> *"became...the best utilizer of information to control absentee ownerships that there's ever been. Which gave him the ability to open as many stores as he opens, and run them as well as he runs them, and to be as profitable as he makes them."[20]*

Learn from Mentors

Just out of college, he went to work for J.C. Penney[21], **finding a mentor** in Duncan Majors, his very successful store manager. He'd learn from Duncan at the store six days a week, then go to Duncan's house on Sundays with his associates to play ping-pong and cards and talk about retailing.

Learn from Books and Publications

During a stint in the army, he was posted in Salt Lake City. **He checked out every book on retailing in their library** and **studied a nearby department store.**

He would read every retail publication he could find and would later refer to himself as an "avid student of management theory."[22]

Learn from Company Training Classes

After the army, he bought a Ben Franklin variety store in Newport, Arkansas.[23] **The company put him through a two week training class,** which taught him the basics of running a store. He would use their accounting system well into his Wal-Mart years.[24]

Learn from Your Competition

Once he started working at his first store, his unique spin on education came into play. He soon discovered that the store he'd just bought was "a real dog." His competition across the street had an excellent manager and was doing twice the business in sales. According to Walton,

> *"I learned a lesson which has stuck with me all through the years: you can learn from everybody. I didn't just learn from reading every retail publication I could get my hands on, I probably learned the most from studying what John Dunham was doing across the street."[25]*

So Walton became a student of his competitor, always hanging out across the street, checking out Dunham's prices, how he displayed his merchandise, learning everything about why he was successful.

According to associate Charlie Cate, "I remember him saying over and over again: go in and check our competition. Check *everyone* who is our competition. And don't look for the bad. Look for the good. ...everyone is doing something right."[26]

He especially checked out Kmart stores, which were far ahead of them in those early years.[27]

He was even so bold as to visit the headquarters of other retailers. He could get away with it, since his operation was small at the time and his competitors didn't consider him a threat. Walton says,

> *"I probably visited more headquarters offices of more discounters than anybody else – ever."[28]*

Get Outside Input

Walton once asked other discounters who weren't in competition to come to his stores and critique them. Being outsiders, they had a different perspective from insiders. According to Walton,

> *"These guys…just ripped our stores apart, telling us how poorly we did everything."*

It shocked them. But Walton considered it "a turning point in our business." It geared them up to compete with Kmart.[29]

Learn from Your Workers

Walton learned from everyone in his stores, regardless of status:

> *"Great ideas come from everywhere if you just listen and look for them. You never know who's going to have a great idea."[30]*

He especially loved to talk to the truck drivers. According to Lee Scott,

> *"For a long, long time, Sam would show up regularly in the drivers' break room at 4 A.M. with a bunch of doughnuts and just sit there for a couple of hours talking to them."*

According to Sam,

> *"It's amazing to me how many ideas they always have for fine-tuning the system."[31]*

He'd grill them, asking, "What are you seeing at the stores?" "Have you been to that store lately?" "How do the people act there?" "Is it getting better?"

Walton said,

> *"I'd still say that visiting the stores and listening to our folks was one of the most valuable uses of my time as an executive. But really, our best ideas usually do come from the folks in the stores. Period."[32]*

Learn from Associations

Walton joined the National Mass Retailer's Institute and the discounters' trade association[33] so he could learn from others in his industry.

He'd **ask questions** of anyone in the know. One day, the executive vice president of the discounters' trade association was minding his own business in his New York office, when Sam Walton arrived. Here's how Walton worked him over:

> *"So in comes this short, wiry man with a deep tan and a tennis racket under his arm. He introduced himself as Sam Walton from Arkansas. I didn't know what to think. When he meets you, he looks at you – head cocked to one side, forehead slightly creased – and he proceeds to extract every piece of information in your possession. He always makes little notes. And he pushes on and on. After two and a half hours, he left, and I was totally drained. I wasn't sure what I had just met, but I was sure we would hear more from him."[34]*

Innovate, Swim Upstream, Constantly Experiment with New Ideas

Many people are good at learning, but have a hard time *applying* what they learn. After Walton learned something new, he'd experiment with the best ideas in his own store.[35] According to Walton,

> *"I think my constant fiddling and meddling with the status quo may have been one of my biggest contributions to the later success of Wal-Mart."[36]*

A pattern emerges in Walton's autobiography. First, grab ideas from anybody you can. Second, shake things up in your stores and your life by innovating. Learn something else. Innovate. It became a lifelong obsession.

According to Sol Price, founder of Fed-Mart and Price Club,

> *"He was notorious for looking at what everybody else does, taking the best of it, and then making it better."[37]*

According to Walton,

> *"After a lifetime of swimming upstream, I am convinced that one of the real secrets to Wal-Mart's phenomenal success has been that very tendency."[38]*

Learn from Your Mistakes

Not all of his ideas worked. The minnow buckets didn't sell. People in Wisconsin didn't go for his Moon Pies.[39]

But when he saw he was wrong, he admitted his mistake and went on to try something else. And he wanted his associates to be the same way. He'd get them together on Saturday mornings to share their successes and admit their failures. That culture of candor produced a great environment to capture ideas.

It helped that he had "very little capacity for embarrassment."[40]

Travel Far and Wide for Great Ideas

He'd travel the world to get an idea. In his early career, he read an article about how two stores in Minnesota had gone to self-service – which nobody else was doing. Typically, employees would follow customers around, helping them get what they wanted. In the newfangled self-service stores, customers picked out their own stuff and checked out at the cash registers at the front of the store. So he rode the bus all night to visit the stores, liked what they were doing and changed his store to self-service.[41]

He was always out looking for new merchandise. Once he came back from New York with some unique sandals called "flip-flops" or "thongs." The clerk said, "No way will those things sell. They'll just blister your toes." They sold like crazy.[42]

Before Walton, very few stores concentrated on buying low, selling cheap and making their profit by selling huge quantities. When Walton heard of a few discounters, he ran around the country from the East to California, studying the concept. Everywhere he went, he visited stores and scribbled ideas on his yellow legal pad.[43]

According to his brother Bud,

"There's not an individual in these whole United States who has been in more retail stores...than Sam Walton. Make that all over the world. He's been in stores in Australia and South America, Europe and Asia and South Africa. His mind is just so inquisitive when it comes to this business. And there may not be anything he enjoys more than going into a competitor's store trying to learn something from it."[44]

Capture Your Ideas

Wherever he found himself, he'd visit stores, look around and ask questions. At first, he wrote down all his ideas on his yellow pad. Later, he used a little tape recorder.[45]

Develop an Idea-Driven Culture

Sam didn't want to be the only idea-hunter. He wanted to get everyone in on the act. Once a week, he'd gather his managers to critique each other – evaluating one another's failures and successes.[46] Each reported their "Best Selling Item."[47]

To add the thrill of competition, they set up a contest for the best volume-producing item.[48]

He'd also invite the hourly associates who came up with the best money-saving ideas and present them with a cash award. He estimates that these ideas have saved Wal-Mart $8 million a year.[49]

These days, their 18 regional managers pile into airplanes every Monday morning to look at stores, with the charge to come back with some idea good enough to pay for the trip. Then, they get with senior management, who also should have been visiting stores, to report in their Friday morning merchandising meeting.[50]

Don't Worry Who Gets the Credit

According to Walton,

> *"...most everything I've done I've copied from somebody else...."*

To get the best ideas, you've got to be humble enough to learn from everyone and give credit where credit's due.

As Claude Harris says,

> *"He was always open to suggestions, and that's one reason he's been such a success."[51]*

Debriefing

Kramer: So what can we learn from Sam Walton's education?

Akashi: I'll bet some of those college classes were helpful to him. But my GPA is so bad that I don't know if I could ever get in.

Kramer: If the front door's closed, go in the back door.

Akashi: There's a back door?

Kramer: Sure. I had to use it. My rote memory was so poor that I couldn't pass foreign languages in high school. That put me in the tech track. So I went one year to a local technical school and then applied to four-year college as a transfer. When they knew I could handle college level work, they were glad to accept me.

Although the average multi-millionaire surveyed by Stanley had a "C" average, most of them did graduate from a four-year college. I think something about that education benefited them. In general, people with more education make more money.[52]

But don't discount one and two year degrees from technical schools. If you can get a degree in a specific skill, you may find yourself making more than four-year students with general degrees.

James: Walton's appetite for reading in his field of interest reminds me of Buffett's early reading. I need to read up more on successful businesses.

Akashi: Much of his learning wasn't too traditional. I mean, wandering around in your competition's stores and bugging the owners with questions isn't much like sitting in a class.

James: I suppose that's where his boldness and competitive spirit came in handy. I don't think that just anybody could talk to people like that, although Akashi could!

Amy: I think we learn best in an area we're excited about. Walton was excited about retailing. Let's apply it to something *we're* excited about. If I started a band and wanted to promote it, I'd be eager to read up on promoting bands and would talk to everyone I know who's been successfully promoting their bands. It's easier to talk to people in your field of interest.

James: Come to think of it, I get a charge out of people coming up to me and asking me all about my car. I feel like somebody's appreciating all that time I put into it. When I see someone who's restored an old muscle car to perfection, it's natural to ask 20 questions about how they did it. I never really thought of that as education, but I've learned a lot from talking to others about cars.

In fact, I'm a member of a club at school that gets together, talks cars and goes to car shows. I suppose that's sort of like Walton's associations.

Kramer: In my opinion, finding and hanging around people with similar vocational interests makes success a whole lot easier. If you start talking to your friends about vocations they are interested in, you might start sharpening each other more than boring each other. Remember, Walton seemed to be able to learn something from anybody, not just the big shots.

By hanging around sharp people, you get ideas. You get charged up. It's a pattern I've found in most successful people. **Just think about:**

- **The world's best known theoretical physicist:** Twenty-two year old Albert Einstein and like-minded friends met frequently in each other's homes or talked on hikes, sometimes all the way through the night. These conversations had an enormous impact on his future work. They called themselves "The Olympia Academy."[53]

- **The most successful entrepreneur:** Fifteen-year old Bill Gates met regularly with other computer enthusiasts who called themselves "The Lakeside Programmers Group."[54]

- **One of the wisest men of all time:** Benjamin Franklin met every Friday for decades with a diverse group of civic-minded thinkers called "Junto." Many of his great accomplishments were a result of cross-pollination from this group.[55]

- **Two of the most popular writers:** J.R.R. Tolkien (*Lord of the Rings*) and C.S. Lewis (*The Chronicles of Narnia*) met with "The Inklings" on a weekday morning in a pub and Thursday evenings at Lewis' house, often reading their manuscripts aloud to get input.[56]

Kramer: So, how can this apply to your lives?

Life Application

Akashi: I need to find a group like that. Most of my friends just hang out, doing nothing. Rather than whining about the colleges I can't get into, I'm gonna start looking into what colleges I *can* get into. If I need to go to a four-year college, I'll look for back doors.

Antonio: A mid-week home group from my church gives me that motivation and accountability.

Kramer: I meet with a group of investors once a month. I also take occasional classes at Kennesaw State University. Someone said that the greatest influences on your life are the books you read and the people you hang around. As basketball great Kareem Abdul Jabaar put it, "Don't let those who are going nowhere influence your opinions." Hang out with people who are going somewhere.

Amy: I once heard someone say, "Know something about everything and everything about something."

James: That's cool. If I become an expert in my field, I'll be indispensable at work.

Amy: Walton had lots of work experience before he got his own store. Most employers I saw on Monster.com wanted experience as well. I think I need to find my next job in a field that's related to my long-term interests, even if it's part time or volunteer, just to get the experience.

Kramer: Because of his grades, Steven Spielberg couldn't get into the great film school he wanted to attend. So he went to another school that didn't have as many film classes, but was close to Universal Studios. He was able to work there, watch the process, make contacts and get experience.[57]

James: This is cool, motivational wisdom about Walton. If I wanted to go into the retail business, I'd want to interview people like him. Since I'm interested in cars, I need to interview people who've made it in the automotive industry.

Akashi: Basically, we need to become scavengers for wisdom in our field of interest. Read articles, listen to motivational tapes, talk to everybody we can, get experience.

Kramer: Find the learning methods that work best for you, and go for it!

Never stop learning. Never stop learning! NEVER, NEVER, *NEVER* STOP LEARNING!

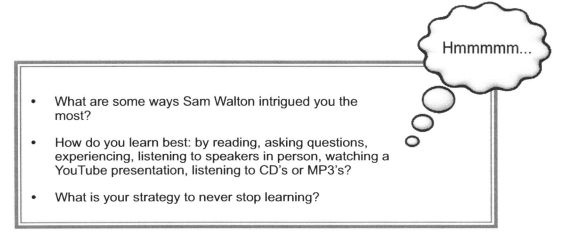

- What are some ways Sam Walton intrigued you the most?

- How do you learn best: by reading, asking questions, experiencing, listening to speakers in person, watching a YouTube presentation, listening to CD's or MP3's?

- What is your strategy to never stop learning?

Resource to Take You Deeper

Sam Walton with John Huey, *Sam Walton: Made in America* (New York: Doubleday, 1992). Emulate Walton in your field of endeavor and you'll likely go far.

Assignment
Between Breakfasts

1. Take your favorite job descriptions from www.careerbuilder.com and www.monster.com, or dream up your own job description. Now plan out an education that could help you land the job and excel in it.

2. Think of five things you could do to learn more about a field of interest.

3. Find a group of people with the same interests (consider www.meetup.com) and begin to meet regularly with them.

4. Talk to friends and family about the best ways to pursue a lifetime of happiness.

5. Put this riddle on the refrigerator and discuss it with your family. Answer the question, "Why was Frank happy and Fred miserable?

A Tale of Two Childhoods

It was the best of times, the worst of times.
For **Frank**, life rolled out his dreams:
A mountain view from his comfortable home
in earshot of cascading streams.

His teachers were decent, his parents were kind,
Friends not hard to be found.
"I'm the luckiest kid," he told all who'd hear,
"To be raised in this home and this town."

For **Fred**, it was the worst of times,
his parents a bore.
His hovel in the country
an embarrassment to the core.

He never had what others had,
Fine clothes and toys and such.
His face told a story of sour regret
For a childhood that lacked so much.

Their stories seem trite, I know,
Until one truth you see:
Frank and Fred were brothers,
Growing up in the same family.

PART FOUR

ENJOYING MONEY

Breakfast #15: Look for Happiness in the Right Places

"Everything you know is wrong
Black is white, up is down and short is long
And everything you thought was just so
Important doesn't matter."

—"Weird Al" Yankovich

Introduction: Successful, but Miserable

Kramer: It's great to have Hash, Carmen and Travis back for this last breakfast! Let's jump right in, and we can socialize later.

See that guy at the far table? He's the reason I asked you to show up early.

Amy: The one eating alone?

Kramer: Don't all look at the same time! He'll think we're talking about him.

Antonio: We *are* talking about him.

Kramer: (rolling her eyes) He's an incredible investor, worth millions. That's his 10-year-old pick-up out front. He works hard, lives well beneath his means, invests wisely. He's scanning the classifieds for bargain properties.

Akashi: Sounds like our kind of guy. So you're inviting him over to chat?

Kramer: Not this guy. Although he's a brilliant money manager and investor, I don't think he's ever asked the "What for?" question.

Akashi: "What for?"

Kramer: Right. All his great effort to work and accumulate wealth. What's it all for? Is it just the fun of accumulating? Is it the superior feeling he gets knowing that his bank account is fatter than others? Is he super-competitive and uses money to keep score? Who knows?

Whatever the motivation, he's 100 percent about his work and his money. But when you're 100 percent for something, there's nothing left for anything else. No time for giving. No time for service. No room for his family. That's why they left him.

When his faithful workers got older and needed more money to live, he fired them for cheaper help. Now, as far as I can tell, it's down to him and his money. Blinded by his materialism, he keeps hoping that his next million will make him happy.

Sure, he's successful at accumulating money, but look at him. He's sad, lonely, pitiful. Remember that face.

Akashi: Reminds me of the wealthy guy who was asked, "How much money does it take to satisfy?" He replied, "Just a little bit more."[1]

Encounter with a Genie

Kramer: Close your eyes with me.

Akashi! Stop looking at the lonely man, and close your eyes!

You're hiking in the Blue Ridge Mountains on a warm, summer day and stop to refresh your feet in a crystal clear, cascading stream. Staring aimlessly at the far stream-bank, a glimmer from the sun bounces off an object, arousing your curiosity.

You wade across to find an old bottle, buried except for the tip. You pull it out, and as you dust it off to look for a label, a strange fog emerges – transforming into a huge genie!

Now being a rather stingy genie, he grants you not three wishes, but one, with the standard limitations and provisos that you can't ask for more wishes or make someone fall in love with you. What will you ask for? And don't get all warm and fuzzy and ask for world peace. It's all about you. Feel free to be a bit selfish.

Akashi: An unlimited income. I'll never have to worry about money again!

James: I want my Porsche 911 Carrera.

Kramer: Good! Some people who know what they want out of life! You've given me enough to work with.

Digging Deeper

Reflecting on your responses, let's do a little dialogue where I play Socrates – the famous philosopher. He liked to ask people questions to help them think more deeply about their beliefs and values.

> **Socrates:** James, why would you want that Porsche?
>
> *James:* Because it's awesomely cool!
>
> **Socrates:** So why would you want something that's awesomely cool?
>
> *James:* Because everyone would think *I'm* cool, including many hot girls.
>
> **Socrates:** So why would you want everyone to think you're cool?
>
> *James:* Well, people would think I was successful and important…. You know…I'd get some respect.

Socrates: And why do you want respect?

James: Hmmm. I suppose that getting people to respect me and getting girls to notice me would make me happy.

Socrates: So, you're telling me that you don't want the car just to have the car. If you knew the car would make you miserable, you wouldn't want it. You want the car because you think it will make you happy.

James: Right.

Kramer: Akashi, if I had this same dialogue with you about your wish for unlimited income, would it end the same way?

Akashi: Of course! If I knew that unlimited money would make me miserable, I wouldn't want it. I want unlimited income because I think it will make me obscenely happy.

Kramer: Can't we extend that to most of the things we want in life? Don't we want a certain kind of job because we think it will bring the most happiness to ourselves and those we love? Don't people want to win the lottery because they think it will make them happier?

Hey, happiness is so important that our *Declaration of Independence* proclaims:

> ***"We hold these truths to be self-evident, that all men are created equal, that they are endowed by their Creator with certain unalienable Rights, that among these are Life, Liberty and the pursuit of Happiness."***

The pursuit of happiness…. I'll bet that the deeper reason you wanted to start these meetings was more about your pursuit of happiness than about finances. You feared that if you grew up managing your money like your parents, you'd face the same miseries they face. You thought that if you could learn to handle your money better, you'd be happier. Am I right?

James: Sure. I feared that if I never found financial freedom, my future wife and I would constantly argue about money, she'd leave me and I'd live a lonely existence, like that guy at the end table.

Studying Happiness

Kramer: If happiness is so important, I wonder why people don't spend more time studying it.

Antonio: You can *study* happiness?

Kramer: Sure. Psychologists used to spend most of their time studying miserable people, to discover why they were so miserable.

Then, particularly in the 1980's, social scientists decided to study happy people, to find out why they were happy. Now scientists can tell us a lot more about finding happiness.[2] Some of their findings are…

Akashi: Let me guess. Counterintuitive?

Kramer: Startlingly so! And since so many who write about building wealth seem to assume that more money will make us happier, we'd better make sure we're on the right track to happiness.

Some people work like crazy to get something they think will make them happy; but when they get it, they find that they're no happier than they were before. **It's like they spend their entire lives climbing the ladder to success, only to find that it was leaning against the wrong wall.**

Put these scientific findings into your thinking pipes and smoke them for awhile:

- In one study, **there was no difference between the happiness level of 22 lottery winners and comparison samples of average people or even paraplegics.**

- "Surveys have found **virtually the same level of happiness between the very rich individuals on the Forbes 400 and the Maasai herdsman of East Africa."**

- **"Compared to 1957, we are now 'the doubly affluent society'—with double what money could buy back then.** We have twice as many cars per person. We eat out two and a half times as often. In the late 1950s, few Americans had dishwashers, clothes dryers or air conditioning; today, most do."

  If more things make us happier, people today should be twice as happy as people were then. But are they? No. **Compared to people in the 1950's, statistics find us less happy, with three times the number of teen suicides and many more depressed people.**

- **People who strive most for wealth tend to be less happy than others. Those who strive for "intimacy, personal growth and contribution to the community" have a better quality of life.**[3]

Kramer: How do these studies strike you?

Debriefing

Akashi: That's bizarre! No difference in happiness between lottery winners and paraplegics? I'd think there would be a gap the size of the Grand Canyon, with the lottery winners deliriously happy and the paraplegics on the brink of suicide.

Antonio: So money and things don't necessarily make us happier. In fact, striving too hard after wealth might just make us *less* happy.

Kramer: Don't get me wrong. You need a certain amount of money to live. Those who have enough money to afford food and shelter are generally happier than those who lack these basics. Also, people who have enough to save and invest have less to worry about. **But beyond taking care of the essentials, just making $10,000 more or $1,000,000 more doesn't do much for our happiness.**

Rich and Miserable

Kramer: Here's a story to think about. Christina Onassis got Akashi's wish of unlimited income as much as anyone I know. Born into the lap of luxury, her dad was Aristotle Onassis − the richest man on earth at the time. She visited the earth's most beautiful destinations on the largest yacht in the world, which was named after her: the "Christina."

It had a large heated pool and a crew of 60 to cater to her every whim. She wintered in Paris and later lived luxuriously on an island they owned in Greece. When she got out on her own, she had a tax-free income of a million dollars a week!

Akashi: Now you're talking!

Kramer: If she wanted it, she could get it. Example: she liked Diet Coke, but it wasn't available locally. Also, she felt that even though it was canned, it lost some of its freshness if stored too long. Her solution? She paid a private jet to fly ten cases of Diet Coke from America to her European home every month, to the tune of $3,000 per case!

Sounds like a fun life. How many would like to trade lives with her?

All: Of course!

Kramer: Not so quickly. You need to hear the rest of the story.

In the midst of luxury, her relationships made her miserable. While she was growing up, her mom had an open affair on the yacht. Her dad retaliated by having his own open affair and divorcing his wife. Christina would never recover from these strained relationships.

She'd get so mad that she'd throw her dad's clothes out of portals into the ocean. She couldn't get along with her parents or the new stepparents, often getting even by bringing them trouble. Neither could she get along with her own string of husbands.

Eventually, a miserable Christina attempted suicide. Her sister Tina succeeded. Those who knew Christina weren't surprised to hear that she died at the age of 37. She relied on drugs to get her through each day and probably died of an overdose.[4]

James: Point well taken. A steady stream of millions won't necessarily make us happy. But what does? This is so incredibly important! I can't believe I've never been taught it in school.

Kramer: Here's a taste of what social scientists have learned, based upon large studies that often spanned many countries. I'll put it in a handy acrostic (**H.A.P.P.I.E.R.**) to help us remember.

Keys to Happiness (According to Recent Scientific Studies)

HELP OTHERS (Bringing happiness to others makes us happy.)

Let's do a little demonstration. Akashi, you and Antonio look across the table and try to get James and Amy to smile. No fair tickling.

(James and Amy keep serious for about 10 seconds, then break into a laugh after Akashi makes an outrageous face. Akashi and Antonio join in the laughter.)

Kramer: Did you notice what happened?

Antonio: In making them smile, we ended up smiling ourselves. Happiness came to us as a byproduct of making someone else happy.

Kramer: What are some things you've done to help others that give you great satisfaction?

Antonio: At our church, we collect clothes for the needy.

James: I volunteered through the Key Club at school, serving food at a homeless shelter.

Amy: I help tutor students with disabilities in Math.

Kramer: How does it make you feel?

Amy: Getting good grades makes me feel good about myself. But if I'm not careful, it's just a head trip – a way to be cool among a certain crowd. Helping others improve *their* grades makes me feel good in a different, deeper way.

Kramer: Frederick Douglass, a former slave and conductor on the "Underground Railroad," risked his life to free slaves. How do you think his service impacted his personal happiness? According to Douglass,

> *"True as a means of destroying slavery, it was like an attempt to bail out the ocean with a teaspoon, but the thought that there was one less slave, and one more freeman– having myself been a slave, and a fugitive slave – brought to my heart unspeakable joy."*

Kramer: "Unspeakable joy." Isn't that what we're all hoping to find? Douglass found it by helping others.

If you're into religion, you'll probably find that this concept is pretty central to whatever religion you're a part of. One day, Jesus was asked to consider all the Jewish laws and tell which was the most important. He quoted passages from the Jewish Scriptures that could be distilled into four words: "Love God, love people." Notice anything about these two commands?

Akashi: *Other* focused. I wake up in the morning thinking, "What can I do today to make *me* happy?" He's challenging me to ask, "What can I do today to make *others* happy?" It's a major shift from "Me, Me" to "Others, Others."

Kramer: Benjamin Franklin thought this so important that he asked himself each morning, "What good shall I do this day?" Each evening, he reflected, "What good have I done today?"[5]

ATTITUDE CHECK (Count your blessings and be grateful.)

William James, the incredibly diverse intellectual who taught philosophy, psychology, anatomy and physiology at Harvard, called this the greatest discovery of his generation:

> *"Human beings can alter their lives by altering their attitudes."*

Antonio: Hmmm. Is it kind of like the person who said, "I complained that I had no shoes, till I met someone who had no feet?"

What's Going Right?

Kramer: That's it! Normally, we take for granted the things that go well and dwell on things that go wrong. If we can reverse that by rehearsing in our minds the things that are going right, we can change our outlook on life. Let's brainstorm all the things we have going for us today.

James: I'm not in jail on death row.

Amy: My arms and hands work. I'm not in any pain.

Antonio: That moisture around my eyes. I never think about it; but if it weren't there, my eyes would hurt.

Akashi: My hair. First, I've got some hair. Second, as bad a hair day as I had this morning, I don't look like Medusa.

Kramer: Great! Each morning, at every meal, before your head hits the pillow at night, count a few blessings. It can change your day…and your life.[6]

PURSUE QUALITY RELATIONSHIPS (With family and friends.)

Loving things and using people leads to misery. Loving people and using things leads to happiness. Money is a thing, a tool, a *means* to an end – *not* the end. Use it to help people, and you'll enjoy life.

PARDON THOSE WHO WRONG YOU (Don't hold grudges.)

According to Gary McKay, Ph.D., "You have the capacity to choose what you think about. If you choose to think about past hurts, you will continue to feel bad. While it's true you can't change the effect past influences had on you once, you can change the effect they have on you now."

IMMERSE YOURSELF IN SOMETHING (Work and/or play.)

"To love what you do and feel that it matters, how could anything be more fun?"
(Katharine Graham)

Remember our discussion about strengths? Keep looking for things you love so much that you lose all track of time doing them.

Amy: For me, it's playing the bass. I get into this cool zone.

Antonio: Wilderness adventures.

James: I could work on my car all day.

Kramer: Keep trying new things, having new experiences. You'll discover many things you can lose yourself in. Hopefully, one of them will translate into a job.

ENVY NOT (Stop trying to keep up with the Joneses.)

Akashi: I'm amazed at how much a change of viewpoint can change my happiness. Yesterday at school, a student in a brand new car parked next to me. I felt so outclassed and a bit depressed. Then, Antonio parked on the other side and I thought, "At least my car's newer than his!"

Kramer: Perfect! Instead of looking at people who have more and getting envious, look at those who have less and be grateful. Socrates was once asked, "Who was the wealthiest?" to which he replied, "He that is content with the least, for contentment is nature's wealth."[7]

Akashi: So doesn't this point and the "Attitude Check" point solve last week's riddle?

Kramer: Explain it.

Akashi: Frank and Fred were brothers. They lived in the same house, had the same parents and probably went to the same school. They lived in a small house in the country. Frank saw the breathtaking view and heard the bubbling brook. He counted his blessings, comparing his circumstances to those who had less and considering himself fortunate. Thus his childhood was "the best of times."

Fred lived in the same house but was materialistic, envying those who had more. He moped around each day feeling sorry for himself, rather than enjoying his family and the beautiful scenery. For him, it was "the worst of times."

Kramer: Exactly!

RELIGION CAN HELP

An extensive, recent study found religious young people reporting higher levels of happiness than the irreligious.[8] Many people report that connecting with God gives them a source of joy that carries them through even the most difficult of circumstances.[9]

Akashi: Another counterintuitive. I suppose I bought the popular conception that religious people miss all the fun, going to boring meetings and feeling guilty all the time.

Kramer: Studies found deeply religious teens experiencing less guilt, significantly less depression and much more happiness.[10]

Travis: I didn't grow up in a religious family. Havin' a drunk earthly father, the last thing I thought I needed was some big, almighty Father. But some things about investin' made me curious about God.

You see, it's been fashionable in recent years for top investment thinkers, the university types, to argue that nobody can really beat the market. It's called the "Efficient Market Theory." To them, people like Buffett aren't smarter than others – just luckier. But here's the funny thing: some of those who argued hardest against Buffett's ability to outsmart the market, *hedged their bet* by investing in Berkshire Hathaway, Buffett's company, *just in case they were wrong!*[11]

Now that reminded me of the anti-church thinker Voltaire, who, at the end of his life, had himself baptized by the church, *just in case he was wrong.*[12]

I thought, "Now that's a lot like Buffett and Graham's *margin of safety* - what Graham called the three most important words of investing."[13] Even after Graham's meticulous research led him to believe that one company would outperform the market, he still waited for a bargain price, givin' him a margin of safety – *hedging his bet, just in case he was wrong.*

"*Just in case I'm wrong…*" I kept thinkin'. No matter how sure I was that God didn't exist, I thought, "I have no margin of safety. A significant proportion of groundbreaking scientists are believers.[14] The most knowledgeable student of philosophy I know is Frederick Copleston, who devoted himself almost single-mindedly to the study of philosophy for six decades and wrote the most comprehensive history of philosophy ever written – in seventeen books on my shelves – and he's a believer. Isn't it just possible that Copleston's right and I'm wrong?[15]

Blaise Pascal, the French scientist and philosopher, put it in the form of a wager.[16] To oversimplify,

> **Let's say I bet *on* God and lose.** During this life, I worship Him and try to live a good life. Even if I lose the bet and it turns out He doesn't exist, I wouldn't have lost much. If there's no afterlife, then I'm no worse off after death than the atheist. Actually, I just might get more happiness in *this* life by following sound religious teachings, which are startlingly consistent with the lifestyle that scientists have found to lead to happiness.

> **But if I bet *against* God and lose**, I just might make Him mad and... well...I doubt that would be so good for either this life or the next.

Puttin' it like a wager appealed to my investment philosophy. Didn't want to throw my *money* into high risk ventures. Didn't want to throw my *life* into high-risk ventures. Too risky to bet against God. Not enough margin of safety.

So I began to seek God more seriously, readin' smart people who defended God and religion.

I was surprised that, once I found a place of worship that suited me, I got a lot out of the services and the people I met there. Made life less shallow. It's the ultimate of living for others rather than myself. Definitely makes me happier.

Kramer: Just don't choose a place of worship that asks you to put your mind on "Stand By." If it stimulates your mind and motivates you to worship God and serve others, it's more likely to be a healthy faith community. You may also want to read a daily devotional to help you personally connect with God.

This is incredibly important stuff. What can you take away from these scientific findings?

Summary

Akashi: I've never known about the relationship between religion and happiness. Makes me want to check it out.

James: I'm startled that "Huge Income" doesn't even rank as securing happiness. I need to start thinking of salary as more of a means to an end, rather than the end itself.

Also, I need to start asking the "What for?" question. I need to think more deeply and ask myself *why* I want to retire so early with a million dollars.

Antonio: I've always enjoyed doing service projects through school and my church. We've done yard work for old folks, served food to the homeless, etc.

Honestly, I *started* volunteering because my guidance counselor said it would look good on my job resumes and college applications. But I *kept* volunteering because it was so fun, so rewarding. Kicking butt with Halo was fun, but the fun I had doing a service project was much deeper and longer lasting.

Now I see *why* it's fun to help others. I need to think through how this impacts my decisions concerning vocation and lifestyle.

Amy: If I'm shooting for personal happiness and the happiness of others, I can't climb a ladder to success that's leaned against the wall of extravagant living. I need to make a living, but *making* a living isn't *living*. I need to live for something bigger.

I suppose my purpose for pursuing financial success should include:

• Making enough to avoid mooching off others.

• Making enough to provide for my family.

• Making enough to help the less fortunate and support other worthwhile causes.

The Payoff

Kramer: Let's keep in touch over the years and do some more breakfasts. But since this is our last official meeting, I've got a little gift for each of you in these envelopes.

Akashi: I don't get it. Is this $265 check for real?

Kramer: Sure. That first week, I knew that at $5.00 each per week, you'd have paid me, as a group, over $1,000 by the end of the year. So I shopped Certificates of Deposit in local banks and put $1,000 into a 12 month CD for one year at six percent interest. Now it's worth $1060, or $265 each.

So here's what you paid me, with interest. It's yours to do with as you please. But what I'd *like* you to do is to put it in a savings account at a local bank. Add to it each week or month until you have enough to purchase a mutual fund for a long-term investment with a higher rate of return. I'll help you find a solid company and fill out the paperwork. If you keep adding to it, you'll be surprised how fast you can save up enough to retire.[17]

James: But sometimes the money went to your guests, like Hash Brown or Travis.

Kramer: They didn't want any money from the start. I convinced them to take it so that we could give it back at the end. This is from all of us.

Amy: If that $265 gets 10 percent interest, doubling every seven years for 50 years, you just gave us $32,000 each in future money! If we add a little each month, it can grow into a fortune!

Akashi: But...why? You don't have a huge salary. You could have used that $1,060...for a neat vacation or something really cool for yourself.

Kramer: Don't you get it? Sure, driving out here every Saturday was a sacrifice. But it was also fun. I'll never forget James and Carmen shopping for stool softeners, the constant soap opera of relationships, watching you scatter when I did the ketchup bottle act.

Much more than that, I have the deeper satisfaction of knowing that I may have spared you guys some heartache and given you some valuable wisdom.
The gift occurred to me that first meeting. When you reluctantly parted with your cash for my breakfast, I began dreaming of the looks on your faces if I were to give it all back at the end. Every week, as you gave, my anticipation built for my little surprise at the end of the year.

And I'm not disappointed. For the last month, I've been counting down the days. Sure, I could have used the money toward a trip to China's Great Wall, which I've always wanted to see, but that trip wouldn't hold a candle to this last breakfast.

Besides being incredibly fun for me, I hope it's an object lesson you'll never forget. As an educator, I knew that this gift would teach you more about giving and growing your money than any chit-chat over breakfast.

It was just a piddling five dollars per week for crying out loud. You'd have blown it on a hamburger! But through saving and investing, it grew to $265 in a year.

Every time you add to that investment; every time you look at how it's grown, remember how it started. Not because of your great wisdom or hard work. It started as a gift, an act of grace from someone who cared.

Akashi: (Tearing up) Nobody's ever given me a gift like that...I don't know what to say.

Kramer: Say that you'll remember this feeling and aspire to make others feel the same way.

Akashi: I will.

Kramer: That's all I want in return. Now it's your turn. You've got to answer the "What for?" question for your own life. I can only hope that it includes the thrill of helping others.

Hmmmmm...

- Do you more often reflect on what you have or what you lack? Could thinking positively lead to a better life?

- Is your life more self-centered or other-centered? What's a good balance between caring for self and caring for others? What specific changes could lead to a more fulfilling life?

- What activities allow you to lose all track of time? How could you find more activities like this? Is there a way to make a living with them?

Assignment
After Breakfast

1. Make a list of things you're thankful for, with columns for "people," "things" and "other" (e.g. freedom, talents, experiences, etc.) Quote aloud from the list several times per day for a week. Does it positively affect your attitude?

2. Imagine your funeral. What do you want people to say about you and your life? How should this exercise impact your life purpose, long-term goals and short-term goals?

3. Write a mission statement for your life.

Resources to Take You Deeper

David G. Myers, *The Pursuit of Happiness* (New York: Avon Books, 1992). Myers is a social psychologist who also wrote *Psychology*, the most widely used text in his field. In *The Pursuit of Happiness*, he brilliantly pulls together hundreds of studies on human happiness and presents them in a readable fashion.

For those interested in exploring spirituality, ask a local pastor or rabbi to recommend a devotional book for daily reading. Entertaining a new spiritual thought each day is a good way to direct our gazes beyond temporal matters. Many recommend *The Purpose-Driven Life* by Rick Warren (over 25 million copies sold). If the potential conflicts between religion and science trouble you, consider starting with a recent, popularly written book by one of today's most highly distinguished physical scientists, Dr. Henry F. Schaefer. He found God while teaching at Berkeley. His book is called *Science and Christianity: Conflict or Coherence?*

Epilogue: Where Are They Now?

Larry Wiersbe

Larry was the best worker that Hash Brown had ever hired. When Hash retired, he paid off Larry's credit cards and put him over the entire operation. Larry promptly cancelled his credit cards, punched holes in them and hung them around his neck as a conversation starter and grim reminder of their power. He married one of his waitresses and lives with her in an almost paid-off condominium.

Carmen

After a journalist discovered Carmen and made her famous for her "Blitz Shopping" techniques, Hollywood called and gave her a permanent spot on "The Shopping Network," showing people how to get more for less.

James

After graduating from KSU's *Coles College of Business*, he landed a job as a salesman at a Porsche dealership, moving up quickly to senior manager. He promptly assigned himself the responsibility of driving each of the new Porches home, adequately testing their performance before selling them. This responsibility occasionally took him to Germany, to drive them on the no-speed-limit *Autobahn*.

He made retirement by age 45, spending his days playing basketball at the Y and volunteering at an inner city soup kitchen.

Unfortunately, he fell for a hot money-grabber, who, after their fifth year of marriage, ran his credit cards to the limit and divorced him for his best friend.

James, grateful that his friend had done him such a favor, relished the new challenge of salvaging half his fortune and multiplying it again. Two years later, he fell in love with a fellow volunteer at the soup kitchen, which they bought and ran together.

Antonio, Amy, Akashi and Travis

Antonio never excelled at making money, but succeeded at living beneath his means. He lived in a small cabin with no debt and a paid off Jeep. He continued to work for *Extreme Wisdom Wilderness Adventures*, helping troubled teens find meaning in their lives. His bumper sticker read, "My Other Car is a Horse."

Akashi never got over her compulsion to outperform all the "A" students who made her look bad in high school. So she hired them and started a "Fortune 500" clothing company, donating time and money to helping students with disabilities.

She took regular retreats to the Montana Rockies, volunteering with Antonio and *Extreme Wisdom Wilderness Adventures* to relieve the stress of corporate life.

One day, Akashi popped the question and Antonio said "Yes!" She immediately went into semi-retirement, ran a T-2 line to the cabin for her internet games and video conferencing and took a corporate jet into New York twice a month for important meetings. Antonio never again worried about either making money or making decisions.

Amy runs market research for Akashi's "alternative" market on Mondays through Thursdays, reserving long weekends to counsel teens at the local detention center with **Travis** and playing gigs with her latest punk band, "The Misfits." Travis proposed over a Blizzard at Dairy Queen. Amy eagerly accepted. The prenup specified that the hound dogs would live outside and Amy couldn't drive his Charger.

Mrs. Kramer and Hash Brown

At age 80, after months of declining health, Mrs. Kramer checked herself into a large assisted living center in Atlanta. Disgruntled that the cheap management refused to upgrade their cable to receive "The Discovery Channel," "The Travel Channel," and "MTV Europe," she persuaded the other residents to pool their savings and purchase the majority stock in the home. They promptly fired the management and made their own decisions.

A year later, she felt somewhat better and disappeared for a few weeks. Her rehabilitated son checked her blog to find a new posting, including a picture of herself, wearing a long white dress and sporting a mischievous grin, waving from the back seat of a Harley with old Hash in front. The caption read: "Departing Shang Hai for The Great Wall."

The blog listed her 10 year goals, including visiting the sites of Indiana Jones' travels and taking a correspondence course in Chinese.

Appendix A: Adult Spending Sheet (Budget)

Add or Subtract Categories to Personalize It.

Amount Left to Save and Invest (income minus expenses): _____

   Income (total): _____

      Salary: _____
      Investment Income (rental income, interest, dividends): _____
      Other Income (child support, etc.): _____

   Expenses (total of below categories): _____

      Food (total): _____

         Groceries (include all purchases: paper towels, toiletries, etc., typically made at the grocery store): _____
         Eating Out: _____

      Auto (total): _____

         Gas: _____
         Payments: _____
         Repairs: _____
         Upkeep (change oil, washing, detailing): _____
         Insurance: _____
         License and Tags: _____
         Saving to Buy Next Car: _____

      Body Upkeep (total): _____

         Health Insurance: _____
         Doctor Visits: _____
         Dentist: _____
         Medicine: _____
         Haircuts/Nails/Tanning/Health Club: _____
         Other (_____): _____

      Insurance:

         Life Insurance: _____
         Disability Insurance: _____

      Clothes and Accessories: _____

Entertainment (total): _____

    Movies (rental and theater): _____
    Video Games (rental, purchase and online gaming): _____
    Dates and Socials: _____
    Vacations: _____
    Activities: _____
    Magazine/Newspaper Subscriptions: _____
    Other (_____): _____

Education: _____

    Tuition: _____
    Textbooks: _____
    Other Books: _____
    Online Subscriptions: _____
    Other (_____): _____

Media and Communications (total): _____

    Phones: _____
    Internet Service: _____
    Television (Cable, Dish, etc.): _____
    Other (_____): _____

Housing (total): _____

    Mortgage or Rent: _____
    Electricity: _____
    Gas: _____
    Water: _____
    Garbage Service: _____
    Homeowner's Insurance: _____
    Repairs: _____
    Upkeep (Lawn, Painting, Cleaning): _____
    Improvements: _____
    Neighborhood fees: _____
    Property Tax: _____
    Other: (_____): _____

Debts (total, not including housing or auto): _____

    Credit Cards: _____
    Loans: _____
    Other monthly payments on furniture, appliances, etc.:
    _____

Miscellaneous:

> **Laundry, cleaning:** _____
> **Allowances, lunches:** _____
> **Gifts (include Christmas):** _____
> **Child expenses (tuition/day care/transportation)**
> **Other (_____):** _____

Taxes (state/federal/FICA): _____

Giving: _____

Appendix B: Example Spending Sheet (Budget) for 17-Year-Olds

PERSONALIZE IT FROM THE ADULT BUDGET.

Amount Left to Save and Invest (Income minus expenses): _____

Income (total): _____

Salary from Work: _____
Allowance: _____
Income from Investments: _____
Other Income (Lawn mowing, extra chores, babysitting, etc.): _____

Expenses (total of below categories): _____

Food (total): _____

Eating Out: _____
Soft Drinks and Snacks from School Machines:
_____

Auto (total): _____

Gas: _____
Payments: _____
Repairs: _____
Upkeep (change oil, washing, detailing): _____
Insurance: _____
License and Tags: _____
Saving to Buy Next Car: _____

Body Upkeep (Haircuts and Beauty Supplies): _____

Clothes and Accessories: _____

Entertainment (total): _____

Movies (rental and theater): _____
Video Games (rental, purchase and online gaming):
_____
Dates and Socials: _____
Activities: _____
Other (_____): _____

Cell Phone: _____

Debts (total): _____

> **Pay mom for football equipment:** _____
> **Pay dad for loan on computer:** _____

Miscellaneous (total): _____

> **Gifts (include Christmas):** _____
> **Other (_____):** _____

Taxes (state/federal/FICA): _____

Giving: _____

Acknowledgements

"The 100 Experts"

These are the 100+ great investors, financial writers and other authors I read on personal finance, business and general success. While all were helpful, I kept returning to Warren Buffett, his mentor Benjamin Graham, Jason Zweig, John Bogle, Thomas Stanley and William Danko. Your painstaking research, sound reasoning, remarkable insights and abundant personal experience produced a vast well of wisdom from which to draw. Standing upon your broad shoulders allowed me to see beyond the sensationalist nonsense and propaganda that permeates this field. (I'm writing free summaries of select books at www.enjoyyourmoney.org.)

"Thousands of Years of Experience"

These "Second-Halfers" (people over fifty years old) generously offered their wisdom gained from abundant life experiences. Many were much older than fifty and retired. All were eager to tell their stories. Why don't we ask our parents, grandparents and the elderly more often for their wisdom, before they take it with them forever? Your "view from the other side of life" was often hopeful, sometimes heart-rending, but always insightful. (I'm posting the results of these interviews on my site.)

"The 40"

These generous souls gave freely of their time to comment on my early drafts. Among them are great business leaders, CPA's, financial planners, professors, employees of the Small Business Administration's Small Business Development Center, fellow writers and just good, sharp folks with abundant financial experience and common sense. You added important insights, gently pointed out errors and encouraged me with your excitement for the project.

I want to especially thank Robert Martin, Dr. Dwight "Ike" Reighard, Larry Winter, William C. Lusk, Dr. Ken Walker, Jamerson Maddox, Dr. Bryan McIntosh, Anthony Daniel, Philip Miller, Mark Hannah, Dr. Phillip Page, Frank Rodriguez, Mark Hoerrner, Dr. Keisha Hoerrner, Richard Miller, Mike Barker, Fred Jones, Tia Amlette and her advanced writing class, Sam Schuessler, Britney Cole, John Joyce, Harold Baker, Jim Wells, Randy Elster, Steven Lange, Chace Wheaton, Nathan Dickinson, Chris Stanley, Alan and Julie Buckler, Demetrius Kloussadis, Ann Miller, Nick Person, Brad Parkhurst, Tim and Bethany Harmon, Dave Hasty, Andy Fried, Katie White, and "The Diehards" investment club.

Financial Mentors

My parents, Joe and Ann Miller, modeled wise financial management throughout their lives. Thanks for showing me the purpose of it all: to help others along the way. If a picture is worth a thousand words, role models are worth millions of words. The longer I live, the more I appreciate you.

Wayne King and Del Bonnette greatly impacted my early views of money and life. Thanks for being there for me during those impressionable years.

Ed Owen, my uncle, drilled into us nephews the wisdom of investing and living beneath your means. I can still hear you passionately telling us, "Nobody understands the power of compounding interest!"

Granny, I'm sure glad you're still with us at age 103! Your lifetime of selfless service to others inspires us all.

Solomon

Your *Proverbs* are as astoundingly relevant to finances today as they were 3,000 years ago.

My Publishing Team

Many thanks to the folks at Wisdom Creek Press and their publishing partners, who shared my excitement for this project and made the journey to print a joy. Callie Brown's keen editing eye improved the manuscript significantly. Your enthusiasm for the project kept me moving forward. John Mark Schuster expertly guided me through the publishing process. Carole Mauge-Lewis delighted us with her cover design. Sue Cochran and Lisa Russell of Callisa Ink & Company laid out the interior in such a way that even poor readers could progress swiftly through the book. Blythe Daniel, my literary agent and Colorado publicist, provided wisdom and expertise at many junctures. Stephanie Richards, my Georgia publicist, has also been a key player and a joy to work with.

My Wife: Cherie

Where would I be if I couldn't bounce every new thought off of you? Your voracious reading, business savvy and writing expertise sharpened me every step of the way. I love you!

Our Children: Steve, Josh, Andrew, Benji, Mark, David and Paul.

I wrote this book with you in mind. Our conversations about life and money enrich me daily. I love you guys!

Although I received input from many, please don't blame them for inaccuracies that remain. The final decisions were mine alone. Please point out errors I need to correct or ideas I should incorporate in future editions. You may e-mail suggestions to jstevemiller@gmail.com. The last word about finances has yet to be written. Think of this book, and all books on finance, as a springboard for your thinking rather than a collection of undeniable data.

 **Endnotes**

Preface

¹ John C. Bogle, *Bogle on Mutual Funds: New Perspectives for the Intelligent Investor* (New York: Dell, 1994) 3.

² To compare the advice of many personal finance books, see my book summaries at www.enjoyyourmoney.org.

³ Thomas J. Stanley, *The Millionaire Mind* (Kansas: Andrew McMeel, 2001) 33ff. Thomas J. Stanley and William D. Danko, *The Millionaire Next Door* (New York: Pocket Books, 1996) 27-69.

⁴ Peter Drucker states, "The task of management is to make people capable of joint performance, to make their strengths effective and their weaknesses irrelevant." Peter F. Drucker, with Joseph A. Maciariello, *The Daily Drucker* (New York: HarperCollins, 2004) 47. On the importance and implementation of strengths, see Marcus Buckingham and Donald Clifton, *Now, Discover Your Strengths* (New York: Free Press, 2001). See also Marcus Buckingham and Curt Coffman's earlier book on management, *First, Break All the Rules: What the World's Greatest Managers Do Differently (New York: Simon & Schuster, 1999),* along with many other books on this theme at the Gallup Press: http://www.galluppress.com/content/?CI=17473 .

⁵ See especially David G. Myers, *The Pursuit of Happiness: Discovering the Pathway to Fulfillment, Well-being, and Enduring Personal Joy* (New York: Avon Books, 1993).

Breakfast 1

¹ From survey of 401 retirees released 3/10/05. Of 600 workers over 45 years of age, 97 percent said they regretted how they spent their money, seeing how much they could have saved. *National Survey Reveals Boomers Have Unrealistic Expectations; Oppenheimer Funds' Research Identifies Four "Retirement Savings Profiles" Among Baby Boomers,* PR Newswire (New York: March 10, 2005).

² According to an AC Nielsen study, "Nearly one-quarter (22 percent) of U.S. respondents said that once they have covered their basic living expenses, they have no money left over." From http://www2.acnielsen.com/news/20060913.shtml.

³ "…40.8 percent reported that they save regularly." Brian K. Bucks, Arthur B. Kennickell, and Kevin B. Moore (of the Federal Reserve Board's Division of Research and Statistics), *Recent Changes in U.S. Family Finances: Evidence from the 2001 and 2004 Survey of Consumer Finances*, p. A7.

⁴ *Savings At Lowest Rate Since Depression: Americans Spent Everything They Made Last Year – And Then Some* (CBS News/Associated Press, February 1, 2007). They cited the Commerce Department for 2005 and 2006, reporting a negative one percent savings rate and negative 0.4 percent savings rate. They also cited Peter Russo of Vanderbilt University for comparisons with 10 years prior and 25 years prior.

⁵ That's the average for the decade ending in 2007. Alan Zibe, *Personal Bankruptcy Filings Rise 40%* (Washingtonpost.com, Associated Press, Jan. 4, 2008) D07.

⁶ This figure derived by adding their college loan debt ($19,300) to their credit card debt ($2,864 for final year students). An average graduating couple contemplating marriage would face a joint debt of over $44,000. On credit card debt, see *Undergraduate Students and Credit Cards in 2004: An Analysis of Usage Rates and Trends* (a study by Nellie Mae, published May, 2005): http://www.nelliemae.org/library/research_12.html . On college loan debt, see Susan P. Choy and C. Dennis Carroll, *Debt Burden: A Comparison of 1992–93 and 1999–2000 Bachelor's Degree Recipients a Year After Graduating* (a report by the US Department of Education, March, 2005): http://nces.ed.gov/das/epubs/pdf/2005170_es.pdf.

[7] *The Facts on Saving and Investing: Excerpts from recent polls and studies highlighting the need for financial education* (Office of Investor Education and Assistance, Securities and Exchange Commission).

[8] Tim Boyle, *Consumer Spending Drives Two-Thirds Of U.S. Economy* (Chicago: Getty Images, 2004).

[9] Oseola McCarty, *Simple Wisdom for Rich Living* (Atlanta: Longstreet Press, 1996). See also Nancy Dorman-Hickson, *The Amazing Grace of Miss McCarty, Southern Living* (Feb., 1998) 33-34.

[10] Jack Welch with Suzie Welch, *Winning* (New York: HarperCollins, 2005) 25ff. Welch states, "I have always been a huge proponent of candor. In fact, I talked it up to GE audiences for more than twenty years. But since retiring from GE, I have come to realize that I underestimated its rarity. In fact, I would call lack of candor the biggest dirty little secret in business. What a huge problem it is. Lack of candor basically blocks smart ideas, fast action, and good people contributing all the stuff they've got. It's a killer."

[11] *Simple Wisdom*, Ibid. 25.

Breakfast 2

[1] Roger Lowenstein, *Buffett: The Making of an American Capitalist* (New York: Main Street Books, 1995) 8-10. What was the source of his drive to make money? His parents weren't passionate about money. Perhaps it came from insecurities brought about by the Great Depression, or, as his younger sister Roberta surmised, "I think it was in his genes." (Ibid. 10.)

[2] Ibid.

[3] Ibid. 4.

[4] Ibid. 10.

[5] Ibid. 4, 16.

[6] "How Much is That Worth Today?" calculator, at http://eh.net/hmit/ppowerusd/.

[7] Lowenstein, op. cit. 20.

[8] Ibid. 23.

[9] Ibid. 26.

[10] Ibid. 24, 25.

[11] Ibid. 24.

[12] Ibid. 34.

[13] *Homes of the Billionaires* (www.forbes.com).

[14] Lowenstein, op. cit. 73.

[15] Ibid. xvi, xvii. See also Wikipedia on Warren Buffett.

[16] *Buffett Spreads the Wealth*: Astonishing $30-billion Gift Could Spark a Revolution in Philanthropy, *Los Angeles Times* (June 27, 2006); Carol J. Loomis, *Warren Buffett Gives It Away, Fortune* (July 10, 2006) 57ff.

[17] CPA and financial counselor Larry Winter says that historically, until the 1950's, our schools taught the 80/10/10 principle in personal economics: live on 80%, save 10%, give 10%. (Personal interview with Larry Winter, 2007)

[18] Allen Hadidian, *Successful Discipling* (Chicago: Moody Press, 1979) 43.

[19] Ibid.

[20] More precisely, about 10.2 percent per year through 2001. Bonds returned 5.3 percent during the same period. Why begin tracking in 1926? We simply don't have reliable data before that year. John C. Bogle, *Bogle on Mutual Funds* (New York: Dell Publishing, 1994) 6-7. See also John Coumarianos, *The Lessons of Market History for Novice Investors*, www.morningstar.com).

[21] Charles Schwab, *Charles Schwab's New Guide to Financial Independence* (New York: Three Rivers Press, 2004) 49.

[22] Janet Lowe, *Warren Buffett Speaks* (New York: John Wiley & Sons, 1997) 128. Quoted from a speech by Warren Buffett at the New York Society of Security Analysts, Dec. 6, 1994.

[23] Concerning "the power of the last double," investment and retirement manager C. Michael Barker says that in his seminars and counseling, the light often comes on when he suggests, "If you decide to wait to invest, decide how many doubles you're willing to give up. You don't understand the power of that last double!" (Personal interview with Michael Barker, 2008)

[24] Nancy Dorman-Hickson, ''The Amazing Grace of Miss McCarty,'' *Southern Living*, Feb.,1998, 18.

[25] See survey results from PayScale at http://www.payscale.com/research/US/All_K-12_Teachers/Salary.

[26] Lowenstein, op. cit. xvi.

Breakfast 3

[1] Janet Lowe, *Warren Buffett Speaks* (New York: John Wiley & Sons, 1997) 67, quoting from *Expert on Investing Plans to Slow Down, Omaha World-Herald*, Feb. 25, 1968,1 (Quote modified later in Buffett's letter to Janet Lowe).

[2] John C. Bogle, *Bogle on Mutual Funds* (New York: Dell Publishing, 1994) 3.

[3] "Gather people around you who are brutally honest. Most surround themselves with 'yes' people. I call at least three people before I make an investment decision. I can't tell you how many times I've been certain about a decision, then one person questioned it and I changed my mind." (From 2007 personal interview with C. Michael Barker, CRPC, CFS, Investment and Retirement Manager, Chatsworth, Georgia).

[4] http://www.roadrunnerrecords.com , News Archive, *Ozzy Osbourne: New Live Album on the Way?* June 10, 2003.

[5] Dave Ramsey, *The Total Money Makeover* (Nashville: Thomas Nelson, 2003) 102, quoting *Money* Magazine as saying that 78 percent of us will experience a major negative event in any given ten-year period.

[6] Rick Sharga, a Vice-President at RealtyTrac, as quoted by Joel S. Hirschhorn in *The Progress Report: The American Dream is More Than Just Barely Surviving, Foreclosure USA*, 2006, at www.progress.org.

[7] *National Underwriter*, May 2002.

[8] The drop in value from \$20,000 to \$12,600 would be consistent with the market's 37 percent decline in the bear market of 1973-1974. Benjamin Graham, *The Intelligent Investor*, revised edition (New York: HarperCollins, 2003) 80.

[9] Barker (op. cit.) calls this "Murphy's Law of Stock Picking," – "The first stock you purchase will always go up so that you get overconfident and lose your shirt on your next picks." Research found that "Professional stock analysts who forecast a company's earnings accurately just four times in a row then go on to make progressively riskier predictions that end up 10% worse than average." Jason Zweig, *Your Money and Your Brain: How the New Science of Neuroeconomics Can Help Make You Rich* (New York: Simon and Schuster, 2007) 108.

[10] *Warren Buffett Speaks*, op. cit., 112.

[11] Benjamin Graham dedicates his entire first chapter to distinguishing investing from speculating. Graham, pp. 18ff.

[12] Ibid. 255. On our tendency to be overconfident about our investing prowess, see Jason Zweig, op. cit. 85-126.

[13] Graham, p. 150.

[14] Zweig, in *The Intelligent Investor*, p. 149.

[15] Graham personified the market, naming it "Mr. Market." Somehow, clothing Mr. Market with the often irrational characteristics of the stock market helps us to better understand our need to ignore the emotional ups and downs of the market and its followers, making rational decisions instead. As Graham wrote, "You are neither right nor wrong because the crowd disagrees with you. You are right because your data and reasoning are right." *The Intelligent Investor*, op. cit., 524.

[16] *The Intelligent Investor*, Op. Cit., 223.

[17] *The Essence of Great Workplaces*, interview with Wayne Brockbank, on www.growtalent.com.

[18] Back in 1992, Bill Gates said of Microsoft, "Take our 20 best people away and I tell you that Microsoft would become an unimportant company." "Bill Gates," *Forbes*, Dec. 7, 1992).

[19] Sam Walton with John Huey, *Sam Walton: Made in America* (New York: Doubleday, 1992) 45.

[20] Ibid. 49.

[21] Ibid. 80.

[22] Ibid. 103.

[23] Ibid. 104. Wal-Mart's first buyer said, "Really, back early, one bad manager could have pulled us under" (p. 54). According to Sam Walton, "Here's what makes me laugh today: it would have been absolutely impossible to convince anybody back then that in thirty years most all of the early discounters would be gone, that three of these four new chains would be the biggest, best-run operators in the business, that the one to fold up would be Woolco, and that the biggest, most profitable one would be the one down in Arkansas. Sometimes even I have trouble believing it." (pp. 49, 95, 194).

[24] *The Intelligent Investor*, op. cit. 248, taken from Lipper, Inc., looking back 20 years from December 31, 2002, comparing actively managed funds to Vanguard's 500 Index Fund. In studies like this, we need to make sure we're comparing apples with apples. Example: Another study compared the index fund to actively managed funds with low management fees and found the managed funds looking much better than in the above cited study.

[25] *Your Money and Your Brain*, op. cit. 86.

[26] *The Intelligent Investor*, p. 190.

[27] Wikipedia on Enron.

[28] The current version (as I write) of the Wikipedia article on "Technical Analysis" provides a good introduction to the contentions between proponents and scoffers.

[29] *The Intelligent Investor*, op. cit. 45. See also Jason Zweig, *False Profits*, August 1999, www.cnnmoney.com .

[30] Siimon Reynolds, compiler, *Thoughts of Chairman Buffett* (New York: HarperBusiness, 1998) (no page numbering). As Bogle puts it, "In my view, attempting to build a lifetime investment program around the selection of a handful of individual securities is, for all but the most exceptional investors, a fool's errand." And again, "Earning extraordinary returns from the ownership of individual stocks is a high-risk, long-shot bet for most investors." (Bogle, op. cit. vii.)

[31] *The Intelligent Investor*, p. 129.

[32] One of Benjamin Graham's central themes was to buy stocks only when they're selling at a bargain price, giving a comfortable "margin of safety" in case the business doesn't go as well as you'd hoped. See especially chapter 20, "'Margin of Safety' as the Central Concept of Investment" in *The Intelligent Investor*, Op. Cit. 512ff.

[33] Larry Winter (CPA, etc.) uses an analogy to warn clients about risky ventures and investments. To start a fire, you need three ingredients: air, fuel and something to ignite the fuel. In the same way three things lead to disaster in investing: 1) Do it in a hurry, 2) in an area you know nothing about, 3) with borrowed money. (From personal interview in 2007).

[34] Our brains have a bad tendency (bad for investing, at least) to find patterns that don't exist. So I look at the newspaper to find that a stock's gone up. Next week, it's gone up again. My brain gives me a natural high, concluding it's found a recurring pattern. I expect it to happen again, *although there may be no rational reason for that expectation.* This explains, in part, people's tendency to herd into funds and sectors that have been going up for some time. And since the psychological pain associated with loss is much more intense than the pleasure associated with gain, the pressure's on to sell when a stock or fund goes way down. *The Intelligent Investor*, pp. 220,221; *Your Money and Your Brain*, p. 67.

[35] "A top 20 fund's performance in one year has no systematic relationship to its ranking in the subsequent year." *Bogle on Mutual Funds*, op. cit. 86.

[36] Ibid. 87-88.

[37] Ibid. 95.

[38] Tech stocks averaged going up over 20 percent each year from 1995 to 1999. *The Intelligent Investor*, op. cit. 83.

[39] Birkshire Hathaway annual meeting, Omaha, 1996. Modified later (as I quoted it here) by Buffett in a letter to Janet Lowe, as cited in her book, *Warren Buffett Speaks*, Op. Cit. 46.

[40] "Warren Buffett Talks Business," The University of North Carolina, Center for Public Television, Chapel Hill, 1995. As quoted in *Warren Buffett Speaks*, Op. Cit. 143. See also the discussion on the airline industry by both Graham and Zweig in *The Intelligent Investor*, Op. Cit. 6-7.

[41] Bogle notes the "powerful tendency" for total returns of common stocks to "regress to the mean," i.e., "the average historical long-term rate of return." *Bogle on Mutual Funds*, p. 20.

[42] Richard Cole with Richard Trubo, *Stairway to Heaven: Led Zeppelin Uncensored* (New York: Harper Collins, 1992) 42.

[43] Again, our brains excite us (neurons fire) when stocks go up in value, motivating us to buy. But many more neurons fire when our stocks go down, motivating us to sell from the powerful fear of loss. *Your Money and Your Brain*, p. 181.

[44] *The Intelligent Investor*, p. 530.

[45] Ibid. 525.

[46] Gorg Wilhelm Friedrich Hegel, *The Philosophy of History*, Translated by J. Sibree (New York: Dover Publications,1956) 6.

[47] L.J. Davis, "Buffett Takes Stock," *The New York Times Magazine*, April 1, 1990, p. 16. As cited in *Warren Buffett Speaks*, Op. Cit. 97.

[48] *The Intelligent Investor*, Op. Cit. 245.

Breakfast 4

[1] Janet Lowe, *Warren Buffett Speaks* (New York: John Wiley & Sons, 1997) (inside sleeve).

[2] As Benjamin Graham wrote, "If you have formed a conclusion from the facts and if you know your judgment is sound, act on it – even though others may hesitate or differ. You are neither right nor wrong because the crowd disagrees with you. You are right because your data and reasoning are right." Benjamin Graham, *The Intelligent Investor*, revised edition with new commentary by Jason Zweig, (New York: HarperCollins, 2003) 524.

[3] *The Intelligent Investor*, op. cit. 50

[4] One dollar invested in stocks in 1925 would have become $1,775 by 2002. Comparatively, bonds would have become only $59 and treasury bills $17. Charles R. Schwab, *Charles Schwab's New Guide to Financial Independence* (New York: Three Rivers, 2004) 24-25.

[5] "Four months" isn't a magical number. Bogle recommends three to six months. (Bogle on Mutual Funds, p. 258.) Everybody's situation differs. Those with equity in their homes might draw on that equity in an emergency. Those making large house and car payments may need more than four month's salary in reserve.

[6] John C. Bogle, *Bogle on Mutual Funds* (New York: Dell, 1994) 237, 258; Burton G. Malkiel, *The Random Walk Guide to Investing* (New York: W.W. Norton, 2003) 57ff; Schwab, pp. 130-135.

[7] I saw this concept first in George S. Clason, *The Richest Man in Babylon* (New York: The Penguin Group, 1988 - first published in 1926) 19. See also David Chilton, *The Wealthy Barber* (California: Prima Publishing, 1998) 37ff.

[8] By building a relationship with my local bank, I'm able to get free services like

notarizing documents, occasionally waving overdraft fees, lending me money at better rates, etc.

[9] "If your investment horizon is long – at least 25 or 30 years – there is only one sensible approach: Buy every month, automatically, and whenever else you can spare some money. "The single best choice for this lifelong holding is a total stock-market index fund." (Jason Zweig in his commentary on *The Intelligent Investor*, op.cit. 219. Benjamin Graham himself recommended index funds as the best choice for individual investors in his latter years (p. 249) and Warren Buffett says the same: "Most investors, both institutional and individual, will find that the best way to own common stocks is through an index fund that charges minimal fees. Those following this path are sure to beat the net results (after fees and expenses) delivered by the great majority of investment professionals." (p. 249, from the 1996 annual report of Berkshire Hathaway).

[10] *The Intelligent Investor*, Op. Cit. 248, taken from Lipper, Inc., looking back 20 years from December 31, 2002, comparing actively managed funds to Vanguard's 500 Index Fund.

[11] So recommends Jason Zweig, *Your Money and Your Brain*, (New York: Simon & Schuster, 2007) 271; Burton G. Malkiel, *The Random Walk Guide to Investing*, pp. 135-152; John C. Bogle, *Bogle on Mutual Funds*, pp.169-189.

[12] Management costs on bond funds range from .25 percent to 2.25 percent. Let's say you invest in a high-cost bond fund, and your brother invests in a fund that differs only in that its costs are small. Bogle shows that your brother's fund could make 40 percent more per year than yours! *Bogle on Mutual Funds*, p. 104.

[13] *The Intelligent Investor*, p. 252. ("…its star ratings are a weak predictor of future results…")

[14] Roger Lowenstein, *Buffett: The Making of an American Capitalist* (New York: Doubleday, 1996) 59.

[15] *Bogle on Mutual Funds*, p. 222.

[16] David Latko, *Everybody Wants Your Money* (New York: Collins, 2006) xxi.

[17] What percentage should I invest outside the USA? Recommendations vary, since we can't really predict whether US companies will outpace international companies. All we have to go on is the past, and "past isn't prologue." Bogle recommends that your foreign equities not exceed 20 percent of your equity portfolio. *(Bogle on Mutual Funds*, p. 76). Schwab suggests 20-30 percent, or 5-10 percent if you're conservative (*Charles Schwab's New Guide to Financial Independence*, p. 88.) Zweig recommends up to 1/3. (*The Intelligent Investor*, p. 187) Burton Malkiel (professor of economics at Princeton) says that, "Investors of modest means need not diversify internationally," since large American companies obtain revenues internationally and "global stock markets tend to decline together." (*The Random Walk Guide to Investing*, pp. 103-104.)

[18] Schwab, p. 24. He compared the S&P 500 Index for stocks with the Intermediate U.S. Government Bond Index.

[19] Bogle, p. 9.

[20] Ibid. 13.

[21] Researchers at London Business School found American stocks *not* outperforming bonds and even cash in the years 1802-1871, a 69-year period! Graham, p. 82.

[22] Graham, pp. 89-91.

[23] Bogle, p. 239.

[24] Roger Lowenstein, *Buffett: The Making of an American Capitalist* (New York: Doubleday, 1995) 331. The exact quote reads, "Only two people understand that. Both of them live in Switzerland. However, they're diametrically opposed to each other."

[25] The only exception to this would be, according to Graham, "When the general market level is much higher than can be justified by well-established standards of value" (Graham, p. 206). On dollar cost averaging, see Graham, pp. 130-132; Bogle, pp. 31,32; Malkiel, pp. 106-110.

[26] Graham, p. 87.

Breakfast 5

[1] I met a cashier at a local filling station who did this. He flipped a car approximately every month from his parking space. If I remember correctly, he'd made $20,000 the previous year flipping inexpensive cars. Free parking space. No overhead. Pretty cool. Just make sure you comply with local and state laws when buying and selling used cars.

[2] The millionaires interviewed by Thomas Stanley and William Danko "allocate their time, energy, and money in ways consistent with enhancing their net worth." Thomas J. Stanley and William D. Danko, *The Millionaire Next Door* (New York: Pocket Books, 1996) 45,46,71.

[3] The 10% average return on investment jives with our experience in flipping houses in the metro Atlanta area. For specifics, from a person with much more experience, see Kevin C. Myers, *Buy It, Fix It, Sell It, Profit* (Chicago: Dearborn, 1997).

[4] When Gary Keller collected wisdom from over 100 millionaire real estate investors, he was surprised to discover that "...again and again, throughout our research, investors referred to all the people who helped them succeed. They had relationships with people who sent them opportunities, mentored them, helped them buy and maintain their properties, and in many cases provided services that enabled them to do more while spending less time and effort." Gary Keller with Dave Jenks and Jay Papasan, *The Millionaire Real Estate Investor* (New York: McGraw Hill, 2005) 30.

[5] For example, Zweig, in his commentary on Benjamin Graham's postscript, says, "To be an investor, you must be a believer in a better tomorrow" (Graham, p. 535).

[6] Larry Burkett, *Crisis Control in the New Millennium* (Nashville: Thomas Nelson, 1999) 3.

[7] *New York Times*, Oct. 23, 1929, cited by Burkett, p. 15.

[8] The Bill and Warren Show, *Fortune*, By Brent Schlender; Warren Buffett; Bill Gates July 20, 1998, found on money.com.

[9] Andrew Tobias, *Still! The Only Investment Guide You'll Ever Need* (New York: Bantam, 1987) 148-152.

[10] Burkett, pp. 209ff.

[11] Travis' input gives us another angle on "risk tolerance." Mutual fund advisers often say, "Here's a mix of funds for aggressive investors who have a high tolerance for risk. Those with a lower tolerance for risk might prefer different funds and a different strategy."

Now maybe it's just a guy thing, but to me that means, "If you can stomach the fluctuations, you'll make more money in this riskier portfolio over the long haul. But if you can't take the ups and downs, choose lower risk options and settle for lower returns." It comes across like a "wimp versus a real man" thing. Thus, I react, "Of course I can take the fluctuations! Of course I should go for the higher risk option!"

But any person who's not optimistic about our economy's future will, by necessity, fit into the "lower tolerance for risk" category. Not believing that our economy will forever prosper, he'll shy away from lower quality bonds and younger, unproven businesses. Tolerance isn't just about "the ability to stay in the market when it falls." Travis would generally have a lower risk tolerance, not because of anything psychological and not because of a short investment horizon, but because of his long-term economic outlook.

[12] On paradigms, see Thomas S. Kuhn, *The Structure of Scientific Revolutions* (Chicago: University of Chicago Press, 1996). Compare a thoughtful critique in Ian G. Barbour, *Myths, Models and Paradigms* (HarperCollins,1974). Steven R. Covey applied paradigms to personal success and business in *The Seven Habits of Highly Successful People* (New York: Fireside, 1990).

Breakfast 7

[1] This one little device – not boasting about your accomplishments – allowed Sam Walton to walk into his competition's headquarters and extract all kinds of information about discount retailing. They never suspected that this country guy who had stores in little towns could possibly compete with the big boys. Sam Walton with John Huey, *Sam Walton: Made in America* (New York: Doubleday, 1992) 81.

[2] Richard Edler, *If I Knew Then What I Know Now: Ceo's and Other Smart Executives Share Wisdom They Wish They'd Been Told 25 Years Ago* (New York: Berkley, 1995) 43.

[3] Walton, p. 28.

[4] According to Larry Winter, financial guru Larry Burkett often told the story of counseling three people in the same day, each of which couldn't make ends meet financially. The first was a mill worker who made $12,000 per year. Burkett asked the worker what he felt would solve his problems. He responded that he needed to make $3,000 more per year. The next was a merchant who made about $30,000 per year. He believed that several thousand more per year would solve his financial problems. The third was a doctor who made $100,000 per year. In his mind, he needed $25,000 more per year to make ends meet. This story provokes a lot of deep thought about how our lifestyle grows to consume our income, whatever it is, and how we refuse to consider lowering our lifestyle to solve our financial difficulties.

[5] Thomas J. Stanley and William D. Danko, *The Millionaire Next Door* (New York: Pocket Books, 1996) 1.

[6] Stanley and Danko, pp. 27-69.

[7] Stanley and Danko, pp. 256-258.

[8] The earliest version of this I've heard comes from Benjamin Franklin in *Poor Richard's Almanac*: "A penny saved is twopence dear" which has perhaps been misquoted through the years as "A penny saved is a penny earned." (Wikipedia on Benjamin Franklin)

[9] There's huge resistance on the part of many to keep a budget. If you're teaching this, find ways to make it sound empowering rather than boring. It's taking charge of your money, rather than allowing it to run your life. Why budget for future needs? Financial counselor Larry Winter notes that everything we own is in the process of breaking. So save 2% of the fair market value of your home every year to pay for its falling apart. We're all in the process of dying, so set aside 7 ½ percent of your income for medical, including insurance. What we call "emergencies" are typically a colossal lack of planning. Budgets plan for the known future.

Breakfast 8

[1] Sam Walton with John Huey, *Sam Walton: Made in America* (New York: Doubleday, 1992) 5.

[2] "The Gates Operating System," *Time*, January 13, 1997, as quoted by Janet Lowe in *Bill Gates Speaks* (New York: John Wiley & Sons, 1998) 149.

[3] According to an AC Nielsen study: "Nearly one-quarter (22 percent) of U.S. respondents said that once they have covered their basic living expenses, they have no money left over." Found on http://www2.acnielsen.com/news/20060913.shtml.

[4] My wife, Cherie, knows a young lady who said she was disgusted at her parents buying cheap shampoo. When she got on her own, she bought a case of great shampoo but ran out of money and had to fast a week before her next paycheck.

[5] I get mixed input on budgets. Some counselors tell me that none of their clients can keep a budget. Another counselor says that the only people who gain control of their finances work from budgets. At the very least, writing down my expenses lets me know where my money's going. Most of us have no idea.

[6] In 2003, teens spent "Thirty-three percent of their weekly earnings and allowance

on clothing and an additional 21 percent on food." (Coinstar Poll, "Coinstar Teens Talk Poll: Teens Report on Money, Spending and Buying." Found in Fiscal Notes, August 2005; "Teens Cash In," at www.cpa.state.tx.us).

[7] *Consumer Reports* found generics selling for an average of 42% less than brand names in one grocery chain. Mike Yorkey, *Saving Money Any Way You Can* (Michigan: Vine Books, 1994) 33-37.

[8] See Wikipedia on "Loss Leaders."

[9] Ibid.

Breakfast 9

[1] From *Pudd'nhead Wilson's Calendar* by Mark Twain.

[2] Ron and Judy Blue, *Raising Money-Smart Kids* (Nashville: Thomas Nelson,1992) 120. See also Thomas J. Stanley and William D. Danko's findings on how many prodigious accumulators of wealth patiently look for deals on reliable used cars, then recoop most of their money when they trade in a few years.

[3] Thomas J. Stanley and William D. Danko, *The Millionaire Next Door* (New York: Pocket Books, 1996) 112.

[4] Ibid. 115.

[5] Ibid. 110-112.

[6] Sam Walton with John Huey, *Sam Walton: Made in America* (New York: Doubleday, 1992) 1-3, 76,77.

[7] Stanley and Danko, pp. 109-112.

[8] American Institute for Economic Research (AIER) study, cited by Motor Trend.

[9] Wikipedia, "Transportation in New York City."

[10] This isn't only possible – it's common. Over the last two years, two of my sons have bought reliable, used vehicles in the $3,000 to $5,000 range for at least $2,000 under the *Kelley Blue Book* Value.

[11] According to *Kelley Blue Book*, a 1999 (seven years old from my time of writing) Honda Accord DX in fair condition with 80,000 miles has a private party value of $5,450. After Travis fixed the fender, it would go from fair to excellent condition. A 1996 model of the same car (three years older) in excellent condition with 125,000 miles has a private party value of $3,800.)

[12] 81 percent, according to Stanley and Danko, p. 112.

[13] The average payment is $378 over 55 months. After that, people feel like they "need" a new car and continue the payments on their next car. Dave Ramsey, *The Total Money Makeover* (Nashville: Thomas Nelson, 2003) 32, quoting from *USA Today*, Feb. 23, 2005.

[14] See www.fueleconomy.gov – from the U.S. Department of Energy and the Environmental Protection Agency. Figures based on the Honda using the recommended regular gas @ $2.50 per gallon and the Bugatti using regular gas (although Premium is recommended) for 15,000 annual miles. Based on 45 percent highway driving, 55 percent city driving.

[15] See www.clarkhoward.com .

[16] Added to and Revised from *Pilgrim Press* brochure.

Breakfast 10

[1] These figures are based on an actual house, bought by a relative in a Georgia city on that date.

[2] I ran the numbers on a $20,000 new 2005 Ford Taurus. *Kelley Blue Book* values a 2001   Taurus at a private party value of $4,885.

[3] Thomas J. Stanley, *The Millionaire Mind* (Missouri: Andrews McMeel, 2001) 312-359. Eighty percent surveyed never pay the initial asking price for a home. A relative in his early 20's recently purchased a home appraised at $220,000, but paid only $135,000 by

giving a low-ball offer. That one transaction increased his net worth by $85,000!

[4] "When interest rates rose to 18 percent during the Carter administration, it would have been stupid to pay off a 6 percent house loan." (Personal interview with Ann Miller.)

[5] A former realtor of ours actually had this experience!

[6] "The Progress Report: The American Dream is More Than Just Barely Surviving," *Foreclosure USA*, by Joel S. Hirschhorn, from www.progress.org.

Breakfast 11

[1] Janet Lowe, *Warren Buffett Speaks* (New York: John Wiley & Sons, 1997) 85.

[2] Ibid. 106.

[3] A good discussion of recent studies of the brain's relation to marijuana can be found in Timmen L. Cermak, M.D., *Marijuana: What's a Parent to Believe?* (Minnesota: Hazelden, 2003), 43-58. "In 1999, the Treatment Episode Data Set (TEDS) recorded more than 220,000 admissions for primary marijuana abuse to publicly funded substance abuse treatment" (Adolescent Substance Abuse Database).

[4] Thomas J. Stanley, *The Millionaire Mind* (Missouri: Andrew McMeel, 2001) 34.

[5] Ben Stein, *How Not to Ruin Your Life: A Formula for Long-Term Happiness* (California: Hay House, 2002), found posted on www.freerepublic.com.

[6] "Three Lectures by Warren Buffett to Notre Dame Faculty, MBA Students and Undergrad Students," Spring 1991, www.tilsonfunds.com.

[7] Richard Cole with Richard Trubo, *Stairway to Heaven: Led Zeppelin Uncensored* (New York: HarperCollins, 1992), See especially pp. 367-372. He eventually came clean of both (p. 377).

[8] Ibid. 1-4.

[9] Statement made April 29, 1962 at a dinner honoring 49 Nobel Laureates. James B. Simpson, *Simpson's Contemporary Quotations* (Boston: Houghton Mifflin, 1988), from *Public Papers of the Presidents of the United States: John F. Kennedy*, 1962, p. 347.

[10] On Jefferson's debts, see Joseph J. Ellis, *American Sphinx: The Character of Thomas Jefferson* (New York: Alfred A. Knopf, 2001) 277, 287, 288, 290; Dumas Malone, *Jefferson and His Time: The Sage of Monticello* (Little, Brown and Company, 1970) 301-303,315, 448, 505-512; Willard Stern Randall, *Thomas Jefferson: A Life* (New York: Henry Holt and Co., 1993) 589; Merrill D. Peterson, *Thomas Jefferson and the New Nation* (New York: Oxford University Press, 1970) 989-990.

[11] Haley Settle, "Foreclosures Still High But Slowing Across the Nation," www.DSNews.com 12/11/06.

[12] Proverbs 6:1-5 (New International Version)

[13] http://clarkhoward.com .

[14] Proverbs 22:7.

[15] Gibbs, p 96.

[16] Ibid.

[17] Ibid. 97.

[18] Ibid. 98.

[19] Ibid.

[20] Ibid. .

[21] Ibid.

[22] Ibid. 95, 99-103.

[23] Ibid.

[24] Ibid. 114,115.

[25] Ibid. 113, 118, 123.

[26] Ibid. 193.

[27] Ibid. 194.

[28] Ibid. 123.

[29] Thomas J. Stanley and William D. Danko, *The Millionaire Next Door* (New York: Pocket Books, 1996) 103-108. "Your ability to hire high-grade financial advisers is directly

related to your propensity to accumulate wealth." (p. 105). See also Thomas J. Stanley, *The Millionaire Mind* (Kansas City: Andrews McMeel, 2001) 375.

[30] He was a big spender; his wife was frugal. He was a risky investor; she was more cautious. He finally learned to lean upon her counsel (Gibbs, p. 197).

[31] Ibid. 123. If a bank won't loan money to someone without co-signing, then the bank doesn't believe the borrower has a good chance of paying it off. By signing, I'm helping someone get a loan that the bank determined he shouldn't get.

[32] Ibid. 116-117.

[33] Francis Hartigan, *Bill W: A Biography of Alcoholics Anonymous Cofounder Bill Wilson* (New York: St. Martin's, 2000) 57-63. A man who had tried seemingly everything to defeat alcohol visited the influential Swiss Psychiatrist, Carl Jung, who mentioned several alcoholics who got sober through a religious conversion. Jung suggested that he try it as well, and it worked. When word got back to Bill Wilson, he reluctantly turned to God as his last hope.

[34] On studies showing that religion tends to be a successful preventative of destructive behaviors (which obviously impact our finances), see the results of the most recent large-scale study of youth and religion in Christian Smith and Melinda Lundquist Denton, *Soul Searching: The Religious and Spiritual Lives of American Teenagers* (New York: Oxford University, 2005), especially chapter 7. See also the studies cited by David G. Myers in *The Pursuit of Happiness* (New York: Avon Books, 1993) 177-204.

[35] Gibbs, p. 113. I'm referring to Howard Dayton, president of Crown Ministries.

[36] David W. Latko, *Everybody Wants Your Money* (New York: HarperCollins, 2006) 10.

[37] Benjamin Graham, *The Intelligent Investor*, Updated with New Commentary by Jason Zweig (New York: HarperCollins, 2003) 262.

[38] Stanley and Danko, p. 108. "Choose a financial adviser who is endorsed by an enlightened accountant and/or his clients with investment portfolios that in the long run outpace the market. If you don't have an accountant, hire one."

[39] Latko, p. 11-12.

[40] So says David Hultstrom, who teaches courses for financial advisers. See his helpful article, "Ruminations on Being a Financial Professional," concerning what he'd look for in a financial professional to advise someone he loves: http://www.financialarchitectsllc. com/Ruminations_on_Being_a_Financial_Professional.pdf. David Latko recommends the "Series 7 Registration." It's required by the government to legally sell stocks and bonds. A "Series 6" is merely a permit that allows him to sell mutual funds. Most states require a "Series 65" license to practice investment advising (Latko, p. 34).

[41] Per the advice of David Hulstrom, Larry Winter (Personal Interviews) and David Latko, pp. 45-48.

[42] Latko, p. 37.

[43] The prodigious accumulators of wealth studied by Stanley and Danko don't actively, regularly trade their stocks. Rather, they buy stocks wisely and hold them. "The so-called active investor is one of the more difficult types of millionaires to find for interview purposes." Stanley and Danko, p. 100-101.

[44] Wikipedia on Pete Rose.

[45] The Dowd Report asserted that Rose bet on 52 Reds games in 1987, at a minimum of $10,000 a day.

[46] Wikipedia on the term "Lottery." See also the "Lottery Mathematics" article.

[47] www.taxfoundation.org, January 19, 2006 "Saving for Retirement: The Lottery vs. the Stock Market" by Alicia Hansen.

[48] *Six-figure savings? Most say* 'unlikely' Survey: 20 percent say lottery is most practical path to wealth, by Andrea Coombes, MarketWatch, Last Update: 7:03 PM ET Jan 9, 2006 at www.marketwatch.com.

In a 1999 survey by the Consumer Federation of America and financial services firm Primerica, 40 percent of Americans with incomes between $25,000 and $35,000 − and nearly one-half of respondents with an income of $15,000 to $25,000 − thought winning the lottery would give them their retirement nest egg. Overall, 27 percent of respondents said that their best chance to gain $500,000 in their lifetime was via a sweepstakes or lottery win.

[49] Rewritten from Latko, pp. 19-22.

[50] Wikipedia on Mark Twain.

[51] Mark Twain's business adventures provide a sometimes humorous, often tragic, glimpse into how intelligent people can lose their money trying to get rich quick. For Twain's own candid description of his business dealings, see his autobiography - Charles Neider, ed., *The Autobiography of Mark Twain* (New York: Harper and Row, 1975 edition) 238ff. See also Peter Krass' excellent recounting of Twain's business ventures in *Ignorance, Confidence, and Filthy Rich Friends* (New Jersey: John Wiley & Sons, 2007).

[52] Quoted by Andrew Kilpatrick in "Of Permanent Value."

[53] Thomas J. Stanley, *The Millionaire Mind*, pp. 260-271.

[54] A.M. Best is a leading rater of insurance companies.

[55] See *Disability Insurance: A Missing Piece of the Financial Security Puzzle*, at http:// www.actuarialfoundation.org/consumer/disability_chartbook.pdf.

Breakfast 12

[1] Sam Walton with John Huey, *Made in America: My Story* (New York: Doubleday, 1992) 258,259.

[2] Ibid. xii.

[3] Dan Miller, *48 Days to the Work You Love* (Nashville: Broadman & Holman, 2005) 1.

[4] Thomas J. Stanley and William D. Danko, *The Millionaire Next Door: The Surprising Secrets of America's Wealthy* (New York: Pocket Books, A division of Simon and Schuster, 1996) 240.

[5] Thomas Stanley, *The Millionaire Mind* (Kansas City: Andrews McMeel, 2000) 87-131.

[6] Ibid. 96-97. See also Daniel Goleman, *Emotional Intelligence* (New York: Bantam Books, 1995) 35-49. Thomas Stanley highly recommends Yale professor Robert J. Sternberg's book, *Successful Intelligence* (New York: Simon & Schuster, 1996).

[7] Stanley, pp. 33ff.

[8] Ibid. 41-43.

[9] Peter Drucker quote found on the sleeve of Marcus Buckingham & Donald O. Clifton, *Now, Discover Your Strengths* (New York: The Free Press, 2001).

[10] Dan Miller, p. 4.

[11] Marcus Buckingham and Curt Coffman, *First, Break All the Rules: What the World's Greatest Managers Do Differently* (Simon & Schuster, 1999).

[12] See Marcus Buckingham and Donald O. Clifton, *Now, Discover Your Strengths*, (New York, The Free Press, 2001).

[13] Berkshire Hathaway annual meeting, Omaha, 1988; found in Janet Lowe, *Warren Buffett Speaks* (New York: John Wiley and Sons, 1997) 66. See also Robert G. Hagstrom, *The Warren Buffett Way* (New York: John Wiley & Sons, 1995) 268, where Buffett speaks of "tap dancing in the office." "There is no job in the world that is more fun than running Berkshire…."

[14] Richard N. Bolles, *What Color is Your Parachute?* 2005 Edition (Berkeley: Ten Speed, 2005) 37-39.

[15] Bolles, p. 40.

[16] Bolles, pp. 40-41.

[17] Larry Winter suggests this. If you're out of a job, go to The United Way or another service organization and volunteer ½ day, every day. Also, you can volunteer at that business you love. One person came to Larry's CPA firm and said he'd work for him for six weeks, free of charge. Larry let him and ended up hiring him (From interview with Larry Winter, CPA).

Breakfast 13

[1] Survey from Thomas J. Stanley, *The Millionaire Mind* (Kansas City: Andrews McMeel, 2001) 34.

[2] Quoted by Andrew Kilpatrick in *Of Permanent Value*.

[3] Jack Welch With Suzy Welch, *Winning* (New York: HarperCollins, 2005) 102-103.

[4] *Omaha World Herald*, February 1, 1994.

[5] Feb. 2003, *Quarterly Journal of Economics*, as quoted by Paul Orfalea and Ann Marsh, *Copy This!* (New York: Workman, 2005) 117.

[6] Ibid.

[7] Benjamin Franklin, *The Autobiography of Benjamin Franklin* (New York: Dover, 1996) 63ff.

[8] Jack Welch with John A. Byrne, *Jack: Straight from the Gut* (New York: Warner Books, 2001) ix.

[9] Paul Orfalea, p. 2.

[10] Ibid. 54-56.

[11] Michael White, *Leonardo: The First Scientist* (New York: St. Martin's, 2000) 211, 214, 234.

[12] Jack Welch, *Jack: Straight from the Gut*, pp. 5, 91.

[13] Dale Pollock, *Skywalking: The Life and Films of George Lucas* (New York, Harmony Books, 1983) 24, 148.

[14] Joseph McBride, *Steven Spielberg* (New York: Simon and Schuster, 1997). He was a "C" student (p. 57) and failed to land acting parts in his school plays because he couldn't memorize the lines (p. 98). He applied to two prestigious film schools but was rejected because of his "mediocre academic record" (p. 131).

[15] Denis Brian, *Albert Einstein: A Life* (New York: John Wiley & Sons, 1996). His "teachers thought him dull-witted because of his failure to learn by rote and his strange behavior" (p. 3). His Greek teacher was so exasperated that he told Albert he'd never amount to anything, was wasting his time, and should leave immediately (p. 6).

[16] C.S. Lewis, *Surprised by Joy* (Orlando: Harvest Books, 1966) 12, 137, 186, 187.

[17] Peter Drucker, *People and Performance: The Best of Peter Drucker on Management*.

[18] Gary Keller with Dave Jenks and Jay Papasan, *The Millionaire Real Estate Investor* (New York: McGraw-Hill, 2005) 30, 31.

[19] See, for example, Daniel Goleman, *Emotional Intelligence* (New York: Bantam Books, 1995).

[20] Dale Carnegie, *How to Win Friends and Influence People, Revised Edition* (New York: Pocket Books, 1981) xiv.

[21] Ibid.

[22] Sam Walton with John Huey, *Sam Walton: Made in America* (New York: Doubleday, 1992). Speaking of his college days, Walton said, "I learned early on that one of the secrets to campus leadership was the simplest thing of all: speak to people coming down the sidewalk before they speak to you" (p. 15). A clerk observed Walton practicing this in an early store: "I guess Mr. Walton just had a personality that drew people in. He would yell at you from a block away, you know. He would just yell at everybody he saw, and that's the reason so many liked him and did business in the store. It was like he brought in business by his being so friendly" (p. 34).

[23] Carnegie, p. 54.

[24] Advice from Larry Winter, CPA, in personal interview, 2007.

[25] Leo Tolstoy, *My Religion*, translated by Huntington Smith, chapter 10. Found on Wikisource at http://en.wikisource.org/wiki/My_Religion/Chapter_X.

[26] Quoted by Dan Miller in *48 Days to the Work You Love* (Nashville: Broadman & Holman, 2005) 7.

[27] Joe Griffith, *Speaker's Library of Business Quotes*.

[28] From interview, Feb 23, 2003, MSN Chat Transcript, MSN Live.

[29] Pat Riley, *The Winner Within* (New York: Berkley Books, 1993) 86.

[30] Griffith.

[31] Griffith.

[32] See Wikipedia on Jason Becker and his website at http://www.jasonbecker.com , which contains links to relevant magazine articles.

Breakfast 14

[1] As Benjamin Franklin put it, if a man empties his purse into his head, no one can take it away from him. An investment in knowledge always pays the best interest.

[2] Wikipedia on Wal-Mart.

[3] Sam Walton with John Huey, *Sam Walton: Made in America* (New York: Doubleday, 1992) 13.

[4] Walton, p. 23.

[5] Ibid. 17-18.

[6] Ibid. 40.

[7] Ibid. 116.

[8] Ibid. xiii, 13 According to Sam Walton, Wal-Mart is the story of "ordinary people joined together to accomplish extraordinary things."

[9] Ibid. 11.

[10] Ibid. 4.

[11] Ibid.

[12] Ibid. 16.

[13] Ibid. 15.

[14] Ibid. 16

[15] Ibid.

[16] Ibid. 15.

[17] Ibid.

[18] Ibid. 84.

[19] Ibid.

[20] Ibid. 86.

[21] Ibid. 17.

[22] Ibid. 22-23, 227.

[23] Ibid. 21.

[24] Ibid. 23.

[25] Ibid. 22-23.

[26] Ibid. 63.

[27] Ibid. 81.

[28] Ibid.

[29] Ibid. 192-193.

[30] Ibid. 211.

[31] Ibid. 212.

[32] Ibid. 230.

[33] Ibid. 81, 85.

[34] Ibid. 81-82.

[35] Ibid. 23.

[36] Ibid. 27.

[37] Ibid. 189.

[38] Ibid. 49. "…what we've been doing all along: experimenting, trying to do something different, educating ourselves as to what was going on in the retail industry and trying to stay ahead of those trends" (p. 46). "…in the marketplace, I have always been a maverick who enjoys shaking things up and creating a little anarchy" (p. 48). He was "totally independent in his thinking" (p. 117). "We had very little capacity for embarrassment back in those days. We paid absolutely no attention whatsoever to the way retail said it had to be done" (p. 63).

39 Ibid. 60-61.
40 Ibid. 63.
41 Ibid. 33.
42 Ibid. 34.
43 Ibid. 42-43.
44 Ibid. 190, from Bud Walton. Note also how he traveled to Germany, France, Italy, South Africa, Great Britain, Australia, and South America looking at the global competition in retailing (p. 198).
45 Ibid. 48-49.
46 Ibid. 60-62.
47 Ibid. 56, 57.
48 Ibid. 56-57, 228-229.
49 Ibid. 229.
50 Ibid. 225.
51 Ibid. 56.
52 According to the U.S. Census Bureau for years 1998-2000, the average person with some high school education earns $23,400 per year. That rises to $30,400 for high school graduates, $36,800 for some college, $38,200 for an associate's degree, $52,200 for a bachelor's degree, $62,300 for a master's degree, and $89,400 for a doctoral degree.
53 Denis Brian, *Einstein: A Life* (New York: John Wiley & Sons, 1996) 54,56.
54 Stephen Manes and Paul Andrews, *Gates* (New York: Touchstone, 1994) 40-43, 88.
55 Benjamin Franklin, *The Autobiography of Benjamin Franklin* (New York: Dover Publications, 1996) 45, 46.
56 Humphrey Carpenter, *J.R.R. Tolkien: A Biography* (Boston: Houghton Mifflin, 2000) 152-155.
57 Joseph McBride, *Steven Spielberg* (New York: Simon and Schuster, 1997) 111-113, 135, 141, 151.

Breakfast 15

1 This comment has been attributed to J. Paul Getty.
2 Some of the best works I've read to summarize and document the scientific research on happiness include David G. Myers, *The Pursuit of Happiness* (New York: Avon Books, 1992); David G. Myers, *The American Paradox* (New Haven: Yale University Press, 2000); Jason Zweig, *Your Money and Your Brain* (New York: Simon & Schuster, 2007) 228ff; Daniel Gilbert, *Stumbling on Happiness* (New York: Vintage Books, 2005).
3 Myers, pp. 126-147. See also Marilyn Elias, *Psychologists Now Know What Makes People Happy*, USA Today, Feb. 10, 2002; *Time Magazine*, January 17, 2005; Oliver James, *Children Before Cash*, "The Guardian," May 17, 2003; Now It's a Fact: Money Doesn't Buy Happiness, Forbes, at http://moneycentral.msn.com/content/invest/forbes/P95294.asp and David G. Myers, *Wealth, Well-Being and the New American Dream* http://www.newdream.org/newsletter/pdf/wellbeing.pdf.
4 Jeff Woloson at *The Divas Site* http://www.divasthesite.com/Society_Divas/christina_onassis_a.htm.
5 Benjamin Franklin, *The Autobiography of Benjamin Franklin* (New York: Dover Publications, 1996) 68.
6 This activity would follow Myer's prescription to increase happiness: act in ways consistent with happy behavior. "Going through the motions can trigger the emotions." Saying becomes believing. (Myers, *The Pursuit of Happiness*, pp. 122-126.) For eighteen years, on both the high school and college levels, Hal Urban tried an unusual assignment that required his students to list things they're thankful for and read their list at four different times during the following twenty-four hours. The next day, invariably, they came into class happier. Hal Urban, *Life's Greatest Lessons* (California: Great Lessons Press, 1997) 56-65.
7 *Stob. Flor.* v. 43.

[8] Funded by the *Lilly Endowment, Inc.*, The *National Study on Youth and Religion* was conducted from 2001-2005 through the University of North Carolina at Chapel Hill. They surveyed 3,370 young people across the nation, between 13 and 17 years of age. 54 percent of the spiritually devoted teens described themselves as "very happy," contrasted with 29 percent of the spiritually disengaged. Seven percent of the spiritually devoted teens felt guilty often, compared to 12 percent of the spiritually disengaged. For a report on this research, see *Soul Searching: The Religious and Spiritual Lives of American Teenagers*, by Christian Smith with Melinda Lundquist Denton (New York: Oxford University Press, 2005), especially chapter 7: Adolescent Religion and Life Outcomes.

[9] Ibid. 225.

[10] David Myers sites studies indicating that religious commitment predicts higher levels of happiness (*The American Paradox*, pp. 283-285), integrity (p. 270), decreased hedonism (p. 270), more generous monetary giving (giving over 2 ½ as much as non-attenders of church, p. 271), and giving of time (over double the amount of time as the highly uncommitted, p. 272-273). "In one Gallup survey, highly spiritual people were twice as likely as those lowest in spiritual commitment to declare themselves very happy" (p. 284).

[11] Roger Lowenstein, *Buffett: The Making of an American Capitalist* (New York: Doubleday, 1995) 306-312.

[12] I'm in debt to both Lowenstein (p. 311) and Zweig (in his commentary on *The Intelligent Investor*, pp. 529, 530) for connecting Pascal's Wager with investing.

[13] See this in many sections of Graham's *The Intelligent Investor*, particularly the final chapter.

[14] Tihomir Dimitrov researched several European libraries to compile an abundance of well-documented quotes by top scientists concerning their views of God. It's entitled *Fifty Nobel Laureates and Other Great Scientists Who Believe in God*. Read it, free of charge, at http://nobelists.net .

[15] Copleston liked to study the philosophers in their original languages, including English, French, Greek, and German. He often lectured on Metaphysics in Latin and once lectured on Wittgenstein in Italian. Besides his massive seventeen book *History of Philosophy*, he wrote twelve other books on philosophy. After sixty years of single-minded philosophical reflection, he held that God had revealed Himself to mankind in the Judeo-Christian scriptures. Frederick Copleston, *Memoirs of a Philosopher* (Kansas City: Sheed and Ward, 1993) 206, 220-224.

[16] Blaise Pascal, *Pensees*, Section III.

[17] While many mutual funds require a minimum $3,000 initial investment, some funds allow smaller starting amounts to help young people get started. Example: as I write, Vanguard offers their Star fund for an initial investment of only $1,000. Most states will allow 18 year olds to open their own mutual funds.

Index

S

Made in the USA
Charleston, SC
12 September 2010